# The Disparity of European Integration

This new study revisits the work of the late Ernst Haas, assessing his relevance for contemporary European integration and its disparities.

With his seminal book, *The Uniting of Europe* Haas laid the foundations for one of the most prominent paradigms of European integration – neofunctionalism. He engaged in inductive reasoning to theorize the dynamics of the European integration process that led from the Treaty of Paris in 1951 to the Treaty of Rome in 1957. The Treaty of Rome set the constitutional framework for a Common Market.

Today, a second Treaty of Rome may lay the foundation for a European Constitution that embeds the Common Market in a European polity. Unfortunately, Haas will not be able to witness this path-breaking step in the development of a European political community, which he so aptly theorized almost five decades ago. This is all the more regrettable since students of European integration are more than ever challenged to tackle a major empirical puzzle: After 50 years of European integration, the member states managed to adopt a single currency and to develop common policies and institutions on justice and home affairs. The integration of foreign policy and defence, by contrast, is still lagging behind. This text delivers sharp insights into these issues.

This book, previously published as a special issue of the *Journal of European Public Policy*, will be of great interest to all students and scholars of international relations, the European Union, European politics and Public Policy.

**Tanja A. Börzel** is professor of European Integration at the Otto Suhr Institute for Political Science, Free University of Berlin, Germany.

## Journal of European Public Policy Series

**Series Editor:** Jeremy Richardson is a Professor at Nuffield College, Oxford University

This series seeks to bring together some of the finest edited works on European Public Policy. Reprinting from Special Issues of the 'Journal of European Public Policy,' the focus is on using a wide range of social sciences approaches, both qualitative and quantitative, to gain a comprehensive and definitive understanding of Public Policy in Europe.

Towards a Federal Europe
*Edited by Alexander H. Trechsel*

The Disparity of European Integration
*Edited by Tanja A. Börzel*

# The Disparity of European Integration

Revisiting Neofunctionalism in Honour of Ernst B. Haas

Edited by Tanya A. Börzel

Routledge
Taylor & Francis Group

LONDON AND NEW YORK

First published 2006 by Routledge
2 Park Square, Milton Park, Abingdon, Oxon, OX14 4RN

Simultaneously published in the USA and Canada
by Routledge
270 Madison Ave, New York, NY 10016

*Routledge is an imprint of the Taylor & Francis Group*

Transferred to Digital Printing 2008

© 2006 Taylor & Francis

Typeset in Agaramond by Techset Composition Limited

*British Library Cataloguing in Publication Data*
A catalogue record for this book is available from the British Library

*Library of Congress Cataloging in Publication Data*
A catalog record for this title has been requested

ISBN10: 0-415-37490-1 (Cased)
ISBN13: 978-0-415-37490-3 (Cased)

# Contents

# Preface

In March 2003, Ernst B. Haas passed away. This special issue seeks to pay tribute to one of the greatest thinkers in European integration studies. The idea was born at the American Political Science Convention of 2003, where Peter Katzenstein, Bob Keohane, John Ruggie, and Philippe Schmitter organized a roundtable in honour of Ernst Haas. The four did a wonderful job in accounting for Haas's intellectual contributions to political science. This is particularly true for his work outside the area of regional integration that many of us are less familiar with (cf. Ruggie *et al.* 2005). Without denying the importance of his studies of change at the level of the world polity or of nationalism, Haas will be mostly remembered as the founding father of neofunctionalist theorizing on European integration. Neofunctionalism still inspires countless students in writing their seminar papers, master theses, and Ph.D. dissertations. Given his immense importance to European Union studies, it only seemed logical to organize something like the APSA roundtable, inviting students of European integration with different intellectual backgrounds to reflect on the theoretical works of Ernst Haas and explore whether his neofunctionalist reasoning can still help us to understand and explain core developments of European integration. Most of the contributors to the special issue had attended the APSA roundtable and immediately subscribed to the idea. I approached Jeremy Richardson, who greeted the suggestion with great enthusiasm and offered a publication spot within less than two years! Thanks to the contributors, who dutifully complied with the strict deadlines imposed on them, thanks to the heroic work of the anonymous reviewer who extensively commented on all eight papers in less than a week (!), and thanks to the professional support of Jeremy Richardson and the *JEPP* team, we were able to meet the publication schedule. I am particularly indebted to Diana Panke and Tina Freyburg for their assistance, which made editing this special issue almost a piece of cake.

*Tanja A. Börzel*

## REFERENCE

Ruggie, J.G., Katzenstein, P.J., Keohane, R.O. and Schmitter, P.C. (2005) 'Transformations in world politics: the intellectual contributions of Ernst B. Haas', *Annual
Review of Political Science* 8 (forthcoming).

# Mind the gap! European integration between level and scope

Tanja A. Börzel

Goods can be 'integrated' and maximized, so to speak, anonymously; the integration of foreign and military policies, in a world in which security and leadership are the scarcest of values, means what it has always meant: the acceptance by some of the predominance of others.

(Hoffmann 1964: 1275)

## INTRODUCTION

Forty-five years ago, in his seminal book *The Uniting of Europe*, Ernst Haas laid the foundations for one of the most, if not the most, prominent paradigms of European integration – neofunctionalism. The book engaged in inductive reasoning to theorize the dynamics of the European integration process that led from the Treaty of Paris in 1951 to the Treaty of Rome in 1957.

The Treaty of Rome set the constitutional framework for a Common Market. Today, a second Treaty of Rome may lay the foundation for a European Constitution that embeds the Common Market in a European polity. Unfortunately, Ernst Haas will not be able to witness this path-breaking step in the development of a European political community, which he so aptly theorized almost five decades ago. This is all the more regrettable since students of European integration are more than ever challenged to tackle a major empirical puzzle: on the one hand, the *acquis communautaire* represents a unique degree of political integration beyond the nation state. The Common Market has been crowned with a common currency and consumers have been made citizens with their own fundamental rights and freedoms enshrined in a European citizenship and a Charter of Fundamental Rights. On the other hand, political integration in some sectors has seriously lagged behind. The Maastricht Treaty extended European integration to the last two bastions of national sovereignty: foreign and security policy and justice and home affairs. But the member states created a completely new set of institutions (second and third pillars) to keep the sectors off-limits to the Commission, the European Court of Justice (ECJ) and the European Parliament (EP). While the Amsterdam Treaty moved parts of the third pillar into the first pillar, the common foreign and security policy (CFSP) has remained under the exclusive control of the member states. Other examples of disparate integration are social welfare, culture and education policy, and economic governance. The European Union (EU) still lacks any substantial competencies in these areas. If the member states decide to co-ordinate their activities, they do so often outside the Community framework.

*Why have the member states been willing to fundamentally compromise the core of their sovereignty in some areas (currency, citizen rights) while resisting any substantial cuts in others (security and defence, social welfare, culture and education)?*

The explanation of what Ernst Haas (1958) called 'task expansion' is at the heart of neofunctionalist thinking (Haas 1958). Consequently, the expansive logic of sectoral integration constitutes the cornerstone of Haas's theory of regional integration. The special issue revisits his works in order to explore whether neofunctionalist reasoning can still help us to understand and explain the dynamic process of task expansion in the EU.

The next paragraphs will outline the puzzle to be addressed by the various contributions to the special issue in more detail. The introductory chapter concludes with a brief road map to the edited volume.[1]

## THE PUZZLE: THE DISPARITY OF EUROPEAN INTEGRATION

When analysing the evolution of competencies in the EU, many studies start with the Treaty of Rome instead of the Treaty of Paris. The foundation of the European Coal and Steel Community (ECSC) in 1951 is hardly considered (Lindberg and Scheingold 1970; Schmitter 1996; Pollack 2000; Hix 2004). This is all the more regrettable because no Treaty represents better the core idea of (neo)functionalist reasoning: close co-operation in specific economic sectors is the key to overcoming national sovereignty and achieving European unity.[2] But while the EU today is a true success story of economic integration, its inception was about peace and security rather than economic wealth. In other words, initial attempts of European integration after the Second World War started in the area of 'high politics'. Once the negotiations on the Council of Europe had dwarfed federalist hopes for a United States of Europe, efforts to eliminate the risk of war in Europe embarked on a less glamorous path shaped by the plan of Robert Schuman and Jean Monnet to place the coal and steel production of France and Germany in particular under the common control of a supranational authority. The failure to establish a European political community, that would have united the ECSC with a newly founded European defence community in the early 1950s, made once again clear that successful integration would have to follow a functionalist rather than federalist logic. The focus shifted to the low politics of economic integration paving the way for the European Atomic Energy Community and the European Economic Community established by the Treaty of Rome in 1957. Throughout the following five decades, the European Community subsequently managed to expand its tasks culminating in the creation of an economic and monetary union by the Treaty of Maastricht in 1992. Political integration, by contrast, has seriously lagged behind. This is particularly true for foreign and security policy, but also parts of other policy areas, as we will see below.

The literature has developed different ways to map the task expansion of the EU. Some studies draw on Lindberg and Scheingold's definition of integration in terms of *scope* and *locus* (level) of decision-making (Lindberg and Scheingold 1970: 67–71). While *scope* relates to the initial expansion of EU authority to new policy areas, *locus* stresses 'the relative importance of Community decision-making processes as compared with national processes' (1970: 68). As a measurement, Lindberg and Scheingold take the *level* at which decisions are formally taken. Others, by contrast, have focused on policy outputs at the EU level as measured in legislation (Directives, Regulations) and/or budgetary expenditures (Pollack 1994, 2000; Wessels 1997; Fligstein and McNichol 2001). Sometimes, the two measurements tend to become blurred when the level of decision-making is not only determined by the allocation of competencies in the Treaties but by the extent to which supranational institutions make use of their competencies (e.g. Schmitter 1996).[3] While it may be interesting to look at legal output, it is not the best indicator for task expansion. First, the numbers of legal acts adopted by the EU do not say anything about their substantive content and relevance. Second, many Directives and Regulations expire after a number of years and are no longer in force.[4] Third, in order to assess the relative weight of EU legislation, we would have to compare the legal output of the EU with those of its member states. Finally, legal output is strongly influenced by the institutions in which legal acts are adopted. Owing to unanimous decision-making, there were some noticeable exceptions to the core of the Common Market, such as transport and energy, where hardly any policy decisions had been taken at the EU level till the 1990s (Schmitter 1996: 124). If institutions have a strong impact on policy output, for the latter of which reliable data are hardly available, the former provides a better indicator for the task expansion of the EU.

Given the various measurement problems, I suggest focusing on formal decision rules rather than legal output or expert estimates to trace the task expansion of the EU. The following analysis draws on the formal allocation of competencies and the institutional decision-making procedures as they evolved in the various treaty reforms. Following Lindberg and Scheingold, the *level* (breadth) of integration refers to the locus where the competence for policy decisions resides. It is operationalized by the number of issues in a given policy sector for which the EU has the power to legislate. Unlike Lindberg and Scheingold, the *scope* (depth) of integration is not understood as the initial expansion of EU tasks into new issue areas. This aspect is already covered by measuring the level of integration every time treaty revisions formally changed the allocation of competencies between the EU and its member states (principle of conferral).[5] Rather, scope is operationalized by the procedures according to which policy decisions are taken focusing on the involvement of supranational bodies and Council voting rules (Figure 1). This conceptualization of scope borrows heavily from Fritz Scharpf's work on institutional decision rules and modes of governance in the EU (Scharpf 2001, 2003).[6]

For each of the two dimensions, a five-point scale is applied. In order to come to a more differentiated assessment, the scale also allows for half points. Table 1 lists the scores for level and scope individually.

Mapping the task expansion of the EU runs the risk of becoming an 'impressionist exercise' (Hix 2004: 18). In order to ensure some 'inter-coder reliability', I based my analysis on the reading of the Treaties rather than using secondary literature or expert assessments. Another problem in analysing the task expansion of the EU is the changing definition of issue areas both in the literature and in the Treaties. The list of policy fields as they are presented in Table 1 follows the analysis of Simon Hix (Hix 2004).

My overall findings do not seriously contradict those of similar studies (Hix 2004; Hooghe and Marks 2001; Donohue and Pollack 2001; Schmidt 1999; Schmitter 1996; Lindberg and Scheingold 1970). Yet, distinguishing between scope and level allows us to refine the puzzle of the disparity of regional integration and challenges at least partly the ways in which the literature has portrayed the EU's task expansion. Drawing on Lowi's distinction between regulatory, distributive, and redistributive policies many studies come to rather similar accounts (e.g. Pollack 1994: 108–13; Hix 2004: 8).

In the 1950s, the overwhelming majority of competencies still resided at the national level, while the EU held some responsibilities for market making (old regulatory) policies in order to dismantle national barriers to the free movement of goods and services, including competition and industry. In the 1960s and 1970s, however, the EU increasingly employed its market making powers to extend its competencies into the realm of market correcting (new regulatory)

*Level of authority*

breadth (number of issues which fall under EU competence)

    1 = *exclusive national competencies* (0% EU)
        competencies for all policy issues at national level

    2 = *shared competencies 'light'*
        competencies for most policy issues at national level

    3 = *shared competencies 'medium'*
        competencies for policy issues split between national and EU level

    4 = *shared competencies ' strong'*
        competencies for most policy issues at EU level

    5 = *exclusive EU competencies* (100% EU)
        competence for all policy issues at EU level

*Scope of authority*

depth (involvement of supranational bodies and Council voting rule)

    0 = *no co-ordination at EU level*

    1 = *intergovernmental co-ordination*
        (European) Council as executive and legislative body, acts by unanimity
        no right of initiative of European Commission
        no involvement of European Parliament
        no judicial review by European Court of Justice

    2 = *intergovernmental co-operation*
        Council as main executive and legislative body, acts by unanimity
        right of initiative of European Commission shared with Council
        consultation of European Parliament
        restricted judicial review by European Court of Justice

    3 = *joint decision-making I*
        exclusive right of initiative of European Commission
        co-legislation by Council acting by
        (a) unanimity and consultation of European Parliament    (3.0)
        (b) unanimity and co-decision procedure OR
            majority and consultation of European Parliament    (3.5)
        full judicial review by European Court of Justice

    4 = *joint decision-making II*
        exclusive right of initiative of European Commission
        co-legislation by Council acting by majority and European Parliament via
        (a) co-operation    (4.0)
        (b) co-decision procedure    (4.5)
        full judicial review by European Court of Justice

    5 = *supranational centralization*
        unilateral decision of European Commission/European Central Bank
        no involvement of Council and European Parliament
        full jurisdiction of European Court of Justice

*Figure 1* Mapping the task expansion of the EU

policies. Since national standards on environment, consumer protection, industrial health and security, or labour markets often work as non-tariff barriers to trade, the need for harmonization at the EU level became increasingly evident. A dynamic interpretation of the Treaties – particularly of Art. 28 (ex-Art. 30 ECT)

Table 1 Scope and level of European integration

| Issue area | | 1958 Treaty of Rome 1957: European Economic and Atomic Energy Community | 1987 Single European Act 1986 | 1993 Maastricht Treaty 1992 | 1999 Amsterdam Treaty 1997 | 2003 Nice Treaty 2001 | 200X Constitutional Treaty 2004 |
|---|---|---|---|---|---|---|---|
| **External Relations** | | | | | | | |
| Political | L | 1 | 1.5 | 2.5 | 3 | 3 | 3 |
| | S | 0 | 0.5 | 1.5 | 1.5 | 2 | 2 |
| Economic | L | 2 | 2 | 3.5 | 4.5 | 4.5 | 4.5 |
| | S | 1.5 | 1.5 | 3.5 | 3.5 | 3.5 | 3.5 |
| **Justice and Home Affairs** | | | | | | | |
| Criminal/Domestic Security | L | 1 | 1 | 2 | 2.5 | 2.5 | 2.5 |
| | S | 0 | 0 | 1 | 2 | 3 | 4 |
| Civil | L | 1 | 1 | 2.5 | 3 | 3 | 3.5 |
| | S | 0 | 0 | 3 | 3.5 | 4 | 4 |
| **Socio-cultural Affairs** | | | | | | | |
| Environment/Consumer Protection | L | 1 | 3 | 4 | 4 | 4 | 4 |
| | S | 0 | 3 | 3–4.5 | 3–4.5 | 3–4.5 | 3–4.5 |
| Occupational Health and Safety Standards | L | 1 | 3 | 3 | 4.5 | 4.5 | 4.5 |
| | S | 0 | 4 | 4 | 4.5 | 4.5 | 4.5 |
| Labour | L | 1 | 1 | 2 | 2 | 2 | 2 |
| | S | 1 | 1 | 3.5 | 4 | 4 | 4 |

| | | | | | | |
|---|---|---|---|---|---|---|
| Culture | L | 1 | 1 | 1 | 1 | 2 |
| | S | 0 | 1 | 1 | 1 | 4.5 |
| Welfare | L | 1 | 1.5 | 1.5 | 1.5 | 1.5 |
| | S | 0 | 3 | 4 | 4 | 4 |
| Research and Development | L | 1.5 | 1.5 | 1.5 | 1.5 | 1.5 |
| | S | 3–4 | 3–4 | 3.5–4.5 | 3.5–4.5 | 3.5–4.5 |
| **Economic Affairs** | | | | | | |
| Economic Freedoms | L | 2 | 4.5 | 4.5 | 4.5 | 4.5 |
| | S | 2 | 3.5 | 3.5 | 3.5 | 3.5 |
| Competition and Industry | L | 2.5 | 3 | 3 | 3 | 3 |
| | S | 2 | 3 | 3 | 4 | 4 |
| Energy and Transport | L | 1.5 | 1.5 | 1.5 | 1.5 | 3.5 |
| | S | 2 | 2 | 2 | 2 | 4 |
| Macroeconomic Policy and Employment | L | 1.5 | 1.5 | 2 | 2 | 2 |
| | S | 1.5 | 1.5 | 3.5 | 3.5 | 3.5 |
| Agriculture | L | 4 | 4 | 4 | 4 | 4 |
| | S | 3 | 3 | 3 | 3 | 4.5 |
| Territorial (Regional), Economic and Social Cohesion | L | 2 | 4 | 4 | 4 | 4 |
| | S | 1–2 | 3–3.5 | 3–4.5 | 3.5–4.5 | 3.5–4.5 |
| Monetary Policy | L | 1 | 4 | 5 | 5 | 5 |
| | S | 0 | 4 | 5 | 5 | 5 |
| Tax | L | 1.5 | 1.5 | 1.5 | 1.5 | 1.5 |
| | S | 1.5 | 1.5 | 1.5 | 1.5 | 1.5 |

which prohibits quantitative restrictions on imports and all measures having equal effect – and the use of Art. 94 (ex-Art 100 ECT) which allows for the harmonization of national regulations that directly affect the establishment or functioning of the Common Market allowed the EU to incrementally expand its task into issue areas that the Treaty of Rome had not defined as Community competence at all (e.g. Pollack 1994: 122–31; cf. Stone Sweet and Sandholtz 1997). The Single European Act (SEA) in 1986 codified this incremental process of 'creeping competencies' (Pollack 1994) and established what has become the 'constitutional settlement' of the EU (Hix 2004: 19). Subsequent treaty reforms in Maastricht, Amsterdam, Nice, and the Constitutional Convention consolidated the allocation of competencies laid out in the SEA: the EU holds exclusive competencies for market making (old regulatory) policies (including external trade) to ensure the free movement of goods, services, persons, and capital. It shares with the member states responsibilities for market correcting (new regulatory) policies that involve the harmonization of national standards on environment, consumer protection, industrial health and security, labour markets, etc. The member states collectively co-ordinate at the EU level their competencies for macroeconomic policies, justice and home affairs, and foreign and security policy. Finally, they remain by and large exclusively responsible for redistributive policy, including taxation and expenditure with some constraints agreed upon at the EU level.

Yet, a closer look reveals some important deviations from the neat picture that seems to portray the EU as a 'regulatory state' (Majone 1994). First, EU policy-making is not confined to regulation. True, the EU's redistributive capacity is small compared to its members with their well-entrenched welfare states. It is currently limited to 1.27 per cent of the gross domestic product (GDP) generated by all member states (de facto, however, it lies at only 1.09 per cent). To put these figures into context, a spending power comparable to the German federation, for example, would correspond to a share of about 20 per cent of European GDP (cf. Börzel and Hösli 2003). Nevertheless, the EU transfers significant resources through its budget, including the common agricultural policy (CAP), regional policy, cohesion policy, and research and development policy. The CAP constitutes more than 60 per cent of the EU budget, and the structural and cohesion funds amount to 5 per cent of the GPD of some member states (Hix 1998: 42).

Second, market making and market correcting policies of the EU constrain the capacity of the member states for redistribution (Scharpf 1996, 1997). Next to state aid, competition rules, and the dynamics of regulatory competition according to which high labour costs may become a serious competitive disadvantage, the convergence criteria and the Growth and Stability Pact have put further constraints on the expenditure policies of the member states. This has created some pressure for what Haas would call a functional spillover from regulatory into redistributive issue areas. While the economic and monetary union (EMU) curbs the capacity of the member states for national macroeconomic stabilization, the EU as a whole does not possess these instruments. Asymmetric 'shocks' occurring in one part of the EMU, which might, for example, sharply increase unemployment in some EU member states, are difficult to address by the collective strategies of the centralized institutions (e.g. the European Central Bank (ECB)). Interest rates are now determined collectively for all EU states participating in EMU. The EU may face difficulties in achieving econ-omic efficiency as long as national business cycles in the EMU area are not yet developing in a harmonized way (cf. Börzel and Hösli 2003). While the member states seek to retain exclusive competencies in areas of taxation and expenditure, they have intensified their attempts to co-ordinate their macroeconomic policies at the EU level (Luxembourg, Cardiff, Cologne processes). Moreover, as long as their domestic constituencies have a strong preference for maintaining the high level of social regulation and societal redistribution that characterizes the Euro-pean (continental) welfare state, member state governments have strong incen-tives to harmonize national standards at the EU level in order to avoid competitive disadvantages to their domestic industries. Thus, for example, both the French and the German governments have repeatedly called for a certain degree of European tax harmonization in order to avoid 'tax dumping'. Enlargement may reinforce the pressures for both direct and indirect redistribution by the EU going beyond mere 'side-payments' in larger cross-sectoral bargains among the member states (Pollack 1994). According to the neofunctionalist logic, member states will sooner or later need to expand the EU tasks in the area of redistributive policies, if they wish to secure their achievements in market integration.

Third, there is a clear divergence or disparity with regard to internal and external security. Interestingly enough, none of the two policies fits the Lowi typology. While Lowi had initially included foreign policy as a separate type (Lowi 1964: 689, fn. 17), he argued later that foreign policy could be dissected in its regulatory, redistributive, and distributive effects and, hence, be subsumed under the other three types (Lowi 1967a: 298–315). He replaced it by another type, constituent policy, affecting 'the structure, the composition, and the oper-ation of a regime or system' (Lowi 1967b: 239; Lowi 1972). Constituent policy covers the history-making decisions of the EU (Peterson 1995) impacting its overall architecture, including the constitutional-legal order and geographical parameters (Bulmer, cited in Pollack 1994: 113). But constituent policy does not comprise what Hix calls 'citizen policies', i.e. 'rules to extend and protect the economic, political and social rights of the citizens', including internal security (police and judicial co-operation in civilian and criminal matters), EU citizenship, and border control (asylum and immigration) (Hix 2004: 8).

In any case, studies on European policy-making have always treated external and internal security as separate issues from regulatory, distributive and redistri-butive EU policies. Defence and war pertain to the core of state sovereignty. So do law and order, which are merely the domestic flipside of the legitimate monopoly of force of the modern state. Both firmly belong in the realm of high politics where, according to functionalist reasoning, integration is most unlikely to occur (see below).

Indeed, political integration of external and internal security issues has significantly lagged behind. Since the second half of the 1990s, however, we can observe an increasing divergence in the task expansion between the two policies, particularly with regard to the scope of integration.

Member states started to co-ordinate internal and external security policies at an informal level, outside the institutions of the EU. After several attempts to institutionalize a CFSP had failed in the 1950s and 1960s, the member state governments established the European political co-operation (EPC) in 1970 as an informal framework in which they could co-ordinate their foreign policy activities. The EPC was an entirely intergovernmental process, 'outside the treaties, agreed among governments and managed by diplomats' (Forster and Wallace 2000: 464). Sixteen years later, the SEA ended the exclusion of security and defence issues from the European Treaties and brought the EPC under the institutional framework of the European Council. And in 1992 the Maastricht Treaty created the CFSP – including the perspective for a common European defence and security policy (Art. J.4) – as the second of the three pillars of the EU.

Internal security co-operation has evolved in a similar way. As in the area of external security, a working model of intergovernmental co-operation emerged at an informal level and was subsequently brought into the Treaties. In 1975 the member states initiated a co-operation of their law enforcement agencies in order to fight terrorism and transnational crime. The so-called Trevi group later became part of the EPC and formed various ad hoc working groups on issues of immigration, asylum, and police and judicial co-operation. Moreover, in 1985, France, Germany, Belgium, the Netherlands, and Luxembourg agreed to subsequently abolish their border controls. At the same time, they decided to establish a uniform control of the EU's external borders, including the harmonization of visa, asylum, and refugee policies. In the early 1990s, Spain, Greece, Portugal, and Italy joined the so-called Schengen Agreement, and a few years later Austria, Denmark, Sweden, Finland, Norway, and Iceland (the latter two countries not being members of the EU) followed suit. The Maastricht Treaty summoned the multiple networks of transgovernmental co-operation in the field of justice and home affairs (JHA) under the third pillar.

With the three-pillar structure, the member states clearly intended to restrict co-operation on internal and external security to the realm of intergovernmental decision-making. To prevent any dynamics of 'creeping competencies', the institutional rules and procedures of the second and third pillars sealed off both CFSP and JHA from the reach of supranational actors. This was a clear indication of the intense tensions between sovereignty and integration in these two fields. Nevertheless, the trajectories of the two policy areas soon started to diverge. While CFSP remained firmly rooted in the realm of intergovernmentalism, JHA issues were subsequently moved into the first pillar.

After the Maastricht Treaty had firmly placed JHA under the procedures of intergovernmental co-operation, the scale of activity within the third pillar steadily increased. Policy-making resulted in a number of intergovernmental conventions (EUROPOL, Fraud, External Frontiers, Schengen). Yet, the majority of activities fell under so-called 'soft law' – non-binding recommendations, resolutions, and conclusions made it easier to reconcile member states' diverging interests and legal cultures (cf. Monar 1997: 326–9). Despite – or because of – the cumbersome decision-making procedures, the Amsterdam Treaty substantially changed the institutional framework of JHA. Article 61 envisioned the creation of an 'Area of Freedom, Security and Justice'. Within five years after the enactment of the Amsterdam Treaty, persons should move freely within the EU without facing any border controls. In order to ensure internal security, visa, asylum, immigration and other policies related to the free movement of persons were 'communitarized'. This also applied to the judicial co-operation on civil matters. The scope of integration, however, remained restricted for the five-year transitional period; Articles 64, 67, and 68 made decisions subject to unanimity in the Council, limited the Commission's power of initiative, offered the EP only consultation rights, and restricted the ECJ's power of judicial review. In 2004 at the earliest, the Council could vote by unanimity to bring all or some issues under the co-decision procedures of Art. 251 (*passerelle*). Police co-operation and judicial co-operation in criminal matters, by contrast, remained within the third pillar. But the Schengen conventions and *acquis* entered the Treaty, with an opt-out for Denmark, the UK, and Ireland. While the Nice Treaty brought only some minor changes to JHA and failed to incorporate the Charter of Fundamental Rights into the Treaty, the European Council of Tampere passed in 1999 a whole programme of measures towards 'a Union of Freedom, Security, and Justice' including mutual recognition of judicial decisions, better access to justice across the EU, closer co-operation against crime (EUROPOL and EUROJUST), and several directives against different forms of discrimination. The Constitutional Treaty (Chapter IV), finally, places the vast majority of JHA issues under ordinary legislative procedure (former co-decision), including parts of the police co-operation and judicial co-operation in criminal matters. Where intergovernmental decision-making still holds, the possibility for enhanced co-operation exists.

While JHA has undergone progressive supranationalization during the last decade, task expansion in CFSP has been far less dynamic. Member states engaged in a number of joint initiatives after the conclusion of the Maastricht Treaty, partly driven by the Yugoslav crisis and the Bosnian conflict. The Petersberg Declaration, for instance, gave the Western European Union (WEU) for the first time a role in undertaking peacekeeping and peacemaking operations. But EU action proved ineffective in responding to external challenges. Unlike in the case of JHA, the member states were unable to agree on any major changes to the institutional framework. The Amsterdam Treaty defines the CFSP as covering all aspects of foreign and security policy, including matters with defence implications. While the level of integration was broadened, the scope remained confined to intergovernmental co-operation. The introduction of 'constructive abstention' and a limited extension of qualified majority voting (Art. 23) did little to increase the use of the foreign policy instruments established by Title V of the Treaty on European Union (TEU) (common positions, joint actions). Member states retained the right to block decisions 'for important and stated reasons of national policy' (Art. 23.2). The creation of a High Representative (Art. 18, 26) contributing to the formulation and implementation of the Council's policy decisions marked the largest step forward but kept the CFSP firmly in the intergovernmentalist framework. The European Council received the explicit role of setting the guidelines for the CFSP and for adopting Common Strategies (Art. 13). The Commission became fully associated but had no right of initiative (Art. 18.4). The role of the EP was only marginally strengthened by obliging the Council Presidency to consult it on the main issues and basic choices of the CFSP (Art. 21). The ECJ still had no authority in this field. Given the limited progress on decision procedures the member states were able to agree upon, the 'capability–expectation gap' (Hill 1993) between what the EU was legally entitled to do and what it was actually capable of doing widened. The Cologne and Helsinki Councils of 1999 and the Nice Treaty of 2000 further extended the level of integration towards a common European security and defence policy (CESDP) by establishing a Rapid Reaction Force and by finally taking over the tasks of the WEU. But the institutional framework stays largely unchanged. It remains to be seen whether the Union Minister for Foreign Affairs, who combines the posts of the High Representative and the Commissioner of External Relations, will sufficiently deepen the scope of integration to close or at least narrow the expectation–capability cap.

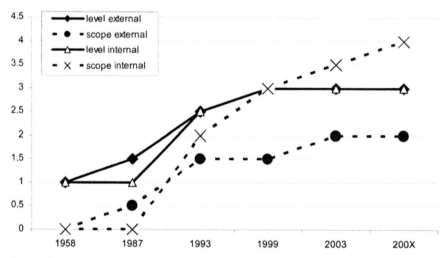

*Figure 2* The disparity between internal and external security integration – scope and level

In sum, since the beginning of the 1990s, we have witnessed a significant task expansion of the EU into the areas of both external and internal security. The achieved *level* of integration is rather similar – under the CFSP the EU can examine all aspects of foreign and security policy, and its competencies in JHA cover the most important issues that the member states deal with in this area. But the *scope* of integration differs significantly. While JHA has subsequently been brought under the supranational framework of the first pillar, the CFSP is still firmly confined to the realm of intergovernmentalism.

## HOW TO SOLVE THE PUZZLE: EXPLAINING THE DISPARITY OF EUROPEAN INTEGRATION

Students of European integration long ago agreed that defence and war, currency, and domestic law and order belonged to the realm of 'high politics'. Since these issues lie at the core of state sovereignty, they have been considered cases in which integration would be the least likely to occur (Mitrany 1966: 25; Haas 1967: 323; Lindberg and Scheingold 1970: 263–6; Mattli 2005). Likewise, '[e]ffective integration in any of these fields … would mark the crucial transition from political community to federation' (Forster and Wallace 2000: 490).

After fifty years of European integration, the member states managed to adopt a single currency and to develop common policies and institutions on JHA. The integration of foreign policy and defence, by contrast, is still lagging behind. These diverging paths of integration seem all the more puzzling if we compare the EU to other federal systems where foreign and defence policy were among the first areas brought under the (exclusive) jurisdiction of the (con)federation whereas economic integration often took much longer to evolve (Sbragia 2004; Donohue and Pollack 2001). How can we account for this disparity of European integration *within* the realm of high politics which relates to the *scope* rather than the *level* of integration?

Inspired by neofunctionalist thinking, Mark Pollack argued in his study on 'creeping competencies' in the EU that member states 'agree to harmonize their national legislation in order to, and only in order to, ensure the proper functioning of the common market' (Pollack 1994: 118). He is quick to point out that functional linkage to the Common Market is the only necessary condition for task expansion – functional needs can go unmet. His argument offers two potential explanations for the disparity of integration between internal and external security. Either, unlike JHA, the CFSP is not functionally linked to the maintenance of the free movement of goods, services, capital and labour. Or the pressures for common policies generated by the Common Market have gone unmet so far.

The linkage between market integration and internal security is rather obvious. The establishment of a common market and an economic and monetary union implies the removal of national barriers to the free movement of goods, services, capital and labour. This process has not been limited to legal, technical, and fiscal barriers but has also led to the increasing elimination of physical border controls creating significant negative externalities for internal security, such as illegal immigration, organized crime, and transnational terrorism. The 'functional' linkage between economic integration and domestic law and order is exemplified by the considerable overlap between the competencies of the EU under the first and the third pillar in the Maastricht Treaty; for example, regarding visa policy or combating drug addiction. The communitar-ization of JHA has been largely driven by the need for common policies on internal security issues, such as immigration, asylum, or criminal prosecution and law enforcement.

However, similar linkages can be found in the area of foreign and security policy. A common market requires a common external trade policy, which has indeed been one of the first exclusive competencies of the EU since the very beginning of European integration. External trade policy, in turn, is an integral part of foreign policy in any state. So it is in the EU. Take the EU's pol-icies for democracy promotion, for example. Economic sanctions form part of the instruments with which the EU can enforce political conditionality prin-ciples. The decision to institute economic sanctions falls under the CFSP in the 'second pillar'. Implementing economic sanctions, however, is a 'first pillar' question, and, thus, the Commission's task. Such processes of cross-pillarization clearly carry the potential for functional spillover. Additional pressure for a common foreign and security policy emanates from 'negative externalities' created by political and economic instability in the EU's immediate neighbour-hood. Ethnic and religious conflicts, migration of refugees and asylum seekers, transnational crime and terrorism, environmental pollution pose a serious challenge to the EU and its member states, particularly since the EU has been extending its borders into the east and south-east of the continent. As a result, the EU has started to develop a comprehensive programme for promo-ting good governance, human rights, democracy, and the rule of law governing its external relations with third countries. This includes the so-called 'circle of friends' and the 'neighbourhood policies' towards Russia, the newly indepen-dent states, the Balkans, the southern Mediterranean countries, but also EU relations with Africa, Latin America, and Asia (cf. Börzel and Risse 2004).

Thus, one could argue that the functional imperatives for an EU's task expan-sion into the last resorts of high politics are in place. And they have indeed not gone unmet. The member states have equally broadened the integration of external and internal security issues by transferring competencies to the EU level in the 1990s. What has given rise to the growing disparity between the two policy areas is their reluctance to deepen the scope of foreign, security and defence policy integration by making the exercise of EU competencies subject to supranational decision-making. In other words, in both areas of high politics, we have seen quite substantial functional spillover. But unlike in JHA, in the CFSP and European security and defence policy functional spillover has not been followed by the 'Communitarization' or supranationali-zation of decision-making rules and procedures.

The diverging degree of scope in external and internal security is even more puzzling since member state interests have been equally diverse in both areas (cf. Boer and Wallace 2000). Moreover, the Commission has been in a much better position to exploit functional linkages under the CFSP than under JHA. While the latter has been only weakly institutionalized within the Commission, the CFSP has enjoyed the advantage of a well-staffed Directorate General (DG Relex) headed by two senior Commissioners and experienced diplomats (van den Broek, former Dutch foreign minister, followed by Chris Patten, former British High Commissioner of Hong Kong). Yet, the Commission has been largely unable to foster the 'upgrading of the common interest' in the second pillar.

So the question remains: Why have the member states responded to functionalist imperatives by broadening and deepening integration of internal security but keep struggling when it comes to increasing the scope of external security integration? Neofunctionalism seems to be ill-equipped to solve the puzzle – not so much because it failed to specify its micro-foundations or has been unable to systematically account for external factors driving regional integration (see the criticisms raised by the various contributions in this volume). The problem lies with the dependent variable, since neofunctionalism – as most of the other integration theories – does not clearly distinguish between the level and the scope of integration (for an exception, see Schmitter 1970). The transfer of tasks from the national to the European level is only part of the story. As long as the member states can firmly control the exercise of their former competencies, losses of sovereignty remain limited. The puzzle as to why member states voluntarily give up power to a new political centre has been solved. Now, we need to explain why member states seek to contain the loss of sovereignty rights in some areas but not in others. The distinction between high and low politics no longer provides a convincing answer (if it ever did).[7] Finally, my analysis does not only show that level and scope do by no means co-vary. Unlike as suggested by JHA, broadening the level of integration does not necessarily precede the deepening of scope. In some highly sensitive policy areas, such as culture and welfare, the number of tasks delegated to the EU level is still fairly limited. But if the EU is entitled to take action, supranational actors are fully involved in the decision-making and the Council decides by qualified majority.

## THE STRUCTURE OF THE SPECIAL ISSUE

Ernst Haas has inspired many students of European integration in their attempts to theorize the dynamics of European integration. His neofunctionalism has been adopted, interpreted and further developed by several generations. While the wide scholarly attention has significantly enriched neofunctionalist reasoning, the theoretical core has become somewhat blurred. Therefore, the volume starts with two attempts to reconstruct the origins and the evolution of Haas's neofunctionalist thinking elaborating on its main assumptions and causal claims. After having laid out the basics, the remaining five contributions explore the strengths and weaknesses of Haas's neofunctionalism, particularly with regard to explaining the disparities between level and scope of European integration.

Ben Rosamond traces the evolution of neofunctionalist theorizing in a broader disciplinary context. Arguing against the often static and stylized reading in the literature, he portrays Haas's neofunctionalism as a dynamic theory that resonates well with contemporary approaches in EU studies and comparative regionalism, such as multi-level governance and sociological institutionalism.

While Ben Rosamond provides an overview of the disciplinary context in which Haas's neofunctionalism originated and evolved, Philippe Schmitter revisits the timeless core of neofunctionalism, reconstructing its main ontological assumptions and hypotheses. He then reviews the historical evolution of European integration and identifies several developments that challenged the explanatory power of neofunctionalism. On the basis of this analysis, Schmitter draws up a balance sheet of the strengths and weaknesses of neofunctionalism. Among other things, he criticizes neofunctionalism for focusing too much on the level of European integration, thereby overlooking very significant extensions of the scope.

This is exactly what Henry Farrell and Adrienne Héritier seek to accomplish. Their contribution focuses on changes in the scope of regional integration. They start from Haas's work on the role of technical and expert knowledge of epistemic communities. Criticizing Haas for failing to specify conditions under which epistemic factors matter, Farrell and Héritier develop a negotiation-centred approach that conceptualizes regional integration as endogenous institutional change. While power-based bargaining accounts for the extension of scope, the level of integration appears to be influenced by both the bargaining power and the epistemic knowledge of EU decision-makers.

Unlike Farrell and Héritier who adopt a rationalist-institutionalist perspective, Thomas Risse employs a social constructivist approach to account for the disparities regarding scope and level of European integration. He argues that the preference for both transferring competencies to the EU level and making them subject to supranational decision-making procedures strongly correlates with the territorial structures of the member states. Federal states, in which power is divided and shared between different levels of government, are more inclined to give up sovereignty. Risse argues that collective understandings about the meaning of sovereignty provide the causal mechanism linking territorial structures to national preferences for the scope and level of European integration.

Gráinne de Búrca approaches the neofunctionalist work of Haas from a legal perspective. In principle, neofunctionalism resonates well with legal scholarship. But in paying tribute to the importance of law, neofunctionalists have tended to change their dependent variable from political to legal integration. As a result, the role of law in political integration has been largely neglected. De Búrca specifies five different ways in which law can affect the level and scope of European integration. Some of her arguments come close to constructivist accounts focusing on the constitutive effects of law on actors' identities and preferences.

Walter Mattli explores the strengths and weaknesses of neofunctionalism from the perspective of comparative regional integration. Focusing on Latin America, he argues that the failure of regional integration with regard to advancing both level and scope can be best explained by the early works of Ernst Haas and does not require the modifications he added on later making his theoretical framework less parsimonious – except for one major puzzle. In order to explain the initial success of the Central American Common Market, Mattli draws on his own work, pointing to the importance of institutional leadership.

Andrew Moravcsik concludes with some rather sceptical reflections on the future of European integration with regard to both level and scope. He starts by criticizing Haas's neofunctionalism for lacking micro-foundations. Moreover, its explanatory power is restricted since Haas over-emphasized the endogeneous dynamics (spillover) of the integration process. Moravcsik highlights the importance of functional trends and crises, for extending the level and scope of integration. Since such factors are unlikely to emerge for the foreseeable future and are, in any case, mitigated by the institutional design of the EU hostile to reform given the large number of veto players, any changes are likely to remain within the current constitutional settlement – 'what we see now is what we get!'

**Address for correspondence:** Tanja A. Börzel, Otto-Suhr-Institute for Political Science, Center for European Integration, Free University of Berlin, Ihnestr. 22, 14195 Berlin, Germany. email: boerzel@zedat.fu-berlin.de

## NOTES

1 I thank Diana Panke, Thomas Risse, and Andrew Moravcsik for their comments and criticisms on earlier versions of this article. Maike Gorsboth provided invaluable research assistance on tracing the EU's task expansions throughout the various treaty reforms.
2 Cf. the preamble to the Treaty establishing the ECSC, 18 April 1951.
3 Schmitter adopted a similar approach to Lindberg and Scheingold, using 'projections based on existing treaty obligations and on obligations undertaken as the result of subsequent policy decisions' (Lindberg and Scheingold 1970). He complemented their study, however, by estimations of five political scientists. Despite the largely subjective nature of the approach, Schmitter's index has been widely used by other students of European integration (see e.g. Pollack 1994; Hix 2004).
4 Pollack (1994, 2000) focuses on policy output but confuses legislation in force with legal output. While the EU provides good data on the number of legal acts adopted in each year, there is no reliable database on the legislation in force for a given year. EURLEX only reports on the number of laws that are currently in force.
5 According to the principle of conferral, the EU has no competencies by right – all its competencies are voluntarily conferred to it by its member states. As a result, any issue areas not explicitly agreed in the treaties remain the domain of the member states.

6  In his 'revised theory of regional integration', Schmitter distinguishes between scope and level, too. However, he refers to scope as the number of issues that member states decide to 'resolve jointly' and level as the authority of regional integration (Schmitter 1970). I decided to follow the definition of level advanced by Lindberg and Scheingold, since it has been widely used in the literature, including by Schmitter himself (1996).
7  For a critical view, see already Hoffmann (1982).

## REFERENCES

Boer, M. den and Wallace, W. (2000) 'Justice and home affairs', in H. Wallace and W. Wallace (eds), *Policy-Making in the European Union*, Oxford: Oxford University Press, pp. 493–519.

Börzel, T.A. and Hösli, M. (2003) 'Brussels between Bern and Berlin. Comparative federalism meets the European Union', *Governance* 16(2): 179–202.

Börzel, T.A. and Risse, T. (2004) 'Making democratic governance work! EU policies for the promotion of human rights, democracy, and the rule of law'. Paper presented for the Workshop on Democracy Promotion organized by the Center for Development, Democracy, and the Rule of Law, Stanford University, 4–5 October 2004.

De Búrca, G. (2005) 'Rethinking law in neofunctionalist theory', *Journal of European Public Policy* 12(2): 310–26.

Donohue, J.D. and Pollack, M.A. (2001) 'Centralization and its discontents: the rhythms of federalism in the United States and the European Union', in K. Nicolaidis and R. Howse (eds), *The Federal Vision: Legitimacy and Levels of Governance in the United States and the European Union*, Oxford: Oxford University Press, pp. 73–117.

Farrell, H. and Héritier, A. (2005) 'A rationalist-institutionalist explanation of endogenous regional integration', *Journal of European Public Policy* 12(2): 273–90.

Fligstein, N. and McNichol, J. (2001) 'The institutional terrain of the European Union', in W. Sandholtz and A. Stone Sweet (eds), *European Integration and Supranational Governance*, Oxford: Oxford University Press, pp. 59–91.

Forster, A. and Wallace, W. (2000) 'Common foreign and security policy: from shadow to substance', in H. Wallace and W. Wallace (eds), *Policy-Making in the European Union*, Oxford: Oxford University Press, pp. 461–91.

Haas, E.B. (1958) *The Uniting of Europe: Political, Social, and Economic Forces 1950–1957*, Stanford, CA: Stanford University Press.

Haas, E.B. (1967) '*The Uniting of Europe* and the uniting of Latin America', *Journal of Common Market Studies* 5(4): 315–43.

Hill, C. (1993) 'The capability–expectations gap, or conceptualizing Europe's international role', *Journal of Common Market Studies* 31(3): 305–28.

Hix, S. (1998) 'The study of the European Union II: the "new governance" agenda and its rival', *Journal of European Public Policy* 5(1): 38–65.

Hix, S. (2004) *The Political System of the European Union*, London: Palgrave.

Hoffmann, S. (1964) 'Europe's identity crisis: between the past and America', *Daedalus* 93(4): 1244–97.

Hoffmann, S. (1982) 'Reflections on the nation-state in Western Europe today', *Journal of Common Market Studies* 20(1–2): 29–37.

Hooghe, L. and Marks, G. (2001) *Multi-Level Governance and European Integration*, Lanham: Rowman & Littlefield.

Lindberg, L.N. and Scheingold, S.A. (1970) *Europe's Would-Be Polity*, Englewood Cliffs: Prentice-Hall.

Lowi, T.J. (1964) 'American business, public policy, case studies and political theory', *World Politics* 16(4): 677–715.

Lowi, T.J. (1967a) 'Making democracy safe for the world: national politics and foreign policy', in J.N. Rosenau (ed.), *The Domestic Sources of Foreign Policy*, New York: The Free Press, pp. 295–331.

Lowi, T.J. (1967b) 'Party, policy and constitution in America', in W.N. Chambers and W.D. Burnham (eds), *The American Political System*, New York: Oxford University Press, pp. 238–176.

Lowi, T.J. (1972) 'Four systems of policy, politics and choice', *Public Administration Review* 32(4): 298–310.

Majone, G. (1994) 'The rise of the regulatory state in Europe', *West European Politics* 17(3): 77–101.

Mattli, W. (2005) 'Ernst Hass's evolving thinking on comparative regional integration: of virtues and infelicities', *Journal of European Public Policy* 12(2): 327–48.

Mitrany, D. (1966) *A Working Peace System*, Chicago: Quadrangle Books.

Monar, J. (1997) 'European Union – justice and home affairs: a balance sheet and an agenda for reform', in G. Edwards and A. Pijpers (eds), *The Politics of European Treaty Reform: The 1996 Intergovernmental Conference and Beyond*, London: Pinter/Castell, pp. 326–39.

Moravcsik, A. (2005) 'The European Constitutional Compromise and the neofunctionalist legacy', *Journal of European Public Policy* 12(2): 349–85.

Peterson, J. (1995) 'Decision-making in the European Union: towards a framework for analysis', *Journal of European Public Policy* 2(1): 69–93.

Pollack, M.A. (1994) 'Creeping competence: the expanding agenda of the European Community', *Journal of Public Policy* 14(2): 95–145.

Pollack, M.A. (2000) 'The end of creeping competence? EU policy-making since Maastricht', *Journal of Common Market Studies* 38(3): 519–38.

Risse, T. (2005) 'Neofunctionalism, European identity, and the puzzles of European integration', *Journal of European Public Policy* 12(2): 291–309.

Rosamond, B. (2005) 'The uniting of Europe and the foundation of EU studies: revisiting the neofunctionalism of Ernst B. Haas', *Journal of European Public Policy* 12(2): 237–54.

Sbragia, A. (2004) 'Seeing the European Union through American eyes: the EU as a reflection of the American experience'. Paper presented at the Annual Meeting of the American Political Science Association, Chicago, 2–5 September 2004.

Scharpf, F.W. (1996) 'Negative and positive integration in the political economy of European welfare states', in G. Marks, F.W. Scharpf, P.C. Schmitter and W. Streeck (eds), *Governance in the European Union*, London: Sage, pp. 15–39.

Scharpf, F.W. (1997) 'Economic integration, democracy and the welfare state', *Journal of European Public Policy* 4(1): 18–36.

Scharpf, F.W. (2001) 'Notes toward a theory of multilevel governing in Europe', *Scandinavian Political Studies* 24(1): 1–26.

Scharpf, F.W. (2003) 'Legitimate diversity: the new challenge of European integration', in T.A. Börzel and R. Cichowski (eds), *The State of the European Union VI: Law, Politics, and Society*, Oxford: Oxford University Press, pp. 79–104.

Schmidt, M.G. (1999) 'Die Europäisierung der öffentlichen Aufgaben', in T. Ellwein and E. Holtmann (eds), *50 Jahre Bundesrepublik Deutschland. Rahmenbedingungen – Entwicklungsperspektiven. PVS Sonderheft 30*, Opladen: Westdeutscher Verlag, pp. 385–94.

Schmitter, P.C. (1970) 'A revised theory of regional integration', *International Organization* 24(4): 836–68.

Schmitter, P.C. (1996) 'Imagining the future of Europe with the help of the past', in G. Marks, F.W. Scharpf, P.C. Schmitter and W. Streeck (eds), *Governance in the European Union*, London: Sage, pp. 121–65.

Schmitter, P.C. (2005) 'Ernst B. Haas and the legacy of neofunctionalism', *Journal of European Public Policy* 12(2): 255–72.

Stone Sweet, A. and Sandholtz, W. (1997) 'European integration and supranational governance', *Journal of European Public Policy* 4(3): 297–317.

Wessels, W. (1997) 'An ever closer fusion? A dynamic macropolitical view on integration processes', *Journal of Common Market Studies* 35(2): 267–99.

# The uniting of Europe and the foundation of EU studies: revisiting the neofunctionalism of Ernst B. Haas

Ben Rosamond

## INTRODUCTION

Academic fields of study cannot help but tell stories about themselves. In almost every discipline or sub-discipline, we find tales about antecedents, foundation, consolidation, evolution, progress and – oftentimes – error-strewn blind alleys. It is actually rather unusual to tell these stories via detailed disciplinary histories. Normally, practitioners in given fields have a sense of how their area has developed over time and these accounts are not usually great sources of contention. After all, the cadence of academic discourse is such that we habitually view ourselves as progressing, adding to knowledge and – ultimately – correcting previous misconceptions in ways that bring us closer to a truthful understanding of our object of study. Of course, in the social sciences, we also have to contend with the probability that our very object of study may be undergoing processes of change that perhaps necessitate revisions in the way that we analyse it. Meanwhile, mainstream social science (for want of a better phrase) has long sought to deploy approaches that optimize the chance of uncovering routine dynamics and regularities, which in turn facilitate an explanatory and predictive form of enquiry.

Theoretical approaches within a field are, therefore, usually judged in terms of two sorts of criterion. The first insists that the theory is capable of asking meaningful questions about a given object, while insisting at the same time that a theory's success be judged in terms of its capacity to generate findings consistent with its derivative hypotheses. The second criterion is concerned with the theory's internal consistency and its conformity (or otherwise) to established rules of social scientific practice.

Such has been the fate of Ernst Haas's theoretical legacy to EU studies. There can be few students of the European Union (EU) who are not made aware, at least in passing, about neofunctionalist theory. It is rare to find a textbook on the subject that fails to mention it and even its most trenchant critics feel obliged still to frame their analysis in terms of the shadow cast by neofunctionalism. For many of these, neofunctionalism represents a coherent 'other' against which their own (supposedly preferable) approaches to explaining the EU and elements of European integration can be defined. The symbolic importance of Haas's neofunctionalism should – at one level – come as no surprise. It is not hyperbole to suggest that *The Uniting of Europe* (Haas 1958) represents the founding moment of the field of what we now routinely term 'EU studies'. At the same time, however, neofunctionalism is frequently represented as a theory of EU studies *past* with comparatively little to say to EU studies *present*.

This article presents a re-reading and a re-evaluation of the neofunctionalist theory within which Haas's work is so prominent. It is a re-reading that suggests Haas should be routinely revisited by students and scholars of the EU and comparative regional integration, not least because he has been mis-read to the extent that the commonplace stories told about neofunctionalism tend to draw over-exaggerated boundaries between past and present EU studies, on the one hand, and international relations (IR) and political science, on the other. In so doing they render inadmissible and under-read a remarkably rich literature as neofunctionalism is assigned a very particular, pre-historical and thus somewhat marginal place within the unfolding story of the field.

To the end of re-positioning neofunctionalism as a still salient toolkit for EU studies, this article proceeds in three broad steps. The first involves situating neofunctionalism in its appropriate social scientific context. This carries with it a number of interesting implications for how we might think about the synergies and oppositions within EU studies, but is only a partial move. Thus secondly, the paper interrogates the extent to which neofunctionalism's alleged obsolescence might be attached to an over-reliance on the notion of spillover, which in turn is said to dramatically attenuate the theory's explanatory leverage. The case here is found to be not proven. Indeed and linking with the third section, the paper emphasizes the dynamic – as opposed to static – qualities displayed by neofunctionalism in its period of ascendancy. The paper concludes two things about Haas's neofunctionalism. The first is that the conceptual repertoire of neofunctionalism still has much to say to both EU studies and to studies of comparative regionalism. The second point draws attention to the lessons that should be drawn from neofunctionalism about the ways in which an open, pluralistic EU studies might be continued.

## THE INTELLECTUAL CO-ORDINATES OF NEOFUNCTIONALISM

One route to dismissing the continuing salience of neofunctionalism in contemporary EU studies is to claim that it is a theory emanating from the discipline of IR. The case is made via a secondary claim that IR is congenitally incapable of asking appropriate questions about the EU political system where the prevailing dynamics are said to resemble the Laswellian constants in which (comparative) political science is so well versed. Moreover, because neofunctionalism is a theory of *integration* and because the day-to-day stakeholders within the EU polity are not motivated to act by a primary interest in the politics of integration, EU studies needs to be steered away from the *problematique* that generated neofunctionalist theorizing (Hix 1994). While Haas's self-definition as an IR scholar lends a degree of *prima facie* credence to the argument (see Kreisler 2000), it runs into trouble when the broader intellectual location of neofunctionalism is considered in more detail.[1] And here Haas is neatly lined up as an impeccable Weberian, as a recent evaluation of his work suggests (Ruggie *et al.* 2005). This feeds not only his particular interests – the possibility of the rational displacing the irrational in human life and the interplay between actors and ideas – but also his fundamental take on social science and its possibilities. This is crucial to a proper understanding of the intellectual space within which neofunctionalism arose. It is also important to read Haas and the neofunctionalists contextually. Like all academic projects, neofunctionalism was not solely related to its object of study (European integration/the European Communities), but also to the prevailing mores and cultures of academic discourse during its lifespan. To read the work of Haas purely from the vantage point of EU studies present runs the risk of imposing a 'presentist' reading of the theory, where our claims about the neofunctionalist project have more to do with establishing a coherent and stylized 'other', from which we – inevitably – are differentiated.

Haas described neofunctionalism as emerging as an alternate position to IR's dominant theoretical streams of the 1950s. Realism's tendency to inscribe a power-centred logic on to the international system was as problematic for Haas as liberal idealism's pretence that conflict might be transcended through the creation of a Kantian international legal order (Haas 2004: xiv). Haas's critique of this prevailing academic discourse drew fuel from two primary sources. First, there was a clear intellectual debt to the functionalist thinking of David Mitrany.[2] Haas was clearly attracted by functionalism's emphasis on the idea that post-national institution-building would/should be premised upon a technocratic engagement with human welfare needs. This helped to form an ontological claim of early neofunctionalism: that human governance was becoming a largely managerial exercise and that grand ideological narratives were on the wane (Haas 1964: 30–5; Haas 1968: xix). The most obvious point of departure from functionalism was the neofunctionalists' emphasis on the inherently *regional* quality of institution-building, as opposed to Mitrany's insistence on the flexible and variegated character of post-national institutional forms (a point noted by Mitrany (1965)). This differentiation is explained by the oft-neglected interest of neofunctionalism in the 'background conditions' that provoke institutionalized integration (discussed below).

The second departure from the recurring realist–idealist conversation is rather more significant. Haas (and his colleagues) imported a 'professionalized' social scientific mindset into their studies of European integration and it is here that the boundaries between Haas the political scientist and Haas the IR scholar become fuzzy, if not unsustainable. In this respect Haasian neofunctionalism is of the same intellectual moment that produced Karl Deutsch's transactionalist or communications approach to the integration of security communities (Deutsch 1964; Deutsch *et al.* 1957). The emphasis, in other words, is on the application of agreed intellectual precepts that together provoke a 'rigorous' approach to the construction of theory. This is transcendent of the IR of the 1950s because of its grounding in empirical investigation and its insistence that theory-derived propositions be exposed to robust empirical tests using the latest intellectual technologies. It goes beyond purely empiricist treatments of European integration because of the analytical leverage that is said to follow from a systematic approach to theory-building (see De Vree 1972; Kaiser 1965). The first edition of *The Uniting of Europe* (Haas 1958) is a densely empirical study of the early years of the European Coal and Steel Community (ECSC) and was largely treated as such by its early reviewers (see Rosamond 2000: 74). But a careful reading, particularly of chapters 1 and 8, shows how Haas was positioning his study of the ECSC as an exercise in grounding a set of general propositions about regional integration in the European experience.

Neofunctionalism is also shot through, from the outset, with a definite interest in the expectation that modern industrialized societies are characterized by a tendency towards social pluralism. In this respect Haas's initiation of neofunctionalism coincided neatly with the high tide of the new pluralist political science that so took hold of US political science in the 1950s (Haas 1964: 35–40; Haas 2004: xiv; Lindberg 1963: 9). This positioning has at least five implications for the conduct of neofunctionalist arguments. The first reinforces the argument made above about the style of social science that was inscribed into neofunctionalism from its birth. Pluralist political science does not simply describe a particular privileging of certain sorts of social actors. It is also bound up with the project to place the study of political phenomena on to ground where systematic explanation is the norm. Second, it fuelled Haas's conviction that classical IR was serially flawed. Put simply, he criticized the notion that complex modern societies are straightforwardly and permanently attuned to security imperatives with its corollary that international politics must, therefore, be nothing more than (a national) interest-based

Hobbesian anarchy. Third, it shifted investigative attention away from national executives and international exchange and towards the significance (if not necessarily the primacy) of organized interests and the role that their dynamic interaction might play in the production of integration outcomes. Fourth, the affiliation to pluralism is integral to the very understanding of integration with which Haas's work began:

> Political integration is the process whereby political actors in several distinct national settings are persuaded to shift their loyalties, expectations and political activities to a new center, whose institutions possess or demand jurisdiction over pre-existing national states. The end result is a new political community, superimposed over the pre-existing ones.
>
> (Haas 1958: 16)

Insofar as integration involved an outcome (and it is certainly worth noting Haas's emphasis on process in his definition), then Haas imagined an emergent form of political community that was at least analogous to the domestic pluralist polity. It is also important to note his preference for the phrase 'superimposed over' rather than – say – 'replacing'. This might even be read as an anticipation of the themes of the multi-level governance literature, which speaks of the EU polity in terms of co-existent and overlapping levels of political action where policy stakeholders are relatively mobile between the various tiers of governance (Hooghe and Marks 2001). The key, however, is the emphasis on the dynamism towards integration that follows from the self-regarding activities of political actors whose 'loyalties' are defined in terms of collective perceptions of how their interests might best be served. Such affiliational shifts were also characteristic of earlier functionalist reasoning, but neofunctionalists were rather more interested in the altering cognitions of collective actors than those of mass publics. The fifth implication of the neofunctionalist concern with pluralism is the built-in recognition, later teased out as neofunctionalism developed, that the propensity to integrate is greater among societies that are characterized by pluralist complexity. Here it is important to reiterate that Haas's pluralism did not lead him to conclude that social pluralism was an ever-present feature of all societies. Rather, he hypothesized that those societies characterized by pluralism would be more likely to engage in integration. Moreover, his affiliation to pluralism was emblematic of an attachment to a conception of social science that required the clear specification of variables and the postulation of testable hypotheses.

Haas admitted that the epistemological and ontological cartography of neofunctionalism was not openly acknowledged in its founding texts (Haas 2001: 29, fn 1). His last essays on the study of European integration (Haas 2001, 2004) are perhaps best read as exercises in the retrospective intellectual placement of neofunctionalism that aimed to reveal the theory's continuing salience *via-à-vis* an assortment of contemporary rivals. What Haas achieved in these papers was a very clear presentation of neofunctionalism as a variety of rationalist theory:

> Its ontology is 'soft' rational choice: social actors, in seeking to realize their value-derived interests, will choose whatever means are made available by

the prevailing democratic order. If thwarted, they will rethink their values, redefine their interests, and choose new means to realize them . . . The ontology is not materialistic: values shape interests, and values include many non-material elements.

(Haas 2004: xv)

As suggested already, neofunctionalism is a theory that relies on actors – be they social groups or institutions – taking a utilitarian approach to the fulfilment of their interests. There is obvious differentiation from harder versions of rationalism since Haas's re-presentation of neofunctionalism allows space for the endogenization of interests through ongoing interaction. Hard rational choice – described by one recent intervention as the 'normal science' of EU studies (Dowding 2000) – treats actors' preferences as (a) exogenous to interaction and (b) formally predictable, and institutional exchange as a mechanism for delivering positive sum bargains subject to the formal rules of those institutions (Haas's dispute with hard rational choice is summarized in Haas 2001: 30, fn 4). Most intriguingly, Haas used these final essays to search for affinities between neofunctionalism and (what is now labelled) constructivism. His interest in developing a 'pragmatic constructivism' (Haas 2004) out of neofunctionalism's legacy engaged his work with that of a particular breed of constructivists who – epistemologically at least – share Haas's commitment to the precepts of theory-building. It also opens for scrutiny the extent to which neofunctionalism in its heyday was a theory that took seriously the cognitions of actors to the extent that it was able to link the dynamic pursuit of objectives in conditions of societal pluralism to the capacity to change the identitive qualities of those very actors. Haas reiterated that neofunctionalism was an approach to the question of community-building (2001: 29). In that respect it shares a primary concern with Deutsch's transactionalism, an approach that has also recently become susceptible to constructivist capture (Adler and Barnett 1998). Also, the deployment of constructivist vocabulary allows neofunctionalists to cope with some of the problems that their approach to integration encountered in the light of the experience of the European Communities from the mid-1960s. Consider the following passage from Haas's essay *The Obsolescence of Regional Integration Theory*, which is often (mis)read as an obituary for neofunctionalism:

In large measure the disappointment resulted from not allowing for the possibility that actors' motives change, that interests and values considered salient and positively linked to integration may give way to different interests and to values with a more equivocal impact on integration.

(Haas 1975: 8)

The point is not necessarily that neofunctionalists failed to incorporate a theory of cognitive change into their overall approach, but that it was probably always there within their conception of loyalties, persuasion, the evolution of expectations (Haas 1958: 292) and interests.

What is also striking about the retrospective reminder that neofunctionalism belongs to the soft rationalist family tree is how this allows us to recast the supposed 'great debate' between neofunctionalism and intergovernmentalism, which many appear to take as the (unhelpfully) dominant conversation in EU studies. At a metatheoretical level neofunctionalism and intergovernmentalism (especially as systematized by Andrew Moravcsik (1998)) are pretty much indistinguishable. Haas took this somewhat further in his later essays. He playfully noted that liberal intergovernmentalism's (LI's) 'core assumptions are identical with those of [neofunctionalism] and seem quite compatible with certain kinds of constructivism as well. It is difficult to understand why he makes such extraordinary efforts to distinguish his work from those sources' (Haas 2001: 30, fn 10). Perhaps the key point here is that, from the vantage point of rethinking images of the disciplinary history of EU studies, the supposed 'great debate' between neofunctionalism and intergovernmentalism is not such a great debate after all. This paper has already suggested that neofunctionalism has been narrated into a coherent and stereotypical 'other' to allow particular claims about the appropriate disciplinary identity of EU studies to be made. It may also be the case, therefore, that (liberal) intergovernmentalism has been perhaps premature in casting neofunctionalism as its 'other' and that LI's advancement has been partly conditional on the plausibility of this claim.

## SPILLOVER: NEOFUNCTIONALISM'S INTELLECTUAL ERROR?

Moreover, if Haas was correct to suggest that the familial resemblance between constructivism and neofunctionalism is indicative of the latter's continuing salience, then the work of Haas and his associates should be reintegrated into the field and not simply be treated as a foundational approach that is talked about only as a theory from which we (in our latter day wisdom) have moved on. The foregoing is a reminder that a disciplinary history/sociology of knowledge approach to Haas's work is likely to chip away at the numerous truth claims that are made about neofunctionalism. But a full reinstatement will require a rather deeper analysis. In particular, we return here to Haas's own insistence that his approach to social science is a method of securing analytical leverage and transcending descriptive empiricism.

The neofunctionalist project was from the outset a comparative exercise in regional integration theory. The explicit purpose of the neofunctionalists was to utilize the pioneering European experience of integration to generate hypotheses for testing in other contexts. In short, the plan was to develop not a theory of European integration, but to arrive at a more generic portfolio of propositions about the dynamics of integration in any context (Barrera and Haas 1969; Haas 1961, 1967; Haas and Schmitter 1964). Without this capacity for application beyond the European case, neofunctionalism would become nothing more than (at best) an exercise in dense description. N would be 1 and, as a result, alternative methods of securing analytical leverage would need to be found.[3] The primary problem that is often used to show why neofunctionalism failed in this enterprise is that (again at best) neofunctionalism discovered a series of dynamics that were able to account for the early years of European integration (roughly 1950–1965), but then emphatically failed to account for the evolution of the Communities thereafter. In addition, because these dynamics were specific – both temporally and spatially – there was no way in which neofunctionalism could operate as a general theory.

At the core of this problem, it seems, was Haas's discovery in *The Uniting of Europe* of the process of 'spillover'.[4] Spillover was originally used to capture the process through which the expectations of social actors shifted in the direction of support for further integration. Haas described how key social groups within national contexts came to support deeper and more expansive integration. New supranational institutions became focal points for such actors, not least because these actors were able to envisage these new centres of authority as potential suppliers of outcomes that were consistent with their preferences (Haas 1958: 292). Haas also concluded from his study of the ECSC that an initial decision to integrate was likely to spawn pressures for deeper and wider integration. Moreover, this would happen independently of any overt ideological preference for 'more Europe':

> Sector integration . . . begets its own impetus toward extension to the entire economy even in the absence of specific group demands and their attendant ideologies. Thus, ECSC civil servants speaking for national governments have constantly found it necessary to 'harmonize' their separate policies in order to make it possible for the integrated sectors to function, without necessarily implying any ideological commitment to the European idea.
>
> (Haas 1958: 297)

Spillover was suggestive of automaticity – the idea that the logic of integration is somehow self-sustaining, rational and teleological. In this respect, Haas was arguing along the same lines as emerging theorists of economic integration (notably Balassa (1962)) who saw a decision to initiate a free trade area as potentially unleashing a set of logics that might culminate eventually in the total merger of hitherto discrete national economies overseen by centralized institutions of economic governance. The idea of spillover as an automatic process was reinforced with Leon Lindberg's more formalized definition, which

> refers to a situation in which a given action, related to a specific goal, creates a situation in which the original goal can be assured only by taking further actions, which in turn create a further condition and a need for more action, and so forth.
>
> (Lindberg 1963: 10)

It has often been said that neofunctionalism contained within itself a conception of 'cultivated spillover' (Tranholm-Mikkelsen 1991), that is a specific theory of how, once created, supranational institutions act as strategic advocates on behalf of functional linkage and deeper/wider integration. The idea does not feature as heavily as is sometimes supposed. There are hints in Lindberg's idea that the actions of the new institutions create situations that are only resolvable through spillover (1963: 11). In his essay 'International integration: the European and the universal process', Haas (1961) thought through the circumstances in which contracting national governments would not default to lowest common denominator outcomes. One such condition would be an act of delegation by those governments of a measure of authority to an institution, whose mission would be 'inherently expansive' (Haas 1961: 376). The key to provoking spillover dynamics, as Haas later noted, is the exposure of a sector or a set of tasks to supranational control (Haas 2004: xxi). The initial assumption of both Haas and Lindberg was that the spillover process was inherently expansive and irreversible.

While Haas (1958) and Lindberg (1963) were able to argue that they had detected evidence of spillover within the European Communities, the assumption of automaticity appeared to run into severe empirical trouble in light of the Gaullist recalibration of the European Community into a more overtly intergovernmental direction. Moreover, and perhaps more tellingly as a test of the theoretical purchase of neofunctionalism, spillover appeared to be a phenomenon that was entirely local to the European context. Joseph Nye (1971) expressed the problem in terms of the probability that neofunctionalism had unearthed a genuine phenomenon, but one that was utterly specific to the case and not at all generic to processes of regional integration. A logical extension would be to suggest that a theory with spillover at its core could not survive in the competition to develop a general explanation of integration worldwide.

This line of thinking is reinforced somewhat if we contemplate the circumstances in which neofunctionalism secured a mini-revival during the late 1980s and early 1990s (see *inter alia* Mutimer 1989; Tranholm-Mikkelsen 1991). The so-called *relance* of the integration project under the jurisdiction of the Delors Commission seemed to suggest that spillovers were once again occurring. However, this partial revival did not overcome the objection that spillover was a European specificity, thereby underscoring neofunctionalism's dubious credentials as a theory of integration. Haas (1971) himself acknowledged this problem long before this partial rediscovery of his theoretical apparatus. Nor did it take into account the substantial amount of work undertaken by neofunctionalists in general and Philippe Schmitter (1971, 2004) in particular to refine the concept in ways that took account of the possibility of disintegrative dynamics taking hold and decoupled the ideas of spillover and automaticity.

However, a careful re-reading of the development of neofunctionalist thinking casts a degree of doubt upon the notion that the lack of spillover elsewhere somehow destroys the potential of the theory. Here it is useful to look at those contributions of Haas and others that endeavoured to look beyond the European case and think about the probabilities of regional integration taking hold (or not as the case may be) elsewhere. At this point there is a very clear recognition, within *early* neofunctionalism, that spillover is to be treated as an empirical phenomenon that is found (probably) only in the European Communities. The question then becomes, why did spillover take hold in the European context? As David Mutimer (1989) notes, there is a presupposition in this literature that spillover takes hold only within a set of specified conditions, namely situations where there is an *a priori* interdependence between the component economies. Charles Pentland (1973: 119) reinforces this replacement of the concept of spillover by describing it as 'merely an organizing concept or hypothesis about the likelihood of integration when certain specified conditions are met'.

In other words, the real action in 1960s/1970s neofunctionalism was the search for candidate independent variables that might help scholars to assess the likelihood of either (a) the initiation of regional integration or (b) the success or failure of integration schemes that were already set in motion. Thus the 'failure' of first wave regional integration to take off in the manner of the European Communities was much less of a problem for neofunctionalists than might be imagined. Philippe Schmitter recently pointed out that the capacity to explain non- or dis-integrative outcomes is a unique feature of neofunctionalism in its original guise (Schmitter 2004: 47), and notice how Haas presented the impasse of Latin American integration as a success for neofunctionalism:

> We predicted successfully that regional integration would not readily occur in Latin America and I explained in the preface of *The Uniting of Europe*, 1968 edition, that the explanatory power of NF [neofunctionalism] in leading to new political communities was confined to settings characterised by industrialised economies, full political mobilisation via strong interest groups and political parties, leadership by political elites competing for political dominance under rules of constitutional democracy accepted by leaders and followers.
>
> (Haas 2001: 29–30, fn 2)

In Haas and Schmitter's careful restatement of neofunctionalism, we find a clear hypothesized explanation of why spillover occurs in some situations of integration but not in others. The Haas–Schmitter typology suggests that certain unions are more prone to automaticity and politicization (i.e. to spillover) and that the explanation resides in a cluster of background variables that account not only for motivations to initiate integration schemes, but also for the likelihood of spillover dynamics setting in once initiation has commenced. Thus scholars are directed to the *ongoing* examination of these background variables (rates of transaction between participating units, the adaptability of participant actors to moments of crisis and the prevalence or otherwise within participating units of bureaucratic styles of decision-making) (Haas and Schmitter 1964: 718).

The exploration of 'background conditions' is embedded in some of Haas's earlier work on the subject (e.g. Haas 1961), where societal pluralism, high levels of economic development and ideological convergence among participating units appear as crucial precursors for the formation of regional integration schemes. Having said this, the early attempts at theorizing background conditions did tend towards treating spillover dynamics as a kind of dependent variable (Barrera and Haas 1969; Haas and Schmitter 1964). In other words, the search for reliable independent causal mechanisms was premised on the idea that what was to be explained was the functional and political linkages through which the remit of integration would expand and deepen. The conflation of integration and spillover does appear to have been a problematic quality of a good deal of neofunctionalist work, but a recovery of Haas's original (much less determinate) definition of integration would imply that there could be a disassociation of the dependent variable from localized European discoveries. In particular, as Haas (1971) noted, the recasting of the dependent variable of integration theory as the creation of some form of post-national community could be explained by independent variables other than those originally ascribed by neofunctionalists to the European case. In short, integration theory/neofunctionalism should (a) open itself to numerous possible independent causal mechanisms and (b) think of its dependent variable as 'putative' (1971: 27) and non-teleological. Both *explanans* and *explanadum* could be divorced from their Eurocentric grounding and neofunctionalist reasoning could still prevail. This would necessitate a re-focusing of the neofunctionalist project on to its foundational tenets: that integration (whatever its destination) was an instrumentally driven process that proceeded through the prosaic interactions of stakeholders whose perceptions, cognitions, values and loyalties might change in the course of that interaction.[5]

## THE DYNAMISM OF NEOFUNCTIONALISM

There is a temptation to develop presentational 'snapshots' of theoretical perspectives, where we list a series of foundational propositions, which are then amenable to some form of external critique. The foregoing has already hinted that such a reductionist approach to neofunctionalism carries with it the danger of (a) misreading the intentions of its practitioners and (b) simplifying an otherwise rich and textured theory. To these perils must be added the problem of presenting neofunctionalism as a static theory, thereby ignoring its almost pathological tendency towards autocritique. This is yet another reason why it is important to understand neofunctionalism's epistemological roots. It is precisely because Haas and his colleagues allied themselves explicitly to Weberian social scientific norms that they practised ongoing self-reflection and thought very carefully about the limitations of and the necessary refinements to their theory of regional integration.

We have noted already how Haas and others worked hard to distinguish the empirical discovery of spillover in Europe from the general propositions of their theory. What strikes the reader of these works now is how this group of scholars managed to re-evaluate and reiterate core neofunctionalist ideas in spite of profound empirical and epistemological challenges. This section examines three moments where the dynamic and reflexive qualities of Haas's theory became apparent: the empirical challenges to neofunctionalism posed by the 'Gaullist moment' in the Communities that commenced in the mid-1960s, the extensive epistemological self-critiques of the early 1970s and Haas's heroic attempt towards the end of his life to reinstate neofunctionalist theories of regional integration into academic discourse.

Stanley Hoffmann's (1966) intergovernmentalist engagement with integration theory is probably the best-known example of neofunctionalism coming under sustained pressure. Hoffmann's lengthy critique commenced with a demonstration that de Gaulle's ascendancy as a dramatic actor within the Communities provided evidence of the enduring qualities of national interests and nationalist sentiment, both of which were – in Hoffmann's reading – neglected or by-passed in neofunctionalist reasoning. Along with the later, more social science-oriented intervention of Roger Hansen (1969), Hoffmann developed an argument that emphasized the hard barriers between 'low', technocratic politics and 'high' politics, where non-negotiable issues of national interest came into play. Hence the neofunctionalist prediction of the politicization of functional integration was seriously questioned. To this Hansen added arguments about neofunctionalism's neglect of the role of external structural imperatives in shaping member-state preferences in the direction of positive sum integrationist bargains. He also hypothesized that societal pluralism – for neofunctionalists a precondition of integration – could be responsible for retarding integrative progress as sophisticated societies are better able to receive messages about potential threats (such as those posed by supranational institutions) to their integrity.

Haas worked through many of these objections in the author's preface to the second edition of *The Uniting of Europe* (Haas 1968). While he regretted the apparent bracketing of national sentiment in the original formulation of his theory, he did note that the original technocratic/'end of ideology' assumptions had brought forward the important observation that the idea of 'the nation' was not fixed and immutable (Haas 1968: xiv). Moreover, the impact of de Gaulle in the mid-1960s merely served to illustrate the absence of such 'dramatic actors' at the Communities' point of origin (Haas 1968: xxiv). The institutional and strategic design of the ECSC was inscribed with functionalist, incrementalist and technocratic logics because these were the prevailing ideas of the time. Also, Haas admitted that pluralism is not a static condition and that complex European societies had undergone significant change in the decade and a half that had elapsed since the Treaty of Paris. This meant that societal expectations would develop autonomously of the growth of the Communities and thereby have the capacity to exercise independent effects upon the integration process as it evolved (Haas 1968: xv). Finally, and in anticipation of Hansen's arguments, Haas took the first steps in acknowledging the significance of exogenous stimuli upon the conduct of integration and the constituent states of the Communities. His point – again underlining neofunctionalism's departure from classical IR – was that the imperatives set by the global security structure of the 1940s/1950s did not amount to a sufficient condition for the institutional choices made by European actors at the time (Haas 1968: xiv–xv). He later extended the analysis of external conditions to postulate that variable (perceptions of) exogenous contexts might help to explain why different integration projects might take alternative pathways (Haas 1975, 1976).

Therefore, critiques of the early intergovernmentalist variety allowed neofunctionalists like Haas to clarify their propositions. It is striking how Haas responded to his critics by reasserting the significance of societal, external and ideational preconditions of integration. In so doing he laid the ground for (a) the reorientation of neofunctionalism as a theory of 'background conditions, (b) Schmitter's (1971) efforts to perfect neofunctionalism as a theory of disintegration as much as integration, and (c) Nye's (1971) interest in 'perceptual' background conditions.

Neofunctionalism's second moment of auto-critique was centred around Lindberg and Scheingold's edited volume *Regional Integration: Theory and Research* (Lindberg and Scheingold 1971), a project evidently designed not to plug the holes in a leaky theory, but rather to take it to a new level of analytical sophistication (Rosamond 2000: 86). Haas's personal contribution to the project (Haas 1971) was, as ever, vital. Aside from his hugely important dissection of the dependent variable problem (discussed above), Haas showed how there was an inherent tension between (a) the logic of spillover and the attendant presupposition of the politicization of the integration process and (b) the continuing emphasis on integration as a process inspired by short-run interest fulfilment and shaped by 'muddling through' rather than grand designs and dramatic political acts. The logic of (a) would suggest the downgrading of (b), yet (b) was given primacy in the neofunctionalist account because it helped to explain both conditions of foundation and the conduct of actors once the institutional arena was functioning.

In this respect Haas was joined by others in conceptualizing integration in political systemic terms. This was always present in neofunctionalist writings, a fact that seems to have been forgotten (see Rosamond 2004 for a more detailed argument). Haas's initial definition of political integration (quoted above) together with Lindberg's own brand of neofunctionalism (Lindberg 1965, 1967) tied together notions of integration and system. The common denominator, yet again, was the consequence of societal pluralism and incrementalism as a prevailing political condition. Thus social complexity is not only a background condition; it also defines the parameters of action within a regional integration project once initiated. Lindberg and Scheingold's (1970) Eastonian take on the European Communities explored the conditions by which integrative dynamics might be extended to new sectors and how more expansive networks of actors might be drawn into the web of integration. Meanwhile Haas's concept of 'turbulent fields' (Haas 1976) applied to the Community system a form of policy analysis that anticipated integrative solutions to dilemmas arising in contexts where self-regarding actors operated in a climate of perpetual complexity and imperfect knowledge.

In short, neofunctionalism remained true to its roots as a critique of IR ortho-doxies. Its appropriation of political science and policy analytic ideas of pluralism and incrementalism enabled it – eventually – to reach a plateau where the generic sources of integration could be hypothesized and where the once rather 'Whiggish' idea of spillover was not only subsumed, but also refined to the extent that it became associated with explanation of how actors engineer greater mutual interdependencies. Thus, contrary to some later claims about neofunctionalism, it aspired by the mid-1970s to offer analytical leverage in two comparative directions. The first involved a capacity to formulate a revised theory of regional integration and the second showed the way to thinking about how systemic environments should be conceptualized in conditions of complexity.

Also apparent was a growing recognition of cognitive and ideational variables as key to understanding integrative processes. It is fitting, therefore, that Haas's final contributions to EU studies (2001, 2004) should devote themselves to exploring the connections between neofunctionalism and constructivism. This matter is dealt with elsewhere in this special issue, but for the sake of this paper's argument it is worth emphasizing that Haas's neofunctionalism was shot through with an interest in cognitions, perceptions, the sociological dimensions of institutionalized interaction and what we would now label intersubjectivities.

Having said that, the attempt to consummate some sort of metatheoretical union between constructivism and mature neofunctionalism does present diffi-culties, which – for some – are likely to pose profound problems. In the first place, neofunctionalism and constructivism are different varieties of theory in that the latter is a 'first principles' claim about the social (as opposed to ration-alistic) status of interaction. Thus there are obvious and potentially irresolvable oppositions at an ontological level between theoretical treatments of integration that follow from constructivist premises (see Christiansen *et al.* 2001; Risse 2004) and varieties of rationalist theory (such as neofunctionalism and inter-governmentalism). Perhaps Haas's late moves to look for points of reconciliation between the two approaches can be read as consistent with the claim made by some (notably Fearon and Wendt (2002)) that, while ontological differences between rationalists and constructivists remain deep and insoluble, there is nevertheless a case for the pragmatic 'bracketing' of these metatheoretical disagreements.

## CONCLUSIONS

This paper has tried to offer a re-evaluation of neofunctionalist thinking, paying particular attention to the contributions made by Haas. The core argument, stated simply, is that stereotypical constructions of neofunctional-ism tend to (a) place the theory firmly in a camp labelled IR and (b) treat neofunctionalism rather too statically. The intention here has been to tease out ways in which neofunctionalism continues to speak relevantly to contemporary

EU studies. A re-reading of the work of Haas and his various collaborators and associates is essential to show that the story of neofunctionalism is better told as a tale of theory-building and evaluation that resonates with long-established social scientific norms. The twin ideas that it was defeated by the unravelling realities of the European Communities and a drastic loss of analytical leverage deserve (at the very least) to come under sustained scrutiny. Aside from the obvious bridges between neofunctionalism *circa* 1958–1976 and twenty-first century treatments of the EU polity such as multi-level governance and historical and sociological institutionalism, there are two further lessons to be drawn.

First, if the re-inspection of Haas's work reveals that – in his words – neofunctionalism 'is no longer obsolescent' (Haas 2004: liii), then the candidacy of neofunctionalism for reinstatement within theories of comparative regionalism should be seriously considered. The latter has recently undergone something of a revival, but within this academic discourse neofunctionalism has been treated very much as a component of the 'old' (as opposed to the 'new') regionalism. As Alex Warleigh has recently argued (Warleigh 2004), the drawing of hard boundaries between these two phases of regional integration studies parallels the processes of differentiation that this paper cautions against. The second lesson is more localized to EU studies. The recovery of neofunctionalism from its reputation as a failed academic experiment is rather more than an exercise in academic excavation. The fact that it was buried in the first place is indicative of a tendency within the present scholarly community to produce narratives of the field's history that draw robust boundaries between past errors and present rigour. In the wrong hands this can induce all manner of closures and the establishment of claims that effectively outlaw particular kinds of work. Beyond its (recovered) analytical salience, neofunctionalism was/is a remarkably open-minded intellectual project that drew sustenance from across the spectrum of the social sciences. In this regard, there is no better exemplar for scholars of the EU than Ernst Haas.

**Address for correspondence:** Ben Rosamond, Department of Politics and International Studies, University of Warwick, Coventry CV4 7AL, UK. Tel: +44 (0)24 765 24461. Fax: (0)24 765 24221. email: b.j.rosamond@ warwick.ac.uk


## ACKNOWLEDGEMENTS

I am grateful for the comments on an earlier draft of this article by an anonymous referee and Tanja Börzel. Others who have helped to formulate, clarify and (occasionally) endorse my thoughts on neofunctionalism include Maura Adshead, Ernst B. Haas, Knud Erik Jørgensen, Ian Manners, Alberta Sbragia, Philippa Sherrington, Helen Wallace, Alex Warleigh and Daniel Wincott.

## NOTES

1  The caricature of IR that emerges in such critiques of neofunctionalism is also
   deeply problematic, but largely beyond the scope of this paper (see Rosamond
   2000: ch. 7; Rosamond 2004 for more detailed arguments). Haas himself seemed
   perplexed and somewhat irritated by the debate about whether IR or comparative
   political science should be the appropriate parent discipline of EU studies – a
   debate he dismissed as 'silly' (Haas 2004: xvi, fn 4).
2  Mitrany's work on functionalism spanned some four decades. Many of his key
   works on the subject are gathered in Mitrany (1975).
3  Hix's (1994) rejection of integration theory together with the research agenda
   endorsed by the relatively new journal *European Union Politics* should be read as
   one way in which the *sui generis*, n = 1 dilemma can be resolved. By changing
   the co-ordinates of EU studies to think of the EU as a political system of the sort
   familiar to seasoned political scientists, numerous comparators (i.e. other political
   systems) come to the fore.
4  I note *en passant* that the term 'spillover' does not feature in the index of *The Uniting
   of Europe*.
5  Perhaps the most systematic attempt to re-state neofunctionalist premises in these
   terms is provided by Nye (1971).

## REFERENCES

Adler, E. and Barnett, M. (1998) 'Security communities in theoretical perspective', in
   E. Adler and M. Barnett (eds), *Security Communities*, Cambridge: Cambridge
   University Press, pp. 3–28.
Balassa, B. (1962) *The Theory of Economic Integration*, London: Allen & Unwin.
Barrera, M. and Haas, E.B. (1969) 'The operationalization of some variables related to
   regional integration: a research note', *International Organization* 23(1): 150–60.
Christiansen, T., Jørgensen, K.E. and Wiener, A. (2001) 'Introduction', in
   T. Christiansen, K.E. Jørgensen and A. Wiener (eds), *The Social Construction of
   Europe*, London: Sage, pp. 1–19.
Deutsch, K.W. (1964) 'Communication theory and political integration', in P.E. Jacob
   and J.V. Toscano (eds), *The Integration of Political Communities*, Philadelphia:
   J.P. Lippincott & Co., pp. 46–74.
Deutsch, K.W. *et al.* (1957) *Political Community in the North Atlantic Area: Inter-
   national Organization in the Light of Historical Experience*, Princeton: Princeton
   University Press.
De Vree, J.K. (1972) *Political Integration: The Formation of Theory and its Problems*, The
   Hague: Mouton.
Dowding, K. (2000) 'Institutional research on the European Union: a critical review',
   *European Union Politics* 1(1): 125–44.
Fearon, J. and Wendt, A. (2002) 'Rationalism v. constructivism: a skeptical view', in
   W. Carlsnaes, T. Risse and B.A. Simmons (eds), *Handbook of International Relations*,
   London: Sage, pp. 52–72.
Haas, E.B. (1958) *The Uniting of Europe: Political, Social and Economic Forces,
   1950–1957*, Stanford: Stanford University Press.
Haas, E.B. (1961) 'International integration: the European and the universal process',
   *International Organization* 15(3): 366–92.
Haas, E.B. (1964) *Beyond the Nation State: Functionalism and International Organi-
   zation*, Stanford: Stanford University Press.
Haas, E.B. (1967) '*The Uniting of Europe* and the "Uniting of Latin America"', *Journal
   of Common Market Studies* 5(4): 315–43.

Haas, E.B. (1968) *The Uniting of Europe: Politics, Social and Economic Forces, 1950–1957*, 2nd edn, Stanford: Stanford University Press.

Haas, E.B. (1971) 'The study of regional integration: reflections on the joy and anguish of pretheorizing', in L.N. Lindberg and S.A. Scheingold (eds), *Regional Integration: Theory and Research*, Cambridge: Harvard University Press, pp. 3–42.

Haas, E.B. (1975) *The Obsolescence of Regional Integration Theory*, working paper, Berkeley: Institute of International Studies.

Haas, E.B. (1976) 'Turbulent fields and the study of international integration', *International Organization* 30(2): 173–212.

Haas, E.B. (2001) 'Does constructivism subsume neo-functionalism?', in T. Christiansen, K.E. Jørgensen and A. Wiener (eds), *The Social Construction of Europe*, London: Sage, pp. 22–31.

Haas, E.B. (2004) 'Introduction: Institutionalism or constructivism?', in *The Uniting of Europe: Politics, Social and Economic Forces, 1950–1957*, 3rd edn, Notre Dame: University of Notre Dame Press, pp. xiii–lvi.

Haas, E.B. and Schmitter, P.C. (1964) 'Economics and differential patterns of integration: projections about unity in Latin America', *International Organization* 18(4): 705–37.

Hansen, R.D. (1969) 'European integration: reflections on a decade of theoretical efforts', *World Politics* 21(2): 242–71.

Hix, S. (1994) 'The study of the European Community: the challenge to comparative politics', *West European Politics* 17(1): 1–30.

Hoffmann, S. (1966) 'Obstinate or obsolete? The fate of the nation-state and the case of Western Europe', *Daedalus* 95(3): 862–915.

Hooghe, L. and Marks, G. (2001) *Multi-Level Governance and European Integration*, Lanham: Rowman & Littlefield.

Kaiser, K. (1965) 'L'Europe des savants: European integration and the social sciences', *Journal of Common Market Studies* 4(1): 36–47.

Kreisler, H. (2000) 'Science and progress in international relations: conversation with Ernest B. Haas', October 30, http://globetrotter.berkeley.edu/people/Haas/haas-con0.html (accessed on 19 October 2004).

Lindberg, L.N. (1963) *The Political Dynamics of European Economic Integration*, Stanford: Stanford University Press.

Lindberg, L.N. (1965) 'Decision-making and integration in the European Community', *International Organization* 19(1): 56–80.

Lindberg, L.N. (1967) 'The European Community as a political system: notes toward the construction of a model', *Journal of Common Market Studies* 5(4): 344–87.

Lindberg, L.N. and Scheingold, S.A. (1970) *Europe's Would-Be Polity: Patterns of Change in the European Community*, Englewood Cliffs: Prentice-Hall.

Lindberg, L.N. and Scheingold, S.A. (eds) (1971) *Regional Integration: Theory and Research*, Cambridge: Harvard University Press.

Mitrany, D. (1965) 'The prospect of integration: federal or functional?', *Journal of Common Market Studies* 4(2): 119–49.

Mitrany, D. (1975) *The Functional Theory of Politics*, London: Martin Robertson.

Moravcsik, A. (1998) *The Choice for Europe: Social Purpose and State Power from Messina to Maastricht*, Ithaca: Cornell University Press.

Mutimer, D. (1989) '1992 and the political integration of Europe: neofunctionalism reconsidered', *Journal of European Integration* 13(4): 75–101.

Nye, J.S. (1971) 'Comparing common markets: a revised neofunctionalist model', in L.N. Lindberg and S.A. Scheingold (eds), *Regional Integration: Theory and Research*, Cambridge, MA: Harvard University Press, pp. 192–231.

Pentland, C. (1973) *International Theory and European Integration*, London: Faber & Faber.

Risse, T. (2004) 'Social constructivism and European integration', in A. Wiener and T. Diez (eds), *European Integration Theory*, Oxford: Oxford University Press, pp. 159–76.

Rosamond, B. (2000) *Theories of European Integration*, Basingstoke and New York: Macmillan/St Martin's Press.

Rosamond, B. (2004) '(European) integration theory, EU studies, disciplinary history and the sociology of knowledge', Department of Politics and International Studies, University of Warwick, mimeo.

Ruggie, J.G., Katzenstein, P.J., Keohane, R.O. and Schmitter, P.C. (2005) 'Transformations in world politics: the intellectual contributions of Ernst B. Haas', *Annual Review of Political Science* (forthcoming).

Schmitter, P.C. (1971) 'A revised theory of regional integration', in L.N. Lindberg and S.A. Scheingold (eds), *Regional Integration: Theory and Research*, Cambridge, MA: Harvard University Press, pp. 232–64.

Schmitter, P.C. (2004) 'Neo-neo-functionalism?', in A. Wiener and T. Diez (eds), *European Integration Theory*, Oxford: Oxford University Press, pp. 45–74.

Tranholm-Mikkelsen, J. (1991) 'Neofunctionalism: obstinate or obsolete?', *Millennium: Journal of International Studies* 20(1): 1–22.

Warleigh, A. (2004) 'Towards a conceptual framework for regionalization: a research agenda to bridge new regionalism and integration theory'. Political Studies Association of Ireland, Annual Conference, Limerick, 15–17 October.

# Ernst B. Haas and the legacy of neofunctionalism

Philippe C. Schmitter

In Europe, the scholarly reputation of Ernst B. Haas is inseparably linked to the vicissitudes of something called 'neofunctionalism'. Although during his long career at the University of California at Berkeley he wrote about many other things – learning and institutional transformation in global international organizations and, most prominently, nationalism (Haas 1964, 1997/2000) – it is as the founding father of a distinct approach (he always insisted that it was not a theory) to explaining the dynamics of the process of European integration that he is so well known. While his recent death has deprived scholars working in this field of one of its most original and creative minds, it has to be said that, except for a recent preface to the new edition of his seminal contribution, *The Uniting of Europe*, Haas had made no contribution to neofunctionalism for over thirty years (see the preface to Haas 2004).

As a doctoral student returning to the continent from whence he had fled as a young man, Haas chose to write his dissertation on the European Coal and Steel Community (ECSC). In doing so, he took a considerable risk since the ECSC was an obscure organization that did not fit comfortably within the established categories of the discipline of international relations at the time. 'Realistically' speaking, it should not have existed. 'Idealistically' speaking, it must have seemed irrelevant alongside the much more prominent and promising specialized functional agencies of the United Nations. To my knowledge, Haas never explained specifically why he selected the ECSC. Somehow, as he states in the preface to *The Uniting of Europe*, he recognized that it alone was '*a priori* capable of redirecting the loyalties and expectations of political actors' (Haas 1958).

His interest, however, in the potentiality for integration in Western Europe was shared by others. Indeed, until relatively recently, theory-driven treatments of the subject have been a virtual monopoly of a unique generation of Euro-American scholars – Europeans who had been driven from their various homelands in the old continent to the new one – and who had found there an academic setting that was congenial to such speculation. Karl Deutsch and Stanley Hoffmann come to mind, along with Ernst Haas (see Deutsch *et al.* 1957; Hoffmann 1960).[1] Each fostered a different approach to the topic, but all harboured the same normative objective: how to conceive, design and guide the process of regional integration so that it would transform the European state system in such a way as to make war between its sovereign units impossible. Each, without doubt, thought of himself as an objective and empirical social scientist, but all directed their knowledge to an even higher collective purpose.

## ONE ECLECTIC APPROACH

Haas's approach was, if nothing else, eclectic. From Columbia University where he did his graduate study, he was exposed to the standard literature on international law and organization that was manifestly inadequate for understanding the novelty of Europe's regional integration. He found the potential answer in a synthesis of David Mitrany's conception of 'functionalism' and Jean Monnet's pragmatic strategy for running the ECSC and developing it into the European Economic Community (EEC) – both forerunners of the present European Union (EU). Haas transformed the technocratic vision that Mitrany had of an expanding world system of functionally specialized global organizations run by experts into a political conception of how co-operation was possible on the basis of competing and colluding sub-national, non-state interests. While he never denied the role played by national states pursuing their (allegedly) unitary interests, he was among the first to realize that, by liberalizing flows of trade, investment and persons across previously well-protected borders, regional integration had the potential to transform the inter-state system that had long characterized Europe and been responsible for two recent World Wars. Once he began his extensive schedule of interviews with the actors involved in the ECSC, he inevitably came into contact with Jean Monnet. As he abundantly demonstrates in his *Mémoires*, Monnet was devoted to the task of eliminating the risk of war in Europe and that meant defusing the antagonism between France and Germany (Monnet 1976). After trying and failing to promote direct routes to this end – federalism and military unification – he had hit upon a second-best indirect solution: integrate the two industrial sectors that would be necessary in the event of any future conflict, i.e. coal and steel. With the Marshall Plan and the Organization for European Economic Co-operation (OEEC) behind him and the United States government beside him, he managed to cajole six countries not only into forming the ECSC, but also into endowing its Secretary-General with very modest supranational powers, a position he subsequently occupied. What Haas did initially in his *The Uniting of Europe* (2004) and subsequently and more systematically in his *Beyond the Nation-State* (1964) was to explore the implications (and limits) of this second-best strategy – nicely summarized in Monnet's phrase '*petits pas, grands effets*'.

Neofunctionalism has always been difficult to classify in disciplinary terms, because it intersects the usual assumptions of international relations and comparative politics. It recognizes the importance of national states, especially in the foundation of regional organizations and at subsequent moments of formal re-foundation by treaty, yet it places major emphasis on the role of two sets of non-state actors in providing the dynamic for further integration: (1) the 'secretariat' of the organization involved; and (2) those interest associations and social movements that form around it at the level of the region. Member states may set the terms of the initial agreement and do what they can to control subsequent events, but they do not exclusively determine the direction, extent and pace of change. Rather, regional bureaucrats in league with a shifting set of self-organized interests and passions seek to exploit the inevitable 'unintended consequences' that occur when states agree to assign some degree of supranational responsibility for accomplishing a limited task and then discover that satisfying that function has external effects upon other of their interdependent activities. Haas captured this potentiality dramatically with his concept of 'spill-over'. He hypothesized that, with the help of an active and resourceful secretariat and support from the organized interests affected by such externalities, national governments might (fitfully) learn and (reluctantly) agree to change their original positions. According to this approach, integration is an intrinsically sporadic and conflictual process, but one in which, under conditions of democracy and pluralistic representation, national governments will find themselves increasingly entangled in regional pressures and end up resolving their conflicts by conceding a wider scope and devolving more authority to the regional organizations they have created. Eventually, their citizens will begin shifting more and more of their expectations to the region and satisfying them will increase the likelihood that economic-social integration will 'spill-over' into political integration.

Needless to say, neofunctionalism as articulated by Haas had no specific temporal component. How long it would take for these functional interdependencies to become manifest, for affected interests and passions to organize themselves across national borders and for officials in the regional secretariat to come up with projects that would expand their tasks and authority was left undetermined. Unfortunately for its reception by scholars, many assumed that Haas had claimed that spill-overs would occur automatically and in close, linear sequence to each other. Even a cursory reading, especially of his more systematic presentation in *Beyond the Nation-State*, would have demonstrated these to be fallacious inferences. Moreover, while he did hint at which specific changes had to intervene before spill-over would occur: increase in economic interdependence between member countries, crises of sufficient magnitude due to unintended consequences, development of political competence and autonomy for intervention by regional bureaucrats and emergence of interest associations capable of acting on the regional level independent of national constraints, he never transformed them into explicit hypotheses. Subsequent scholars who only gave his work a superficial reading could complain that Haas had not addressed the crucial question of what contextual conditions were necessary for spill-over to take place. Needless to say, when the integration process in Europe proved to be more controversial, to take more time and to make less continuous progress than expected, his theory was repeatedly declared 'disconfirmed', or 'underspecified'.

## TWO GENERIC SUPPOSITIONS

First, before turning to an evaluation of the past demerits and possible future merits of the way that neofunctionalism attempts to link economic and political integration, we should specify the presuppositions that all approaches/theories of European integration have in common:

1 The process of European integration will be consensual in that no actor – national, sub- or supranational – is likely to use physical force or organized violence to bring about the rules, institutions or policies it prefers. Old-fashioned realists may wince at this, but the EC/EU does constitute a 'pluralistic security community', in the sense of Karl Deutsch (Deutsch *et al.* 1957),[2] within which this strategic alternative is not contemplated by any of its member states, and probably could not be threatened or applied. The same constraint, needless to say, does not necessarily hold for integration processes elsewhere.
2 The actors in the process of European integration will remain for the foreseeable future independent in the formation of their preferences and disregarding of the welfare of each other. In other words, the basic problem is how to make 'Europe without Europeans'. If one could presume that its states, peoples or individuals cared sufficiently about each others' welfare that they would not distinguish it from their own, none of the existing approaches would hold.

## SEVEN WORKING ASSUMPTIONS

Now, let us look briefly at a few of neofunctionalism's most distinctive features. There is no need to provide a full exposition since this has already been done and is readily available in the introductory chapters of Haas's *Beyond the Nation-State* (Haas 1964, also 1958).[3] The following maxims are not necessarily unique to its way of looking at integration processes. Some of them have been subsequently 'borrowed' and inserted into other more ambitious and abstract theories. Taken as a whole, however, they represent a quite considerable critique of the dominant modes of thinking about international relations, in particular, and about political power, influence and bargaining, in general.

1  *States* are not the exclusive and may no longer be the predominant actors in the regional/international system. The fact that they do possess residual sovereignty and, therefore, are the formal co-signatories of the treaties that typically constitute and punctuate the integration process is potentially illusory in that:

A.  Their commitment to treaty terms rests on an imagined predominance of national interest that most likely reflects only a temporary equilibrium among the conflicting interests of classes, sectors, professions, parties, social movements, ethnic groups, etc.;

B.  Their presumed capacity for unitary and authoritative action masks the possibility that important sub-national groups can act independently either to reinforce, undermine or circumvent the policies of national states.

2  *Interests*, rather than common ideals or identity, are the driving force behind the integration process, but this does **not** mean that:

A.  Their definition will remain constant once the integration process has begun and is distributing (usually uneven) benefits. Actors can learn from their experiences in co-operative decision-making, modify their preferences, and even develop common ideals and identities;

B.  Their expression will be confined to the national level once new opportunities for exercising influence have opened up within institutions at the supranational level.

3  *Decisions* about integration are normally taken with very imperfect knowledge of their consequences and frequently under the pressure of deadlines or impending crises. Given the absence of clear historical precedents:

A.  Actors are likely to miscalculate not only their capability to satisfy initial mutually agreed-upon goals;

B.  But also the impact of these efforts upon other, less consensual goals.

4  *Functions or issue arenas* provide the usual foci for the integration process (at least, in Western Europe), beginning with those that are initially considered the least controversial and, hence, easiest to deal with. Given the intrinsic (if uneven) interdependence of these arenas – '*l'engrenage*' is the jargon term – in modern societies:

A.  Advancement toward the solution of concrete problems or production of collective goods in one arena is bound to affect performance and interests in other arenas, and may even lead to demands for their explicit inclusion in the process;[4]

B.  Even where one issue arena can be separated from others, advancement toward the fulfilment of initially consensual tasks may generate increased controversy, thereby widening the range of actors potentially involved.

5  Since *actors* in the integration process cannot be confined to existing national states or their interest groups and social movements (see maxim no. 1 above), a theory of it should also explicitly include a role for supranational persons, secretariats and associations whose careers, resources and expectations become increasingly dependent upon the further expansion of integrative tasks. Even where their nomination or financial support is formally controlled or monitored by national actors, they may:

   A. Develop an increasingly independent *esprit de corps* and interject ideas and programmes into the process that cannot be reduced to the preferences of national or sub-national groups;
   B. Acquire, often as the unintended side-product of problem-solving in discrete issue arenas, increased resources and even authoritative capacities to act in ways that countermand or circumvent the intentions of national authorities.

6  *Strategies* with regard to integration are convergent, not identical. Actors agree upon rules and policies not because they have the same objective, but because their different preferences overlap. This implies that:

   A. When divergences in benefits and external effects emerge from the process, actors will respond with different demands for changes in rules and policies;
   B. From these inevitable conflicts, new convergences based on new combinations of actors can emerge which will redefine the level and scope of common obligations in ways not originally anticipated.

7  *Outcomes* of international integration are neither fixed in advance by the founding treaty, nor are they likely to be expressed exclusively through subsequent formal agreements. They should be recognized as the transient results of an on-going process rather than the definitive product of a stable equilibrium. Which is not to say that all attempts at integration among initially consenting states are equally likely to be successful or to expand functionally, since:

   A. All of the above – the mix of actors, the diversity of their interests, the extent of convergence in their strategies, the interdependence of issue arenas, the degree of knowledge and, hence, potential for miscalculation, the inequalities in benefits and unanticipated consequences – will differ systematically from one experience to another;
   B. These differences will be associated with differences in initial endowment and subsequent performance and will lead, in turn, to differences in outcome, ranging from encapsulated intergovernmental organizations to emergent supra-states. Between these extremes lie a wide variety of intermediary forms of political organization which are no less stable and which may be more likely to emerge.

From these assumptions, Haas and the neofunctionalists who have been inspired by him (which includes myself) have derived most of their more specific concepts and hypotheses. As we shall see, not all of these have proven equally useful or been equally verified by the experience with European integration since its institutional origin in the Coal and Steel Community in 1952. There is evidence to suggest that its perspective overlooked some key variables and focused too much attention on others.

But it is important to note that several of the critiques of neofunctionalism that emerged in the 1970s misrepresented its claims and distorted its arguments. For example, it offered no reason for anticipating that its central process, 'spill-over', would be either automatic or free of conflict. On the contrary, emphasis was placed on the likelihood of increasing controversiality and difficulty in reaching agreement, as the process expanded to affect more actors and adjacent issue arenas. This is called 'politicization' in the neofunctionalist jargon. Nor did it necessarily predict 'transcendence' – the unlimited and irreversible accumulation of tasks by a single regional institution at the expense of national member states. Such a supranational state based on a complete 'transferral of sovereignty' was only one possible outcome – and not the most likely by any means. A good deal of subsequent neofunctionalist effort has been spent exploring the probability of 'entropy' and 'encapsulation' setting in, rather than 'momentum' and 'expansion' inexorably taking over (Schmitter 1970).[5] Finally, the sheer fact that the European Community (EC) had not spilled-over continuously into new issue arenas during the first thirty years of its existence and appeared for some time (roughly from the mid-1960s to the early 1980s) not to be extending the authority of its central institutions did not, in itself, disconfirm the perspective since none of its proponents dared to place a specific timeframe around his or her suppositions. This embarrassing lack of temporal specificity, incidentally, it shares with many other theories of political change – whether at the global, regional or national level.

## EIGHT UNANTICIPATED DEVELOPMENTS

Which is not to say that neofunctionalism emerges blameless from a confrontation with several generations of experience with European integration. Although few, if any, of the close academic observers of the EC were using it when the Single European Act (SEA) was signed in December 1985 – intergovernmentalism, a variant neorealism, dominated their thinking – I doubt if its concepts, maxims and hypotheses would have been of much help. The decision to move toward the so-called 'Completion of the Internal Market' in 1992 with the SEA could not have been spotted using its lenses (although I, personally, am not convinced that neorealist or neorationalist lenses would have been much better for seeing what was coming).

Reflecting *ex post*, I would stress the following features about the event – none of which have attracted much prior attention on the part of neofunctionalists and all of which are likely to continue to be salient in determining the future course of integration:

1 The crucial role of Heads of Government/State, meeting in the European Council, in actually putting the 1992 package together;

2  The impact of economic trends and cycles originating outside Europe and threatening the region as a whole with declining competitiveness and low growth rates;

3  The quiet accumulation of decisions by the European Court of Justice that established the supremacy of Community over national law and set precedents, such as *mutual recognition, proportionality, direct effect,* and *implied powers* that could be used to resolve other disputes;

4  The indirect effect of Community enlargement, first to nine, later to twelve and subsequently to fifteen and now twenty-five members, upon internal decision-making processes;

5  The importance, not just of well-entrenched European-level interest associations, but of *ad hoc* and even *ad personam* informal groups such as the European Business Roundtable;

6  The relatively low level of mass public attention and, hence, of politicization of issues which 'should have' attracted greater controversy;

7  The 'catalytic role' played by the European Parliament when it threatened to shift to a more overtly political or 'federalist' strategy by introducing the Draft Treaty Establishing European Union in early 1984;[6]

8  The indirect, but steady, impact of an ideological shift at the national political level from a predominance of social democratic to a growing hegemony of neoliberal values.

What cannot be questioned is that the putting into effect of the SEA unleashed a veritable avalanche of interdependencies between issue arenas, Eurocratic initiatives, shifts in interest association activity, redefinitions of Community authority, mobilization of sub-national actors, and further expansions of the functional agenda – culminating in the Maastricht, Amsterdam, and Nice agreements.[7] This sequence of treaties may not all have been the product of obvious spill-overs motivated by the externalities generated by functionally linked policies and unevenly distributed benefits or promoted by a joint conspiracy of European civil servants and interest groups that outwitted the entrenched interests of national governments and state bureaucracies, but they have demonstrated *ex post* that, as Ernst Haas put it, neofunctionalism may have been obsolescent but it was not obsolete (Haas 1976).[8]

## ONE DUAL PARADOX

The optimistic expectations of early neofunctionalists that European integration would exploit the latent interdependencies of complex, welfare-oriented societies by inexorably spilling over from one issue arena to another were rather quickly frustrated. The whole approach was rooted in a serious 'dual paradox' which, if not overcome, threatened to confine it to political impotence and academic obscurity.

On the one hand, for the process to begin, existing states had to converge upon some relatively non-controversial and apparently separable issue arena where tangible gains from co-operation were sufficient to warrant giving up some portion of their respective autonomy to a common institution. But if this arena really were so non-controversial and separable, then there was little reason to expect any further expansion. The new regional organization would merely perform its task unobtrusively and, in so doing, reinforce the status and capabilities of the states that composed and continued to control it. The present international system – global and regional – is virtually saturated with such stagnant functional organizations, none of which seems to be contributing much to transforming its basic, i.e. inter-statist, structure. What emerged as distinctive to Western Europe (as opposed to efforts at regional integration elsewhere) was the sheer complexity of multi-layered interdependencies – not only between member states but also policy arenas. This made it unusually difficult to predict the consequences of liberalizing exchanges between them and, therefore, to impose rationally bounded limits on what they had consensually decided to accomplish in common.

On the other hand, if the proponents of integration did manage to select an issue arena with greater potential for '*l'engrenage*', i.e. linkage to other initially unattended arenas, and for eventual 'politicization', i.e. capacity to attract the efforts of a wider set of actors, then they ran the risk that neofunctionalism would become 'self-disconfirming'. National politicians had only to catch on to the strategy (or read the academic analyses) to realize that whatever the immediate benefits they might reap from such international co-operation, these would eventually be overwhelmed by the rising costs in terms of diminished sovereignty and irreversible entanglements. To the extent that they could internalize the implications of such long-term effects and discount the short-term payoffs, they might well rationally choose to refuse to enter such arrangements in the first place or, as seems to have been the case with de Gaulle, pull the plug before the process had advanced too far. Again, the world is full of so-called regional integration schemes whose members have anticipated such a threat and, therefore, designed their institutions to minimize such an eventual outcome.

This is not the time or place to analyse how the founding fathers of the ECSC managed to pick an arena with considerable potential for spill-over and to steer it past national politicians in the early 1950s.[9] Nor to go over again the relatively well-known story of how its successor, the EEC, was more or less stopped in its tracks in the mid-1960s by a combination of increased awareness of its emerging impact upon national sovereignty and the capability of national states to pursue their own macro-economic policies.

## TWO PARAMETRIC SHIFTS

Although it is risky to rely on just a few variables to explain why the neofunctionalist strategy-*cum*-perspective again became relevant, I am convinced that the turnaround in the late 1970s and, especially, the mid-1980s can be attributed *grosso modo* to two changes in the European policy environment:

1 A vague, subjective feeling that Europe as a whole was destined to decline in its competitiveness (and, ultimately, in its relative standard of living) *vis-à-vis* other developed world regions, specifically Japan, the Pacific Basin and North America; and
2 An objective demonstration by the Socialist government of François Mitterrand (1981–83) that measures taken independently by national policy-makers were incapable of attaining desired macro-economic outcomes and could even lead to perverse outcomes in terms of growth and monetary stability.

Only the second of these changes can be said to have any intrinsic connection with neofunctionalism via underlying and increasingly irreversible functional interdependencies and policy entanglements. The first is a parametric and exogenous shift that was not – and could not be – identified by such an approach. At best, its relevance might be spotted *ex ante* by an alert neorealist trained to be sensitive to perceptions of relative power and dependence.

## ONE ELEMENT OF IRONY

The irony of this tale is that Haas himself contributed substantially to the demise of interest in his own theory in both Europe and the United States. He was, no doubt, aware of the validity of the Streeten-Kuhn principle that 'a model is never defeated by facts, however damaging, but only by another model' (Hirschmann 1970: 68). By publicly declaring in print on no less than two occasions that neofunctionalism was 'obsolescent', it became literally impossible for any scholar to take the approach seriously (Haas 1975, 1971). Who could dare to contradict its founder? Moreover, this happened at a moment, the 1970s, when the process of European integration itself seemed stagnant, if not moribund. Leon Lindberg and Stuart Scheingold had just published their *Europe's Would-Be Polity* which concluded that, while it had accomplished a good deal, the (then) EEC had settled into an equilibrium from which it was unlikely to escape for some time to come (Lindberg and Scheingold 1970). Of the ten contributors to that *magnum opus* of theorizing about regional integration that Lindberg and Scheingold edited in 1971 (Lindberg and Scheingold 1971), only one, Donald Puchala, was still writing on the subject by 1980 (Puchala 1981).

Why did Haas lose faith in neofunctionalism? The simple answer embedded in his 'obsolescent' articles was Charles de Gaulle. Not only did de Gaulle put a sudden stop to the gradual expansion of tasks and authority by the Commission and to the prospective shift to majority voting in the Council, but he also made a full-scale effort to convert the EEC/EC into an instrument of French foreign policy. What Haas came to fear more than anything else was that a united Europe could be just as nationalistic and even aggressive as had been its component national states. To put it bluntly, his (implicit) normative assumption that the regional integration process would produce a qualitatively and not just a quantitatively different actor in international politics was shaken. By the time it had become clear that, however much de Gaulle and his successors might have preferred this outcome, it was not to happen, Haas was deeply involved in research on other topics. Just as he had hoped in the late 1950s and 1960s, the EU seems condemned for the foreseeable future to wield 'soft coercion' over its own members and 'civilian power' in the rest of the world. Even now that it is discussing the creation of a capacity for intervention in matters of external defence and internal security, it is clear that Europe has neither the collective will nor the common identity necessary to play a more proactive role.

I do know from personal experience that when I revived my interest in European integration and came to the (not surprising) conclusion that the neofunctionalist approach remained the most insightful and helpful in understanding its underlying dynamics, he seemed neither surprised nor dismayed (Schmitter 2004).[10] I even like to think that he was rather pleased, not just at my efforts, but also those of other European scholars.[11]

For, when interest in the topic picked up rapidly in the mid-1980s with the unanticipated breakthrough of the signature and easy ratification of the SEA, interest in neofunctionalism blossomed in Europe – but not in the United States where (neo)realism continued to dominate the discipline of international relations. When the Berlin Wall fell and the Cold War ended, European scholars interpreted these events as encouraging further spill-overs into functional arenas previously made impervious owing to national security calculations – air traffic control, transport infrastructure, energy, immigration – while American realists declared that the entire *raison d'être* of European integration had collapsed and its nation-states would inexorably return to their previous state system (Mearsheimer 1990).

In a sense, both were wrong (the latter far more than the former). Nevertheless, the calculation that national reunification made it more than ever imperative to bind Germany firmly to the rest of (Western) Europe no doubt played a major role in ensuring agreement on the Maastricht Treaty in 1991. This Treaty committed its signatories to establishing a common currency, something that had been mooted on several occasions, but always rejected as intruding too far, materially and symbolically, into the sovereignty of member states. To the surprise of almost everyone, the introduction of the new common currency produced relatively little resistance and has been a quiet success.

## ONE BALANCE SHEET

Now that we have had more than fifty years of experience with the ECSC/EEC/EC/EU's efforts at promoting regional integration, it does seem possible to draw up a balance sheet of the strengths and weaknesses of the neofunctional perspective:

1　There were, indeed, underlying interdependencies that may have taken some time to mature, but they did serve to compel actors into reaching agreements that were not initially intended. The volume of intra-Community transactions continued to rise relative to the exchanges of its member economies with other countries and this triggered a spill-over into capital markets and monetary affairs at the very core of an increasingly regionalized economic system.[12] Not only was the customs union eventually converted into a more genuine common market, but virtually the entire scope of government functions previously performed exclusively at the national level came within at least the purview of the EC. It is less clear, however, that the roles assigned to Eurocrats in the EC/EU secretariat and to the Euro-associations headquartered in Brussels in this process were so significant in this process of task expansion.[13]

2　This impressive growth in the number and variety of EC activities has meant a vast increase in the frequency with which national representatives meet – for example, the Council of Ministers in its various guises meets over one hundred times a year and the quantity of national expert reunions runs well into the thousands. This seems to have induced important learning effects in the ranks of these representatives and even to have resulted in shifts in conceptions of national interest which may have been more important than the upward shift to regional interest politics predicted by neofunctionalists.

3　Moreover, the policy expansion – when coupled with the persistent increase in commercial, financial and personal transactions between individuals, firms and sub-national groups – has made it not only easier but even imperative to reach complex 'log-rolls' and 'package-deals' sufficient to extend further Community *compétences* and to buy out even the most recalcitrant of opponents. The process may even have crossed 'the threshold of irreversibility' beyond which the threat by any individual member state to defect is no longer credible, just as the previous attainment of the status of a security community had already removed the credibility of using force to impose one's preferred outcome.

4　Which is not to say that the neofunctionalist momentum that Leon Lindberg and Stuart Scheingold failed to find in the late 1960s has necessarily emerged (see Lindberg and Scheingold 1970). Much of what has happened since the mid-1970s can better be attributed to external trends and shocks than to purely internal processes and functional *engrenages*. It was correct to emphasize the declining capacity of national states in Europe to control macro-economic outcomes within their borders, i.e. to couple the loss of external sovereignty with the decline in internal sovereignty, but it is doubtful that this would have had such an impact were it not for the generalized perception that Europe as a whole was declining relative to other competing regions of the world. For example, neofunctionalists were right to stress the underlying interdependence of energy policy with those conditions determining the relative competitiveness of producers within a single market, but very little happened in the energy sector until actors were made aware of the overriding importance of the dependency of the region as a whole upon foreign suppliers by the successive oil shocks of the 1970s. A similar case could be made for European monetary policy in the aftermath of Nixon's 'shocking' decision to take the US dollar off the gold standard in 1971.[14]

5 In their singular concentration on interdependencies rooted in production and exchange and, hence, the roles played by representatives of classes and sectors, the neofunctionalists tended to overlook very significant extensions of the scope and, especially, the level of Community authority that were going on right under their noses – namely, as a result of the deliberations and decisions of the European Court of Justice. Its assertion of the primacy of Community law – in effect, converting the Treaty of Rome into a proto-Constitution for Europe – and its imaginative interpretations of specific (if vague) clauses were crucial for supranationalism.[15] The effective implementation of these new rules, however, depended upon a quite different form of interdependency – that embodied in a common legal profession, doctrines of jurisprudence and respect for the rule of law which extended across intra-European borders into the very entrails of the national state.[16]

6 Finally, neofunctionalists failed to recognize (or, at least, to 'problematize') the significance of the enlargement of the EEC/EC to include new members. Neither it nor any other theory of integration can explain why the Community began with six – rather than seven or nine – subsequently expanded to twelve, has recently reached twenty-five and may even include thirty or more countries before exhausting itself somewhere on the Asian steppes. And yet, it is impossible to deny that increasing the number of participants has had a marked effect on decision-making rules within Community institutions or that increasing the heterogeneity of member interests has had a significant impact upon the functional scope of Community policies. With the EC/EU now facing this issue as never before – there are already two states in the short queue, and another five or more in various stages of application – the absence of any clear guidelines is particularly striking. All the discussion about 'widening vs. deepening' is taking place in a theoretical vacuum that neofunctionalism is incapable of filling.[17]

## ONE ENDURING BUT ENDANGERED LEGACY

So, what has been Ernst Haas's European legacy? His work on regional integration continues to be read and cited – I suspect with increasing frequency since the 1990s. By now, almost everyone recognizes that no single theory or approach can explain everything one would like to know and to predict about the EU. The process has already generated the world's most complex polity and, *pace* the Convention's 'Constitutional Treaty', there is every indication that it will become even more complex now that it has ten new members and has been taking on new tasks.[18]

Moreover, the entire logic of spill-over based on underlying and unanticipated functional interdependencies may have exhausted itself. On the one hand, the EU is already meddling in almost all policy domains. On the other hand, if monetary union is any indication for the future, the designers of the European Central Bank were very careful to insulate it from any relation with the Commission or with organized interests. The same seems likely in the cases of police co-operation and foreign policy co-ordination. Only a common energy policy and certain aspects of transport infrastructure seem capable of igniting latent functional linkages and generating unintended consequences. Moreover, the expansion to twenty-five members of much greater heterogeneity of interests and passions means that it will become much more difficult to respond with an expansive package-deal that will have something in it for everyone. Given such a diversity, it is much less likely that actors will recognize a common need, that experts will agree on what to do, that lessons will be transferred from one experience to another and that citizens will mobilize to demand that the good, service or regulation be supplied by the EU, rather than their national state or sub-national region.

But the real impediment to a revived neofunctionalist dynamic comes from something that Ernst Haas long anticipated, but which was so slow in coming to the European integration process. I have called it 'politicization' (see Schmitter 1970). When citizens begin to pay attention to how the EU is affecting their daily lives, when political parties and large social movements begin to include 'Europe' in their platforms, and when politicians begin to realize that there are votes to be won or lost by addressing policy issues at the regional level, the entire low profile strategy becomes much less viable. Discrete regional officials and invisible interest representatives, in league with national civil servants, can no longer monopolize the decision-making process in Brussels (known in Euro-speak as 'comitology'). Integration starts to generate visible 'winners and losers' within member states, and loses its perception of being an 'all winners' game. Haas had an idiosyncratic term for this. He called it 'turbulence' and there is no question in my mind that the regional integration process in Europe has become 'turbulent'. It will take a major revision of his theory before anyone can make sense of its changing dynamics.

**Address for correspondence:** Philippe C. Schmitter, European University Institute, Via dei Roccettini 9, 50016 San Domenico di Fiesole, Italy. email: Philippe.Schmitter@IUE.it

## ACKNOWLEDGEMENTS

I thank Tanja Börzel and an anonymous reviewer for their helpful comments on an earlier version of this paper. I am also grateful to Tina Freyburg for her assistance in editing this text.

## NOTES

1 One might also include Amitai Etzioni among them, although he is of a younger generation and emigrated voluntarily to the United States from Israel (Etzioni 1965).
2 See also Wangenen (1952).
3 As presented by Haas, neofunctionalism is a 'self-consciously eclectic' effort at explaining the dynamics of change in an international system composed largely – but not exclusively – of established nation-states. It is one of a broader class of middle-range approaches that emphasize the range of possible outcomes rather than those that are most probable or certain; concrete actions and tasks of real politicians at the expense of abstract models or behaviours of stylized actors; rational intentions but also unintended consequences and reactions; real demands and emergent properties, not just imputed preferences or fixed structures; learning and gradual adjustment instead of singular exchanges or dramatic solutions; process and goal-seeking at the expense of equilibrium and goal satisfaction.
4 Elsewhere, I have defined this 'spill-over hypothesis' in the following way: 'Tensions from the global environment and/or contradictions generated by past performance (within the organization) give rise to unexpected performance in pursuit of agreed-upon objectives. These frustrations and/or dissatisfactions are likely to result in the search for alternative means for reaching the same goals, i.e. to induce actions to revise their respective strategies *vis-à-vis* the scope and level of regional decision-making' (Schmitter 1970).
5 For a case study of entropy and encapsulation, see also Schmitter (1969).
6 Joseph Nye was the first to pick this theme up, but his insight remained unexploited (Nye 1968).
7 Someone, I am not sure who, has baptized the Maastricht Treaty that instituted the process of monetary unification as 'the Mother of All Spill-Overs'.
8 At the end of his Introduction to the new edition of his *The Uniting of Europe*, Haas concludes that 'Regional integration theory (i.e. neo-functionalism – PCS) has a new lease on life; it is no longer obsolescent' (Haas 2004).
9 It undoubtedly helped that in the early 1950s an unusually homogenous group of statesmen was governing the six original member states. Their common Conservative and Catholic background and high degree of mutual trust may have made them exceptionally willing to take '*le saut dans l'inconnu*' that such a novel measure implied. Protestant Britain, it will be remembered, was governed by Clement Atlee and the Labour Party at the time (Pineau and Rimbaud 1991).
10 Incidentally, this most recent compilation of diverse approaches is 'In memoriam of Ernst Haas who so greatly inspired generations of integration scholars'. All but one of the scholars involved in this project are either Europeans or working in a European university. Mark A. Pollack is the American exception. He takes a (modified) rational choice perspective and does not cite once the work of Haas.
11 This is well reflected in the Introduction he wrote for the recent new edition of his *The Uniting of Europe* (Haas 2004).
12 For a particularly prescient analysis of this, see Schmitt (1968).
13 There has been some disagreement among specialists on the specific role that Jacques Delors, President of the Commission, and his staff played in the 'crafting'

of the Single European Act and the Maastricht Treaty. Neorealists and neorationalists, such as Andrew Moravcsik and Geoffrey Garrett, tend to discount it, and
stress the initiatives taken at the European Council Meetings by Kohl, Mitterrand
or their respective Foreign Ministers. For the view of a scholar not contaminated by
an *a priori* theoretical stance who stresses the relative autonomy of the Commission
and, especially, its President (but who may be influenced by his status as a participant observer), see Ross (1992).

14 Recent research by Roy Ginsberg on the foreign policy actions of the EC confirms
this impression. After classifying the causes of Community action as due either to
'integration' (i.e. functional responses stemming from prior EC policies), 'interdependence' (i.e. political or economic linkages to the global inter-state system) or
'self-styled action' (i.e. emanating from the EC's own sense of mission and
independence), he observes an overall tendency for the functional explanations to
decline monotonically and proportionately over time from an initial high in
1976–80 (73 per cent of all foreign policy actions) to 1981–85 (64 per cent) to
1986–90 (57 per cent) – even though their absolute number continues to increase.
More and more of the EC's attention in this field seems motivated either by its own
autonomous initiatives or by global incentives (Ginsberg 1991).

15 Most of what I know about this process I owe to the magisterial article by Joseph
Weiler (Weiler 1991).

16 Ironically, this need to pay more attention to the role of professional norms and
solidarities in the integration process comes close to advocating a return to the
original international functionalism of David Mitrany where a great deal of
emphasis (and hope) was placed on the role of independent experts (Mitrany
1966; originally published in 1943). Recent work on 'epistemic communities'
seems to touch on the same theme, even if the imbrication of national and international lawyers and judges has not (yet) been subjected to its scrutiny.
See, especially, P.M. Haas (1992) and Adler and Haas (1992).

17 At most, there have been inconclusive discussions about the 'limits to Europe' based
on a variety of cultural criteria; virtually nothing about how different mixes of
member states might affect the long-run evolution of European institutions. For
some discussion of this issue, see Galtung (1989). Presumably, if a theoretical
tradition on this subject does develop, it will come from the neorationalists who
can draw on an existing (if not very successful) literature on 'optimal currency
areas' or the 'optimal size of the firm'. For an effort to apply the theory of clubs
and other aspects of economic reasoning to the EEC and other international
associations, see Dosser *et al.* (1982).

18 One very important limitation of neofunctionalism should be inserted at this
point. It focuses attention exclusively on the extension to new tasks and the
expansion of common authority. It says nothing, however, about what has
been one of the major dynamic features of the EU; namely, the incorporation
of new members. Who, how, when, under what conditions and for what reason
a regional organization will expand territorially is simply not contemplated by
this approach.


## REFERENCES

Adler, E. and Haas, P.M. (1992) 'Conclusion: Epistemic communities. World order
and the creation of a reflective research program', *International Organization*
46(1): 367–90.

Deutsch, K.W. *et al.* (1957) *Political Community and the North Atlantic Area: International Organization in the Light of Historical Experience*, Princeton: Princeton
University Press.

Dosser, D., Gowland, D. and Hartley, K. (1982) *The Collaboration of Nations: A Study of European Economic Policy*, Oxford: Martin Robertson.

Etzioni, A. (1965) *Political Unification: A Comparative Study of Leaders and Forces*, New York: Holt, Rinehart & Winston.

Galtung, J. (1989) *Europe in the Making*, New York: Crane Russak.

Ginsberg, R.H. (1991) 'European Community foreign policy actions in the 1980s'. Unpublished paper presented to the Second Biennial International Conference of the European Community Studies Association, George Mason University, 22–24 May 1991.

Haas, E.B. (1958) *The Uniting of Europe. Political, Social, and Economic Forces 1950–1957*, Stanford: Stanford University Press.

Haas, E.B. (1964) *Beyond the Nation-State. Functionalism and International Organization*, Stanford: Stanford University Press.

Haas, E.B. (1971) 'The study of regional integration: reflections on the joy and anguish of pretheorizing', in L.N. Lindberg and S.A. Scheingold (eds), *Regional Integration: Theory and Research*, Cambridge, MA: Harvard University Press, pp. 3–44.

Haas, E.B. (1975) *The Obsolescence of Regional Integration Theory*, Berkeley: University of California Press.

Haas, E.B. (1976) 'Turbulent fields and the theory of regional integration', *International Organization* 30(2): 173–212.

Haas, E.B. (1997/2000) *Nationalism, Liberalism and Progress (Vols 1 and 2)*, Ithaca: Cornell University Press.

Haas, E.B. (2004) *The Uniting of Europe. Political, Social and Economic Forces 1950–1957*, Stanford: Stanford University Press.

Haas, P.M. (1992) 'Introduction: Epistemic communities and international policy coordination', *International Organization* 46(1): 1–36.

Hirschmann, A.O. (1970) *Exit, Voice and Loyalty*, Cambridge, MA: Harvard University Press.

Hoffmann, S. (1960) *Contemporary Theory in International Relations*, Englewood Cliffs: Prentice-Hall.

Lindberg, L.N. and Scheingold, S.A. (1970) *Europe's Would-Be Polity*, Englewood Cliffs: Prentice-Hall.

Lindberg, L.N. and Scheingold, S.A. (eds) (1971) *Regional Integration. Theory and Research*, Cambridge, MA: Harvard University Press.

Mearsheimer, J. (1990) 'Back to the future: instability in Europe after the Cold War', *International Security* 15(1): 5–56.

Mitrany, D. (1966) *A Working Peace System*, Chicago: Quadrangle Books.

Monnet, J. (1976) *Mémoires*, Paris: Fayard.

Nye, J.S. (1968) 'Patterns and catalysts in regional integration', *International Organization* 19(4): 870–84.

Pineau, C. and Rimbaud, C. (1991) *Le Grand Pari. L'Aventure du Traité de Rome*, Paris: Fayard.

Puchala, D.J. (1981) 'Integration theory and the study of international relations', in R. Merritt and B. Russett (eds), *From National Development to Global Community. Essays in Honour of Karl W. Deutsch*, Boston: Allen & Unwin, pp. 145–64.

Ross, G. (1992) 'Russian dolls and resource mobilization. Thoughts on supranational strategies, interstate systems and the European Community after Maastricht'. Unpublished paper prepared for the CES, Eighth International Conference of Europeanists, Chicago, March 1992.

Schmitt, H.O. (1968) 'Capital markets and the unification of Europe', *World Politics* 20(2): 228–44.

Schmitter, P.C. (1969) 'La dinámica de contradicciones y la conducción de crísis en la integración centroamericana', *Revista de la Integración (Buenos Aires)* 5: 87–151.

Schmitter, P.C. (1970) 'A revised theory of regional integration', in L.N. Lindberg and S.A. Scheingold (eds), *Regional Integration: Theory and Research*, Cambridge, MA: Harvard University Press, pp. 836–68.

Schmitter, P.C. (2004) 'Neo-neo-functionalism', in A. Weiner and T. Diez (eds), *European Integration Theory*, Oxford: Oxford University Press, pp. 45–74.

Wangenen, R.W. V. (1952) *Research in the International Organization Field. Some Notes on a Possible Focus* (Princeton University Publication No. 1), Princeton: Center for Research on World Political Institutions.

Weiler, J.H.H. (1991) 'The transformation of Europe', *Yale Law Journal* 108(8): 2403–83.

# A rationalist-institutionalist explanation of endogenous regional integration[1]

Henry Farrell and Adrienne Héritier

## 1. INTRODUCTION: WHAT DRIVES REGIONAL INTEGRATION?

What is at the basis of regional integration and what are the processes that drive integration? Why do integration processes develop faster in some issue areas than in others? These questions are at the heart of our own work, just as they are the driving concerns of Ernst Haas's version of neofunctionalism. While we, unlike Haas, emphasize endogenous processes of institutional change rather than exogenously driven processes of technical needs and spillover, we believe that there is important overlap between our approach and Haas's, as well as areas of disagreement. By exploring these areas of overlap in this article, we hope to empirically illustrate on the one hand how our approach may help to answer questions that Haas's version of neofunctionalism had difficulties with, and on the other how Haas's emphasis on epistemic factors can alleviate some of the blind spots in our own perspective.

Haas argues that deepening integration flows from a process of spillover/ramification. In contrast to Mitrany (1975), he does not conceive of this as an automatic technical process, but as a process driven both by the interest-oriented behaviour of political élites and the impact of expertise and epistemic communities in complex technological policy areas. He provides us with an understanding of the macro-level processes driving European integration. What his work arguably lacks is a specification of the precise processes by which belief systems translate into policy outcomes.

In this article we set out our own model of an endogenously driven mechanism of formal and informal institutional change building on the foundations of negotiation theory. We illustrate how the mechanism works with reference to the empirical example of the early agreements in codecision-based legislation in Europe. While our account may explain the occurrence or non-occurrence of institutional change/integration it could in principle also be applied to the uneven development of integration in different policy areas (see, for instance, for external and internal security policy Börzel (2005)). By including the mechanism of negotiation as part of the causal account it is possible to explain differential degrees of institutional change/regional integration. The depth and speed of integration/institutional change would then depend on the outcome of this negotiation process in which expertise does play an important role, but is subject to a power-driven negotiation process.

However, our emphasis on bargaining might usefully be supplemented with a more detailed examination of the processes through which the parameters of bargaining are set. As we note in our conclusions, Haas provides just such an account of parameter-setting, which is especially relevant to those fields of policy-making where technical knowledge is of importance.

## 2. HAAS'S ARGUMENT

Ernst Haas built on David Mitrany's version of functionalism, extending and revising it in important ways. Mitrany sought to show that transnational ties among experts (rather than politicians) in solving technical problems led to increased collaboration among states and thus to international integration. Successful co-operation in one field would lead to a ramification/spillover, i.e. further collaboration, in other fields. Under this account, integration occurs because of external factors (the technical nature of the problems being solved) rather than an internal dynamic within the regional organization.

According to this early account integration would proceed quasi-automatically. There would be demands for additional integrated services as centralized institutions found themselves unable to satisfy all the demands of the new clients. Activities associated with integrated sectors would 'spill over' into linked sectors not yet integrated, and become the focus of demands for more integration (Haas 1991: 23).

Thus, economic integration would lead to political integration in Europe, integration being defined as a process 'whereby political actors in several distinct national settings are persuaded to shift their loyalties, expectations and political activities toward a new centre, whose institutions possess or demand jurisdiction over the preexisting national states' (Haas 1958: 16). In contrast to Mitrany, however, Haas stressed that technical tasks cannot be separated from political tasks, or welfare from power. 'International integration is advanced most rapidly by a dedication to welfare, through measures elaborated by experts *aware of the political implications* of their tasks and representative of homogeneous and symmetrical social aggregates, public or private' (Haas 1958: 49; emphasis added). The actors become politicized because, in response to initial technical purposes, they consider the spectrum of means considered appropriate to attain them and choose among them (Haas and Schmitter 1964: 707). Hence, it is necessary to specify the conditions under which actors will choose to collaborate. Haas argues that the force driving choice will be the self-interest of political élites. Integration only occurs when political élites consider it to be in their self-interest. Thus, Haas's epistemology rests on the assumption of a goal-oriented actor: 'rather than relying upon a scheme of integration which posits "altruistic" motives as the conditioners of conduct, it seems more reasonable to focus on the interests and values defended by them as far too complex to be described in such simple terms as "the desire of Franco-German peace" or "the will to a United Europe"' (Haas 1958: 13; Haas 1991: 23). As Haas says: 'the ontology is "soft" rational-choice: societal actors, in seeking to realize their value-derived interests, will choose whatever means are made available by the prevailing democratic order ... The ontology is *not* [original emphasis] materialistic: values shape interests and values include many nonmaterial elements' (Haas 1991: 23, 25).

How would Haas then account for the unevenness in speed and depth of regional integration in different policy areas? Two points emerge. First, since Haas argues that spillover is not automatic, the preferences of the political élites will determine whether sectoral integration is taken forward or not. Thus, in the context of the European Community of the mid-1970s Haas expressed reservations regarding the logic of spillover. He did not think that a common monetary policy was imminent. He argued that an integration process based upon expectations of economic gain is an 'ephemeral' and 'frail process, susceptible to reversal' because it is not based upon deep ideological commitments (Haas 1967: 324). Thus, the first explanation for unevenness of integration across sectors, admittedly theoretically not very sophisticated, would be: deepening integration occurs whenever the political élites predominantly prefer it over other possible outcomes.

The second answer to the 'why' of differential sectoral integration can be derived from Haas's argument about epistemic communities and the role of expertise. The influence of problem interdependence and its treatment through the professional knowledge of epistemic communities would favour deepening integration. One of neofunctionalism's core claims is that integration is accelerated in issue areas in which scientists and technicians play a central role. The key causal factor is learning. Epistemic communities, characterized by a high level of technical and expert knowledge, may play a role in accelerating regional integration, because scientific views tend to converge, and facilitate the formation of policy communities. Since collaboration among states takes place under conditions of great complexity, there is uncertainty about means–ends relationships in policy-making in areas such as the environment, energy, industrial policy, research and development, and technology transfer. In the process of gaining control over this complexity and interdependence among policy areas, we may expect convergent problem views and policy solutions, i.e. integration.

> Epistemic communities are associations of professional experts in a particular field who, because of the knowledge they have, have an unusual influence on politicians and bureaucrats, and are, therefore, able to penetrate government departments and make their ideas part of policy... They only operate in fields of policy where science matters. In the field of human rights, forget it ... In environmental politics, it matters a great deal.
>
> (Haas 2000: 10)

Haas argued that if we could say that a given scientific idea or discovery 'or a network of specialists triggered the development of a political consensus, which in turn legitimated a new international program, we could make a definite observation about the impact of science on collective problem-solving' (Haas *et al.* 1977: 9).

However, in his own research Haas noted that, even in the case of complex science-based issues, international epistemic communities have had only modest effects: although states have increasingly been confronted with complex and interdependent problems, the political willingness of political élites to engage in supranational action has not increased accordingly (Haas 1976: 184). Empirically, Haas failed to find unequivocal evidence of this. He concluded that, despite the growth of international institutions and fora for debating scientific issues, the power of these bodies to bring about a policy change has remained weak (Haas *et al.* 1977: 352ff.).

So why is it that epistemic communities and other factors sometimes lead to an acceleration of regional integration and sometimes not? We argue that a proper emphasis on causal processes will help us to arrive at a better answer to this question. Haas does not describe a causal process explaining why the members of epistemic communities do or do not translate their beliefs and preferences into influence over policy outcomes, why some wield influence on bureaucrats or not. Although Haas provides some of the elements of such a theoretical explanation, he does not bring them together into a coherent whole. Haas discusses modes of conflict resolution in a bargaining process when he talks about the three methods of resolving disputes among states, i.e. the methods of the 'lowest common denominator', of 'splitting the difference' and of 'upgrading the common interest' (Haas 1961: 371). However, even if these important elements of a conflict-solving strategy are present in Haas's theory of integration, they are not premised on a fully developed theory of negotiation.[2] Furthermore, the simple claim that epistemic communities' causal beliefs are diffused to and among state decision-makers, and that there is an increasing likelihood of convergent state behaviour and international policy co-ordination, is 'theoretically incomplete' (Sebenius 1992: 356) because it does not specify the mechanism by which the influence of epistemic communities translates into policy outcomes.

We will argue that, by applying negotiation theory, we can account better for when regional integration takes place and when it does not. This negotiation theoretical approach to integration also potentially allows us to accommodate the influence of epistemic communities and their expertise.

## 3. AN ENDOGENOUS DYNAMIC OF REGIONAL INTEGRATION/ INSTITUTIONAL CHANGE THROUGH THE INTERPRETATION OF INCOMPLETE CONTRACTS

In our work we have focused on endogenous causal mechanisms accounting for institutional change, with particular reference to decision-making rules in regional integration, i.e. Europe. The argument as such, however, may be applied to the occurrence or non-occurrence of other types of institutional change such as the delegation of decision-making powers in particular policy areas to a supranational level. Thus, in contrast to Haas we scrutinize the development of integration in terms of its weakening or deepening at the level of *institutions*, i.e. rules of behaviour, in this particular case the rules governing the distribution of competences and authority among formal European decision-making bodies. Further, we present an *endogenous* explanation of institutional change; rather than privileging the specific characteristics of the issues, or focusing on spillover from other issue areas, we concentrate explicitly on processes of institutional bargaining and negotiation.

In a first step, accounting for the *development of informal institutions*, defined as rules of behaviour not subject to third-party dispute resolution, we argue that the creation of informal institutions is driven by the interpretation of formal rules, which we define as written rules of behaviour subject to third-party dispute resolution. Since formal rules are usually ambiguous, actors develop informal rules guiding the daily application of these rules.[3] Actors will have different interests over the content of these rules, in particular when these rules effectively redistribute decision-making weight, each actor preferring those rules that maximize its own decision-making competences. Thus, we suggest that the rule-making process will be driven less by common gains from co-ordination than by conflicts over how these common gains are distributed (Knight 1992).

In a second step, we argue that, under specific conditions, these informal institutions may in turn affect future rounds of Treaty change, i.e. *informal rules may be formalized* and contribute to a further development of integration.

This negotiation-centred perspective suggests that the speed and extent of integration can be explained by negotiations and the relative bargaining power of actors.

Empirically we examine the institutional change in the legislative procedure of codecision, i.e. joint decision-making of the Council of Ministers and the European Parliament. We argue against the one-shot game approach or 'procedural models' (e.g. Tsebelis and Garrett 2000), which posits that the procedural rules of regional integration produce determinate equilibria, and are the product of conscious choice by a small group of actors – the member states. We share with Haas the base assumption that all actors have bounded rationality, and a limited ability to anticipate truly uncertain events. Thus, the member states cannot anticipate all eventualities and cannot create 'complete contracts'. They are constrained in their ability to respond to unexpected outcomes, creating opportunities for other actors to influence the institutional development. Under these circumstances, institutional outcomes will only imperfectly reflect the intentions of the principals (member states) and will be shaped in important ways by the indefinitely iterated exchange among the main actors in the legislative process.

We also argue that these 'procedural models' over-emphasize the formal legal sequencing of decision-making processes at the cost of analysing the impact of informal extra-legal bargaining in decision-making – institutional rules may reflect both power relations and the intensity of preference/saliency of an issue for actors, in a way that is not reducible to the formally defined number of votes, or right to submit a proposal, etc. (Achen 2003).

Thus, we argue that member states do not have complete control over the integration process and stress that power differences affect the re-negotiation of the specifics of ambiguous treaty provisions (Farrell and Héritier 2003, 2004). We assume that actors are goal-oriented and seek to reach institutional outcomes that match their objectives, so that bargaining over the implementation of political procedures may lead to the creation of informal institutions.[4] Bargaining may involve formal negotiations around a table, but this is not necessary – the negotiation of new rules may be tacit, ongoing, and decentralized (Knight 1992; Sebenius 1992: 352). The more powerful an involved actor, in terms of available options should agreement not be reached, i.e. the better the fall-back position, the more likely it is to obtain the outcomes it desires. Based on this argument (Knight 1992), we argue that the following factors may affect the relative influence of actors to achieve the informal rules that they prefer.

1 The formal institutional framework. While formal institutions do not decisively determine the relative power positions of actors, they may have an important influence upon them. Formal institutions grant general competences to actors, and have a substantial effect on their ability credibly to threaten specific kinds of action. Formal institutions' actual effects do not necessarily reflect the intentions of their designers, both because it is impossible to predict all contingencies that these institutions must deal with in advance, and because the third-party dispute resolution provider which provides definitive interpretations of these institutions has considerable

autonomy from the member states (Stone Sweet 1999; Moral Soriano 2002). Indeed, particular formal institutions, such as the unanimity rule, giving the right of veto to every single decision-making participant, invite the emergence of informal institutions to avoid a deadlock situation (Héritier 1999).

2 The fall-back position in the case of non-agreement, as reflected in the factors of:

- differing time horizons. Some actors take a longer view than others. Shorter time horizons may make actors vulnerable to pressure; other actors may be willing to delay decisions for long periods, or to threaten such delay, if this serves their particular interests.
- differing sensitivity to failure. Some actors may be less affected by failure to reach agreement on a specific item of legislation (or legislation in general) than others because of differences in the intensity of preferences, i.e. the saliency of an issue to them. These actors will be better able to make credible threats with regard to this item (or items) of legislation, in order to enhance their overall position in the negotiation of informal rules.

The two factors discussed above are likely to have an important – and differential – impact on the ability of actors to decisively shape terms of interaction that are favourable to them. Over time, a basic *modus vivendi* is likely to be hammered out, consisting of informal rules which provide a basic structure to interactions between actors by co-ordinating expectations, which will reflect the differential power of actors to make credible threats that other actors must take account of. This process of informal institutionalization is likely to affect outcomes in two main ways: (1) informal institutions may modify or even supersede formal procedures; (2) substantive issues may be instrumentalized to establish informal institutional gains.

First, when informal institutions have arisen, these clearly are likely to structure the legislative process. They may have implications for legislative procedures, affecting the practices through which legislation is drafted and amended, modifying, or in extreme cases effectively replacing, the formal institutions governing inter-institutional relations, thus shifting the relative decision-making weight between actors. Second, while actors struggle over informal rules, they may seek to demonstrate their power by delaying or blocking individual items of legislation that are important to others, so as to show that they are willing to endure breakdown (i.e. are obdurate 'types'), and thus increase their overall bargaining strength.

Therefore, our first claim is that there is a process of informal institution creation, which is influenced, but certainly not determined, by the formal institutional framework. Informal institutions will also be affected by power disparities and different intensities of preferences in the negotiation process between actors. In other words, the availability of non-agreement alternatives for actors will reflect not only formal institutions, but also differences in time horizons and differences in sensitivities to failure.

Second, the processes of formal and informal institutional change may become imbricated, so that actors with little direct power over formal institutional change will seek to exercise indirect influence through making their informal co-operation conditional on formal institutional concessions that they desire.

## 3.1 The introduction of informal institutional rules

Within the European Union (EU), we apply these arguments to the codecision procedure of legislative decision-making, which has been the subject of much recent study. The two most important actors engaged in negotiations over the informal rules under which codecision is applied are the Council of Ministers and the European Parliament; while the European Commission plays a role, it is a secondary one.

We argue that:

— *legislative actions will be linked together in a succession of indefinitely iterated interaction (issue) rounds, wherein legislative actors will seek to make their co-operation in one issue round conditional on another;*
— *substantive short-term policy goals will be forfeited in order to obtain long-term institutional goals;*
— *these iterated interactions will give rise over time to informal institutions, which will structure actors' expectations.*

We propose that:

— *informal institutions will reflect the bargaining power of actors, as determined by the existing formal institutions and the factors affecting non-agreement alternatives, i.e. time horizons, sensitivity to failure.*

Or more specifically:

— *Given the equality of the Council and the Parliament under the codecision procedure, the actor with the better fall-back position, i.e. with longer time-horizons and less vulnerability in the case of non-agreement, will have more power to shape informal rules.*

In order to provide an initial 'plausibility probe' for our model, we seek to examine the evolution of the codecision procedure, both in formal and informal terms. If our model provides a first good fit to the data on codecision, one could proceed to a systematic testing of a number of its claims.

*Empirical plausibility probe*

*Case 1: The institutionalization of 'trialogues' and 'early agreements'.* The introduction of the codecision procedure in the Maastricht Treaty led to a series of institutional battles between the Parliament and the Council over how codecision should be implemented (Farrell and Héritier 2003). Fundamental ambiguities in the Treaty text led Parliament and Council to adopt differing interpretations. While the Parliament maintained that the codecision procedure effectively gave it equality with the Council in the process of debating and deciding legislation, the Council initially maintained that it did not need to bargain with the Parliament, and would merely indicate those pieces of legislation that it was prepared to accept or reject, on a 'take it or leave it' basis. Neither side was initially prepared to back down – the Parliament went so far as to threaten to block or slow down legislation in order to increase its negotiating power. After a series of hard-fought legislative battles, the Council gradually came to accept that it did indeed need to negotiate with the Parliament over legislative items that came under the codecision procedure. This in turn gave rise to a series of informal institutions, which instantiated the expectations of both Council and Parliament over how negotiations should proceed, and reduced transaction costs by creating a set of shared expectations among all actors in the legislative process regarding appropriate procedures.

The most important of these institutions involved the process of informal meetings, or 'trialogues' and 'early agreements' (Shackleton 2000). Trialogues allowed the Parliament and Council to meet together after the first reading of a particular piece of legislation in order to discuss points of contention, and to hammer out differences and come to a mutual agreement and avoid the conciliation procedure. The Committee of Permanent Representatives (COREPER) and the Council had to recognize that Parliament had the role of copartner in legislation. The introduction of the informal trialogues enabled both sides to speak more frankly, and to explain in more detail the underlying reasons for the positions that they adopted and, in well over a fourth of all legislative items per year, led to 'early agreements'.[5] In the words of an official from the European Parliament,

> this institutional innovation has . . . served to generate a variety of procedural norms and shared beliefs about how the parties should behave which can only be described as 'rules of engagement'. By the end of the Maastricht era, they had become so self-evident that no one contested them.[6]

In a world where the Parliament was willing and able to block legislation, the Council had a strong interest in ensuring that discussions with Parliament began at an early stage, and were conducted reasonably smoothly. The Council is keen to see legislation passed in time (because of deadlines for legislation set during European Councils). Further, the six-month presidency system means that each member state holding the presidency has a strong incentive to see part of its agenda passed through early agreements within the six months. Also, COREPER 2, which is relatively under-staffed, would face serious problems if each piece of legislation had to pass through the time-consuming and arduous procedure of conciliation. In other words, the non-agreement alternative to early agreements is costlier for the Council than the Parliament. Finally, the Council and member state government representatives are more likely to be blamed in domestic politics for failing to pass particular items of legislation than the individual Members of the European Parliament (MEPs) who are elected in 'second-order elections' which usually revolve around national controversies rather than European issues. The Council, therefore, is more vulnerable *vis-à-vis* the failure of negotiations than the Parliament and has fewer non-agreement alternatives than the Parliament in negotiating the informal rules under codecision. Hence – following our argument – the informal institutions governing codecision should to a larger extent reflect the institutional preferences of the Parliament.

Under our argument, the trialogues and early agreements can be seen as an unexpected informal institutional innovation – they were in no sense anticipated in the Maastricht provisions that introduced the codecision procedure. However, once they had been introduced – because of the Parliament's strong bargaining position – they began to guide day-to-day behaviour under codecision, and demonstrably eased transaction costs. Given the potential veto power of the Parliament over important items of legislation, the member states had some considerable incentive to reach an appropriate *modus operandi*, giving the Parliament important clout in the decision-making process that initially had been denied by the Council.

*Case 2: Establishing an informal rule of 'Council coming to committee'.* Another effort of the Parliament to establish an informal institution has enjoyed considerable success, i.e. the attempt to establish an informal rule that the Council comes to the relevant Committee of Parliament in order to defend its legislative proposals. This is very clearly an effort by the Parliament to extend its power further by building on the model of national parliaments, which have committees that can summon ministers to defend proposed legislation. The Parliament's efforts were initially opposed by many member states (Interview, Permanent Representations 1 and 2). Actors within the Council feared that this would certainly create logistical problems for the Council, given the Secretariat's chronic lack of time and resources; even more pertinently, it would also create internal and external negotiating problems for the Council. Within the Council, it would be more difficult to negotiate on contentious issues if member states' actual positions on an issue were revealed by the Presidency in an 'official' forum (Interview, Permanent Representations 1 and 2, Brussels, January 2001; Interview, MEP, Brussels, March 2001). It would also weaken the Council's negotiating position *vis-à-vis* the Parliament in a possible future conciliation by providing information about the Council's bottom line. Thus, 'it would challenge the way in which Council traditionally operates, searching for agreement outside the public eye and avoiding open discussion of its position' (Shackleton 2000: 12). Most member states would clearly prefer that contacts between the Parliament and the Council remain informal, secretive and voluntary rather than formal, public and obligatory.

As matters currently stand, the Parliament has had some real success in persuading representatives of the Presidency to come to committee. Since the Amsterdam Treaty, the competent ministers of the member state holding the

Presidency appear before the competent parliamentary committee at the beginning or end of their period in office (EP Activity Report July 2000/1: 11). In purely formal terms, the representatives of the Council only offer *information* about the overall position of the Council. They do not openly engage in *negotiations* with the members of the Parliament committee and they do not give explicit information on individual member states' stances. However, informally, the Council has recognized the need to accede to some of Parliament's demands in order to smooth the process of law-making. Thus, the Council now provides the Parliament with documents that effectively allow MEPs to figure out what the main sticking points are – and which member states oppose particular initiatives (Interviews, Council representatives, October 2001). Increasingly, ministers recognize that they need tacitly to negotiate with the committees in question in order to get legislation through. Thus, there is some considerable evidence to suggest that the Parliament is making real progress in its efforts to win concessions.

The Parliament continues to push for this to be extended to a general duty on the part of ministers to defend their proposals to the Parliament, threatening to withhold informal co-operation to persuade the Council to its point of view. 'The Parliament should not develop informal contacts unless the Council is first prepared to make a greater effort to explain its views in committee' (EP Activity Report 2000/1: 29, 52). And: 'on the basis of active Council participation in committee meetings, committees should decide what kind of contacts they are willing to agree to outside this framework e.g. trialogues' (EP Activity Report 2000/1: Appendix V). The Parliament's ability to carry through on these threats is to some extent limited by its own internal disorganization, and inability to organize MEPs to implement collective action (Farrell and Héritier 2004). Thus, the proposed informal rule met with substantial resistance on the part of rapporteurs. In one prominent MEP's words:

> They can write down whatever they want. They write a lot of reports. Nobody will take notice of that ... Those people who are really doing the job, need the contacts and they use the contacts ... I am an independent MEP. I am not one that follows the orders of the Vice President ... There are some people who want such rules, but they have no chance.
>
> (Interview, Rapporteur B, January 2002)

This internal conflict regarding the change of interorganizational rules makes it difficult for Parliament collectively to carry through on its threat, and has therefore reduced the prospects of achieving this institutional revision.

Hence, in terms of the *negotiation of an informal institutional rule* of 'Council coming to committee' the Parliament has obtained real – but somewhat limited – success.

## 3.2 The formalization of the informal institutional rules

In a second step we ask whether the informal institutional rules which have been negotiated will be formalized in subsequent treaty revision rounds. One simple argument that flows from our theory is that the combination of (a) the inability of member states to agree to complete contracts that would cover all possible contingencies, and (b) the decision rules governing formal revision, will mean that it will sometimes be impossible for member states to reverse informal institutional gains, and that indeed under certain circumstances they may wish to incorporate them into the treaty. We can derive some initial hypotheses from this simple framework.

- *When all member states agree that the informal institution in question hurts their interests, and that it can be blocked through formal Treaty changes, they will be able to incorporate new Treaty revisions that seek to undermine the informal institution on the basis of unanimity.*
- *When all member states agree that the informal institution in question has positive (or for those member states at the margin, neutral) consequences, and that transaction costs would be lowered by making it more formal, they will agree to formalize it by incorporating it into the Treaty.*
- *If member states disagree with respect to the benefit of an informal institutional rule, they will not formalize it, but the informal rule will remain as an informal rule.*

However, we note that this argument has clear limits – it does not explain certain kinds of treaty change. Thus, it cannot explain why member states would accept a loss of competences through the formalization of informal rules. In fact, there have been formal institutional developments benefiting the Parliament that cannot be explained by either of our first two hypotheses; a case in point is the elimination of the right to resubmit the Council Joint Decision after a failed reconciliation procedure. In order to account for this, one has to look beyond the preferences/unanimity logic of member state decision-making. Why has the Parliament been successful in extending its formal competences in the revision of macro-institutional rules even when the gains of the Parliament implied a relative loss of competences of the Council?

We suggest that actors, such as the Parliament, which have a limited formal role, or no formal role in the negotiation of treaty changes, may still have informal influence through their formal role in making lower-order rules. They may withhold co-operation at the lower level of rule-making or indeed in a different higher-level rule-making arena where the actor in question does have formal competences.

In the context of the EU we ask whether the Parliament as the actor with no formal rights in higher-order rules revisions will seek to use its informal weight in order to gain formal institutional concessions from the member states. Again we conduct an initial 'plausibility probe' of these arguments by showing how they seem to describe well or less well three cases of the formalization or non-formalization of informal institutions.

*Plausibility probe: the (non-)formalization of informal rules*

*Case 1: The formalization of 'early agreements'.*   During the treaty changes after Maastricht, the Council Secretariat proposed an effective extension of the trialogue procedures that had been negotiated between Parliament and Council, so that it would cover earlier parts of the codecision process. They found considerable enthusiasm among the member states. Accordingly, the Treaty of Amsterdam formally included a new measure, which allowed the Council and the Parliament to begin negotiating at a much earlier stage with regard to dossiers that were either technical in nature, or very time sensitive. This 'early agreement' provision was intended to promote agreement at the stage of the first reading, before Council had reached a formal common position. We see how an informal institution, which was not predicted *ex ante*, provided gains to member states which they formalized in a subsequent round of Treaty negotiations.

*Case 2: A stronger role for the Parliament in Treaty revisions.*   The Parliament only has a right to be heard with respect to Treaty revisions and accordingly issues Resolutions and reports. An important group of member states recognized the need to associate the Parliament more closely with the work of the Inter-governmental Conferences. Resistance to this association could be overcome 'with the help of the political agenda' (Schiffauer 2004: 10f.).

The Parliament used its right of veto over the Northern enlargement (its formal acquiescence was necessary) to push for an increased role, emphasizing that enlargement would only be possible if there were an institutional deepening of the EU. It agreed to support the enlargement decision when in 1996 it was guaranteed a role in the preparatory *groupes de réflection* for the treaty revision. In these *groupes de réflection* the representatives of the Parliament arguably played an 'agenda-setting' role (Schiffauer 2004: 11). This case shows how an actor, who is not formally part of the process of the definition of higher-order rules, by issue linkage may increase its influence by withholding its formal consent in a separate higher order issue arena where it does have a formal say.

*Case 3: A formal role for Parliament in comitology under codecision legislation.*   After the introduction of the codecision procedure the Parliament fought battles on how the codecision procedure should be applied over each individual item of legislation. Besides asserting its role in the codecision process itself, the Parliament had the institutional aim of asserting its position in the comitology process (Bergström 2003: 228; Corbett *et al.* 2000: 258). It used the Open Network Telephony case to underline its demand for a *droit de regard* and a substitution mechanism. The Council did not make any concessions and the conciliation process ended in deadlock. Finally, the Council was willing to consider the exercise of implementing powers under codecision in the Intergovernmental Conference of 1996 and to accept for the intermediate period a *droit de regard* for the Parliament. But, disappointingly for the Parliament, in the Amsterdam Treaty the member states did not formally strengthen the role of the Parliament in the exercise of implementing powers at the Treaty level, but provided for a new Comitology Decision, i.e. a revision of the Council Decision of 1987 (Bergström 2003: 230–56).

Thus, in this case the Parliament's indirect power to block legislation in its role as a co-legislator did not provide it with enough leverage to induce the formal macro-institutional decision-makers to take its views on the shaping of the treaties into account. One reason may be that the Parliament had other important issues at stake in the Amsterdam Treaty negotiations, such as the widening of the application of the codecision procedure and the right to approve the President of the Commission, so that the role in the exercise of the implementation powers did not have the same salience for Parliamentarians as winning an increase in their legislative powers.

## 4. CONCLUSION

In the above, we have argued that our approach, which seeks to identify the causal mechanisms through which deepening integration or other forms of institutional change work, helps to answer some of the questions that Haas's version of neofunctionalism has difficulty in handling. In particular, we suggest that negotiation theory helps us to identify the key causal mechanisms explaining when regional integration/institutional change does or does not occur in a particular instance. Our argument stresses the extent to which regional integration is a function of institutions, as well as the importance of differential bargaining power in accounting for institutional change. Our argument is endogenous in that it posits that institutional change occurs when ambiguities in higher-order rules lead to the negotiation of informal rules, thus allowing institutions to work on a day-to-day basis. The outcome, the informal rule, in turn depends on the relative bargaining power of the actors involved which is linked to their particular institutional position (i.e. the short-term horizon of the Council Presidency and the lesser vulnerability of the Parliament *vis-à-vis* a negotiation failure). While we develop our argument with regard to legislative institutions, we submit that it may be extended to those issue areas where scientific knowledge plays an important part. Accordingly, we suggest that Haas's research agenda, which elaborated the impact of problem interdependence and epistemic communities on the regional integration process, should be supplemented by a bargaining approach. The influence of epistemic communities on policy-making will be mediated by the negotiation processes through which institutions are created and revised. It is not enough to conceive of the impact of epistemic communities in the sense of convergence of policy beliefs as a 'trickle down' or socialization process – a finer-grained attention to the causal processes involved is needed.

Haas argues that the views of epistemic communities diffuse to and among state decision-makers, that there is an increasing likelihood of convergent state behaviour and international policy co-ordination, informed by the causal beliefs and policy preferences of the epistemic community, that the application of consensual knowledge to policy-making depends on the ability of groups transmitting this knowledge to access and exercise bureaucratic power. This is true, but 'theoretically incomplete' (Sebenius 1992: 356–7). Epistemic consensus and empowerment are not sufficient to account for agreement, and key elements are missing from Haas's account. We propose that power-based bargaining and strategic action provide the missing part of the story that Haas is trying to tell.

However, we also wish to conclude by suggesting that while Haas's account is incomplete without a theory of negotiation, so too are negotiation theories of the sort that we employ, if we do not pay attention to the factors that Haas identifies. We do not attempt to lay out a complete argument as to how to integrate bargaining theory with epistemic factors here; this is one of the key challenges facing both rational choice accounts of bargaining (which tend to overlook epistemic factors) and constructivist accounts of negotiation (which tend to underplay the real role that clashes of interests play). Instead, following Johnson (2002), we seek to identify the foundations of a research agenda that might begin to bring Haas's concern with epistemic factors back to bargaining theory, just as we have sought to apply bargaining theory to explain some of the outcomes that Haas's current model has difficulty in explaining.

In particular, we focus on the importance of problematizing the basic notions underlying game theoretic accounts of negotiation. Some aspects of negotiation are well captured by game theory. Others, even if they may be difficult to model in formal terms, are still compatible with the underlying assumptions of game theory. Others still are difficult or impossible to reconcile with the fundamental concepts of game theory as it is usually applied.

Our basic theoretical framework stems in large part from the standard accounts of bargaining in non-cooperative game theory, building both on simple accounts that employ mixed motive co-ordination games (Krasner 1991; Knight 1992) as well as the variants of the Rubinstein bargaining model (Rubinstein 1991). All of these accounts rely on the assumption that actors have *complete information* about the games that they are playing – that is, that they share common knowledge over the underlying structure of the game, including *inter alia* the possible actions that are available to each player at each decision-making node of the game, and the outcomes that are associated with particular combinations of strategies. Games that have incomplete information are, relatively speaking, intractable – while Harsanyi shows that some games of incomplete information may be transformed into games of imperfect information in which Chance takes the first move, his technique still requires that players have complete knowledge over the underlying probability distribution associated with Chance's move.[7]

Recently, it has become popular to argue that constructivist accounts may help to complement game theoretic accounts by explaining how this common knowledge is generated. While this is an important step in the right direction, it still underestimates the importance of uncertainty in explaining bargaining outcomes. In the middle of bargaining, new possibilities of action (or hitherto unknown consequences of particular actions) may be revealed to players (Farrell 2003).

Here, we may see how epistemic factors may play a crucial role, not only in shaping the common frame of knowledge shared by negotiators when bargaining begins, but also in allowing negotiators (and outside actors with specialized knowledge) to intervene in debates for strategic or non-strategic reasons. Epistemic factors may determine bargaining outcomes to the extent that they delineate the range of possible alternatives that are available to actors (Johnson 2002). This means that they will be a key negotiating resource in many contexts. Actors may deploy epistemic resources to foreclose or to disclose new possibilities of action, or to reveal hitherto unsuspected consequences associated with those actions. Thus, epistemic communities may make previously acceptable bargains unacceptable, or vice versa, by changing the common body of knowledge regarding the benefits and drawbacks associated with each available alternative. In short, they may fundamentally reshape the parameters within which political actors bargain – and do this even while bargaining is taking place. As Haas himself would predict, epistemic communities are unlikely to play such a role in the kinds of bargaining that we discuss in our empirical examples, where scientific knowledge has little relevance. However, if negotiation theory is extended to areas such as environmental policy-making, we predict that it will be necessary to pay attention *both* to epistemic factors and to bargaining in order to explain outcomes. We note that this is an important research agenda both for rationalist and constructivist approaches to international relations – understanding exactly how epistemic factors and strategic motivations intersect in situations of negotiation. While we do not pretend to do more here than sketch out the beginnings of this agenda, we feel confident in asserting that it will require attention both to the basics of strategic interaction, as sketched out by game theorists, and the forms of knowledge creation described by Haas.

**Addresses for correspondence:** Henry Farrell, Department of Political Science, Elliott School of International Affairs, George Washington University, Washington DC 20052, USA. email: henry@henryfarrell.net/Adrienne Héritier, Department of Social and Political Science, European University Institute, Via dei Roccettini 9, 50016 San Domenico di Fiesole, Italy. email: Adrienne. heritier@iue.it

## NOTES

1  We thank Yannis Karagiannis, Tanja Börzel and the anonymous reviewer for their comments and suggestions.

2  White presents a convincing analysis of how these core elements of neofunctionalism had important political implications. The methods of resolving disputes developed by Haas were taken up by Lindberg (1965: 12) who talked frequently to Karl-Heinz Narjes (Chef de Cabinet of Walter Hallstein). Hallstein in various lectures expressed the idea of a 'Sachlogik' of an inevitable process of economic and then political integration in Europe (White 2003: 121). The Commission in its famous 'triple deal' which then triggered the 'empty chair crisis' applied this approach of bundling issues when it proposed the financing of the common agricultural policy, but also unexpectedly introduced two new dimensions: to have its own financial resources and to give the European Parliament new authority to oversee the Community budget (White 2003: 124). The triple deal arguably was 'entirely the brainchild of Hallstein ... [It] ... was cooked up by Karl-Heinz Narjes and Ernst Albrecht ... and sold to Hallstein' (White 2003: 125). To be true, the issue of an increase of the supervisory authority of the Parliament linked to an independent source of revenue of the Commission was also supported by the Dutch, Italian and German governments (Bergström 2003: 61f.).
3  See also Stone Sweet (1999) for dispute resolution by courts in the interpretation of ambiguous rules; and Jupille's 'procedural politics' for the selection of lower-order rules under a higher-order rule (Jupille 2004).
4  Informal rules may also specify formal rules in a way that is useful for all actors (win/win informal rules; see Stacey and Rittberger 2003). These informal rules are not subject to negotiation, but emerge spontaneously.
5  Interview with Council Official B.
6  Shackleton (2000).
7  However, see Aumann *et al.* (1995) for an effort to develop an applicable theory of games with incomplete information.

## REFERENCES

Achen, C.H. (2003) 'Institutional realism and bargaining models', in R. Thomson, F.N Stokman, C.H. Achen and T. König (eds), *The European Union Decides: A Model Comparison.* Unpublished manuscript, pp. 95–113.
Aumann, R.J., Maschler, M.B. and Stearns, R.E. (1995) *Repeated Games with Incomplete Information,* Cambridge: MIT Press.
Bergström, C.F. (2003) *Comitology. Delegation of Powers in the European Union and the Committee System,* Oxford: Oxford University Press.
Börzel, T.A. (2005) 'Mind the gap! European integration between level and scope', *Journal of European Public Policy* 12(2): 217–36.
Corbett, R., Jacobs, F. and Shackleton, M. (2000) *The European Parliament,* London: John Harper.
European Parliament (2001) *Activity Report 2000/1,* Brussels, available on htpp://www.europarl.eu.int/code/information/activity_reports/activity_report_2002_en.pdf
Farrell, H. (2003) 'Constructing the international foundations of e-commerce: the EU–US safe harbor arrangement', *International Organization* 57(2): 277–306.
Farrell, H. and Héritier, A. (2003) 'Formal and informal institutions under codecision: continuous constitution building in Europe', *Governance* 16(4): 577–600.
Farrell, H. and Héritier, A. (2004) 'Inter-organizational negotiation and intra-organizational power in shared decision-making: early agreements under codecision and their impact on the Parliament and the Council', *Comparative Political Studies* 37(10): 1184–212.
Haas, E.B. (1958) *The Uniting of Europe,* London: Stevens & Sons.
Haas, E.B. (1961) 'International integration: the European and the universal process', *International Organization* 15(3): 366–92.

Haas, E.B. (1967) '*The Uniting of Europe* and the uniting of Latin America', *Journal of Common Market Studies* 5(4): 315–43.

Haas, E.B. (1976) 'Turbulent fields and the theory of regional integration', *International Organization* 30(2): 173–212.

Haas, E.B. (1991) 'Does constructivism subsume neo-functionalism?', in T. Christiansen, K.E. Jørgensen and A. Wiener (eds), *The Social Construction of Europe*, Thousand Oaks: Sage Publications, pp. 22–31.

Haas, E.B. (2000) Interview by H. Kreisler, Institute of International Studies, University of California at Berkeley, 30 October.

Haas, E.B. and Schmitter, P.C. (1964) 'Economics and differential patterns of political integration', *International Organization* 18(4): 705–37.

Haas, E.B., Williams, M.P. and Babai, D. (1977) *Scientists and World Order: The Uses of Technical Knowledge in International Organizations*, Berkeley: University of California Press.

Héritier, A. (1999) *Policy-making and Diversity in Europe: Escaping Deadlock*, Cambridge: Cambridge University Press.

Johnson, J. (2002) 'How conceptual problems migrate: rational choice, interpretation, and the hazards of pluralism', *Annual Review of Political Science* 5: 223–48.

Jupille, J. (2004) *Procedural Politics: Issues, Influence, and Institutional Choice in the European Union*, Cambridge: Cambridge University Press.

Knight, J. (1992) *Institutions and Social Conflict*, New York: Cambridge University Press.

Krasner, S.D. (1991) 'Global communications and national power: life on the Pareto frontier', *World Politics* 43: 336–66.

Lindberg, L.N. (1965) 'Decision-making and integration in the European Community', *International Organization* 19(1): 56–80.

Mitrany, D. (1975) *The Functional Theory of Politics*, New York: St Martin's Press.

Moral Soriano, L. (2005) 'Public services: the role of the European Court of Justice in correcting the market', in D. Coen and A. Héritier (eds), *Refining Regulatory Regimes: The Creation and Correction of Markets*, forthcoming Edward Elgar.

Rubinstein, A. (1991) 'Comments on the interpretation of game theory', *Econometrica* 59(4): 909–24.

Schiffauer, P. (2004) 'Die Gestaltungskraft des Europäischen Parlaments im Prozess der Entstehung einer Verfassung der Europäischen Union', Europäisches Parlament, Abteilung Internationale und Konstitutionelle Angelegenheiten, Brussels.

Sebenius, J.K. (1992) 'Challenging conventional explanations of international cooperation: negotiation analysis and the case of epistemic communities', *International Organization* 46(1): 323–65.

Shackleton, M. (2000) 'The politics of codecision', *Journal of Common Market Studies* 38(2): 325–42.

Stacey, J. and Rittberger, B. (2003) 'Dynamics of formal and informal institutional change in the EU', *Journal of European Public Policy* 10(6): 858–83.

Stone Sweet, A. (1999) 'Judicialization and the construction of governance', *Comparative Political Studies* 31(2): 147–84.

Tsebelis, G. and Garrett, G. (2000) 'Legislative politics in the European Union', *European Union Politics* 1(1): 5–32.

White, J.P.J. (2003) 'Theory guiding practice: the neofunctionalists and the Hallstein EEC Commission', *Journal of European Integration History* 9(2): 111–31.

## Interviews

Permanent National Representations 1, 2 and 3: six interviews, January and October 2001

Council Secretariat: two interviews, October 2001

# Neofunctionalism, European identity, and the puzzles of European integration

Thomas Risse

Then came along the political project of creating a united Europe, which had the result of creating a myriad of institutions in which very, very many people participated ... These institutions developed a permanence through which both French and German ... learned to do routine business with each other every day. A problem which they experienced was a common problem ... first comes the traumatic lesson, then comes the institution for learning to deal with each other.

(Haas 2000: 16)

## INTRODUCTION

It took four intellectual heavyweights – John G. Ruggie, Peter J. Katzenstein, Robert O. Keohane, and Philippe C. Schmitter – to write an article on the scholarly contributions of Ernst B. Haas, another intellectual giant (Ruggie *et al.* 2005).[1] Thus, writing about 'potential gaps or explanatory weaknesses of Haas's neofunctionalist thinking [to] be compensated by using your own preferred theoretical approach' (the editor's assignment to authors for this special issue) represents quite a daunting task. My own 'preferred approach' is probably meant to be moderate social constructivism, or, in Ernst and Peter Haas's terms, 'pragmatic constructivism' (Haas and Haas 2002; see also Adler 1997, 2002).[2]

To make my task a bit easier, let me first state what I will *not* do in this paper. I will not discuss here whether or not neofunctionalism can be subsumed under social constructivism as its metatheory or, worse, whether Ernst B. Haas was a social constructivist, for two reasons. First, one should not press an intellectual giant into the confines of any 'ism.' Second, Haas himself has already said all there is to say about the subject, first in the volume on the 'social construction of Europe,' and then in the above-quoted article with his son (Haas 2001; Haas and Haas 2002).[3] I take it from these two contributions that Haas pretty much sympathized with those of us sitting on the fence between moderate constructivism and soft rationalism.

What is this article about then? I take as my starting point Ernst B. Haas's famous definition of political integration as 'the process whereby political actors in several distinct national settings are persuaded to shift their loyalties, expectations, and political activities toward a new centre, whose institutions possess or demand jurisdiction over the pre-existing national states' (Haas 1958: 16). Among the more under-explored parts of that conceptualization is the 'shifting loyalties' part which I translate into a statement about collective identity formation, a subject matter dear to social constructivists. The first part of the article then engages in a conversation between Ernst B. Haas's own writing on the subject and most recent progress in the study of European identity. I then go on to use these insights to analyze what identity-related research can contribute to exploring the puzzle of disparities in European integration (see Börzel 2005). I concentrate on two issues which both refer to the scope or depth of integration:

1   How can we explain the continuing and uneasy balance between supranational and intergovernmental solutions in the institutional make-up of the European Union (EU) which has endured since the Treaty of Rome all the way through to the Constitutional Treaty?
2   Why is it that European foreign and security policy remains the one policy area lagging behind in integration, and continues to be based on consensual decision-making by the member states even if the Constitutional Treaty will enter into force?

The article concludes with a summary and an outlook for the future.

## HOW MUCH LOYALTY FOR EUROPE IS ENOUGH?

It is interesting to note that the two founding fathers of integration theory – Karl W. Deutsch and Ernst B. Haas – both include identity-related concepts in their conceptualizations. While Haas talks about 'shifting loyalties' toward supranational institutions (see above), Deutsch includes a 'sense of community' in his conceptualization of integration (Deutsch *et al.* 1957: 5–6, 9). As Deutsch *et al.* put it: 'The kind of sense of community that is relevant for integration ... turned out to be rather a matter of mutual sympathy and loyalties; of "we-feeling," trust, and mutual consideration; or partial identification in terms of self-images and interests' (Deutsch *et al.* 1957: 36; Haas, who was otherwise rather critical of Deutsch's security community argument, quotes this passage approvingly in Haas 1958: 5, fn. 1). Thus, collective identification with institutions beyond the nation-state becomes a major yardstick for measuring integration.

In these initial statements, however, it remains unclear how identity-building relates to integration. For Karl W. Deutsch, collective identification with the community was one of the indicators for the degree of integration (see also Adler and Barnett 1998 on this), i.e. part of the dependent variable. The same holds true for Ernst B. Haas's famous definition of integration, as quoted above. Yet, he never assumed that collective identification with European institutions was the starting point of integration: 'The "good Europeans" are not the main creators of the regional community that is growing up; the process of community formation is dominated by nationally constituted groups with specific interests and aims, willing and able to adjust their aspirations by turning to supranational means when this course appears profitable' (Haas 1958: xiv; see also 1958: 13; Haas 1970: 627). He assumed that more or less instrumentally rational actors oriented themselves toward supranational solutions in order to further their interests. While he was a Weberian 'soft rationalist' insofar as he assumed values and ideas as being an intrinsic part of actors' interests (Haas 2001: 27), he never argued that identification with Europe was a necessary starting condition for integration. Rather, he seems to have assumed some kind of positive feedback loop in the sense that instrumental interests lead to initial integration (transfer of authority to a 'new center') which then leads to increasing identification with the 'new center' ('shifting loyalties') resulting in further integration.

Interestingly enough, in *The Uniting of Europe*, we find some interesting arguments about 'multiple loyalties.' Referring to Guetzkow (1955), Haas argued that 'shifts in the focus of loyalty need not necessarily imply the immediate repudiation of the national state or government' (Haas 1958: 14). According to Haas, actors acquire new loyalties

1  because they value the new center of attachment as an end in itself,
2  because the new center of authority pressures them into conformity, or
3  as a side-product of otherwise instrumental behavior toward another ultimate end.

In *Beyond the Nation-State*, he clarified the third mechanism insofar as he assumed that satisfaction with the organization's performance would lead to shifting loyalties (Haas 1964: 49). 'If the process of developing dual loyalties via this mechanism continues for a sufficiently protracted period, the new central institutions may ultimately acquire the symbolic significance of end values' (Haas 1958: 14–15).

Taken together, the three causal mechanisms can be conceptualized as an ongoing socialization process by which actors internalize the values and norms of the community (on European integration as a socialization mechanism, see Checkel, forthcoming a). When the new supranational institutions acquire 'the symbolic significance of end values,' socialization appears to be complete in that actors have internalized its values and norms as part of their collective identities. Haas seemed to have imagined identification with supranational institutions as an incremental process, that works via both logics of 'consequentialism' and of 'appropriateness' (March and Olsen 1989, 1998).

The first identification mechanism seems to pertain to the 'good Europeans,' i.e. those actors who support European integration for ideational and identity reasons (an 'end in itself'). While Haas himself dismissed this mechanism as largely irrelevant for integration, Craig Parsons has recently argued against both neofunctionalists and liberal intergovernmentalists that we should not overlook the significance of ideational factors in the early days of European integration (Parsons 2002, 2003). The second causal mechanism ('pressure into conformity') could be understood as a process of habitualization. Actors become increasingly used to the supranational institution which then leads to loyalty transfers. These two mechanisms both work via the logic of appropriateness rather than through instrumental utility-maximization.

The third mechanism combines the two logics. The more actors are satisfied with the institution's performance to meet their interests ('logic of consequentialism'), the more they will identify with the institution ('logic of appropriateness'). In David Easton's language, specific support for the institution's output leads to increased diffuse support for the institution as such (Easton 1965). This final mechanism could be regarded as an ideational 'spill-over' process.[4]

Unfortunately, Haas gave up on loyalty transfer later, preferring instead to talk about the transfer of authority and legitimacy (Haas 1970: 633). But he also started asking, '(h)ow do actors learn? Do perceptions of benefits from changing transactions affect the definition of interests? Is there some other process of socialization at work?' (1970: 622; see also Haas's later work on learning, particularly Haas 1990). When Haas abandoned European identity, European integration studies followed suit. Neofunctionalists would battle (liberal) intergovernmentalists and vice versa, but this fight was mainly about chapter 8 in *The Uniting of Europe* ('The Expansive Logic of Sector Integration') focusing on 'spill-over' effects and unintended consequences as well as about the nature and power of supranational institutions. It was lost in these battles that neofunctionalism and liberal intergovernmentalism agreed about theorizing about European integration 'from the domestic bottom up' and shared a soft rationalist ontology, while disagreeing about the process.[5] Then 'multi-level governance' came along as the game in the European town trying to differentiate itself from both neofunctionalism and (liberal) intergovernmentalism (e.g. Hooghe and Marks 2001; Jachtenfuchs and Kohler-Koch 2003). 'Shifting loyalties' as a defining feature of political integration was largely lost as an object of study. Up to the early 1990s, the conventional wisdom simply held that European integration was somehow marching along without any noticeable transfers of loyalty from the nation-states to the European level.

More than forty-five years after the publication of *The Uniting of Europe*, however, exploring European identity has assumed center-stage in European studies. Moreover, and through the combined effort of quantitative sociologists, experimental psychologists, hermeneutic discourse analysts, and political scientists, a new scholarly consensus has emerged that strikingly resembles Ernst B. Haas's original thoughts on multiple loyalties in 1958 (for the following, see particularly Herrmann *et al.* 2004; and also Risse 2003). In fact, Haas was exactly right in his thinking about multiple loyalties. It is wrong to conceptualize European identity in zero-sum terms, as if an increase in European identity necessarily decreases one's loyalty to national or other communities. Europe and the nation are both 'imagined communities' (Anderson 1991) and people can feel a part of both communities without having to choose some primary identification. Survey data suggest and social psychological experiments confirm that many people, who strongly identify with their nation-state, also feel a sense of belonging to Europe (Citrin and Sides 2004). Analyses from Eurobarometer data and other sources show that 'country first, but Europe, too' is the dominant outlook in most EU countries and people do not perceive this as contradictory. The real cleavage in mass opinion consists between those who only identify with their nation and those perceiving themselves as attached to both their nation and Europe. Nationalists are far less likely to support European integration than those who at least partially also identify with Europe (Carey 2002). Moreover, as Marks and Hooghe show, identity is a stronger predictor for support for European integration than economic rationality (Hooghe and Marks 2004).

Thus, Ernst B. Haas had already got it right in the late 1950s that European integration would lead to dual or multiple identities. What is less clear, however, is what the concept of 'multiple identities' actually means. The empirical findings reported above confirm the truism that people hold multiple identities and that Europe and the EU can be easily incorporated in people's sense of community. There are at least two ways in which we can think of multiple identities pertaining to territorial and political spaces.[6] First, identities can be *nested*, conceived of as concentric circles or Russian Matruska dolls, one inside the next. My identity as a Rhinelander is nested in my German identity, which is again nested in my Europeanness. We find the 'Russian Matruska doll' model of European and other identities on both the level of élites and of ordinary people. This model suggests some hierarchy between people's sense of belonging and loyalties. European and other identities pertaining to territorially defined entities can be nested into each other so that 'Europe' forms the outer boundary, while one's region or nation-state constitutes the core.

There is a second way of conceptualizing the relationship between European and national identities which people might hold. We could call it a 'marble cake' model of multiple identities. Accordingly, the various components of an individual's identity cannot be neatly separated on different levels as the concept of nestedness implies. What if identity components influence each other, mesh and blend into each other? What if my self-understanding as German inherently contains aspects of Europeanness? Can we really separate a Catalan from a European identity? Most empirical work on European identity does not explicitly deal with such a 'marble cake' concept. Yet, most of the evidence is actually consistent with it, starting with the 'nation first, Europe second' identification found in the Eurobarometer data.

One corollary of the 'marble cake' model is that European identity might mean different things to different people. EU membership, for example, might lead to an identity change, which impacts upon the previous national identity. Since EU membership identity then interacts with rather different national identity constructions, the overall effect will not be homogenous leading to a generalized EU identity. Rather, Europe and the EU become enmeshed with given national identities leading to rather diverging identity outcomes. This concerns, above all, the content and substance of what it means to identify with Europe. Indeed, our own longitudinal study of political discourses about Europe among the major parties in France, Germany, and Great Britain revealed that the meaning of Europe varied considerably (Marcussen *et al.* 1999; for similar findings, see Diez Medrano 2003). For the German political élites, 'Europe' and European integration meant overcoming one's own nationalist and militarist past. The French élites, in contrast, constructed Europe as the externalization of distinct French values of republicanism, enlightenment and the *mission civilisatrice*. While French and German political élites managed to embed Europe into their understandings of national identity, the British élites constructed Europe in contrast to their understandings of the nation, particularly the English nation. This qualitative analysis is consistent with some quantitative data according to which there is variation in the degree to which even 'nationalists,' who solely identify with their nation-state, support European integration. Portuguese nationalists are still more likely to support the EU than, say, British nationalists (Hooghe and Marks 2004). This can only be understood and explained if we assume that the notion of being Portuguese already contains some attachment to Europe, while this is far less the case for the idea of Britishness.

Haas was also right in his assumption that the EU was and is essentially an élite-driven project – similar to other nation-building projects. No wonder that identification with and support for Europe and its institutions is highest among political and social élites. Eurobarometer data demonstrate an enormous gap between élite support (in fact, élite *consensus*) for the EU, on the one hand, and widespread skepticism among the larger public, on the other (see e.g. Spence 1998). The difference between élite and citizen identification with Europe can be largely explained by how 'real' Europe is for people. Social psychologists refer to the concept of 'entitativity' (Castano 2004). An imagined community becomes real in people's lives when they increasingly share cultural values, a perceived common fate, increased salience, and boundedness. The EU is certainly very *real* for Europe's political, economic, and social élites.

For the citizens in general, the EU is still a more distant community than the nation-state, despite the fact that EU rules and regulations cover almost every political issue-area by now. There are at least three reasons for this. First, while EU law is the law of the land, has direct effect, and overrides national law, EU authorities do not implement European rules and regulations, but national and subnational authorities do. Thus, when citizens are confronted with, say, environmental regulations in their daily lives, they rarely know that these are EU rules. Second and more important, 'Europe' has fuzzy boundaries. While there are plenty of indicators telling me that I have left Germany, it is unclear when I have left 'Europe.' Yet, boundedness is a crucial ingredient for the psychological reality of a community in people's lives. Third, the élite discourse about the EU is ambivalent at best when it comes to 'shared values' and 'common fate.' On the one hand, there is the conscious identity construction of a liberal and civic community emanating from EU institutions. On the other hand, national policy-makers routinely reify the nation-state in their dealings with Brussels. Whenever they charge the EU for some tough decision at home, they adopt a populist rhetoric of conscious blame-shifting ('Brussels made me do it').

But Haas was not that much concerned about mass public opinion and the loyalties of the ordinary citizens, as he regarded European integration as an élite affair. While he was right in general concerning élite attitudes toward the EU – strong support and collective identification as well as multiple loyalties to the EU and the nation-state – it is less clear whether his assumed causal mechanisms, namely some degree of socialization, actually hold (for the following, see particularly Checkel, forthcoming a; forthcoming b). When it comes to the three causal socialization mechanisms identified in Haas's work (see above), the jury is still out.

Let me start with the third mechanism identified above, namely identification as a side-product of otherwise instrumental behavior. Haas seemed to have assumed in this context that those who profit the most from European integration are also more likely to shift their loyalties toward Europe than others. If this were true, two groups should be much more supportive of European integration than they actually are. First, farmers are arguably the one professional group who profit most from the EU which spends by far the largest percentage of its budget on the common agricultural policy (CAP). Yet, there is no indication that farmers identify with the EU to any considerable degree. Their satisfaction with the EU's performance appears also to be rather low. Second, we would expect women to be in general more supportive of European integration than men, given that it was the EU that pushed gender equality, particularly equal treatment and equal pay in the workplace (Caporaso and Jupille 2001). But there is a gender gap in support for the EU, with men being in general more supportive of integration than women (Liebert and Sifft 2003; Nelson and Guth 2000).

As to the first and second mechanisms mentioned above, it remains unclear which of the two causal arrows is stronger: Does strong identification with Europe lead to support for European integration and for EU institutions? Or does involvement and interaction with EU institutions lead to stronger identification with Europe?

On the one hand, Jeffrey Lewis's work on the Committee of Permanent Representatives (COREPER) in particular appears to show socialization effects through strong involvement with European institutions. New members of COREPER are quickly socialized into the rules of the game and many of the national permanent representatives to the EU adopt a 'double hatted' loyalty to their nation-state and to the EU (Lewis 1998a, 1998b; Lewis, forthcoming; see also Laffan 2004).

On the other hand, Liesbet Hooghe shows that the reverse causal arrow also seems to hold. While she finds that Commission officials support European integration much more strongly than national bureaucrats, she sees little socialization at work. Only those who enter the Commission at a relatively young age appear to be socialized in support for the EU, while all others already come to Brussels with strong and positive attitudes toward European integration (Hooghe 2001; Hooghe, forthcoming). Public opinion research also seems to point in the direction that identity strengthens support for the EU rather than vice versa (Citrin and Sides 2004; Hooghe and Marks 2004).

In sum, while Ernst B. Haas was right on target concerning his conceptualization of multiple loyalties, we still do not know for sure whether his assumed causal mechanisms — socialization into stronger identification with Europe combining expected benefits from integration with an incremental habitualization process — hold true. We still know too little about the causal relationship between multiple including European identities, on the one hand, and European institutions, on the other. At least one of Haas's assumed causal mechanisms in both *The Uniting of Europe* and in his 1970 article — perception of benefits from the EU → re-definition of interests → European identity — does not seem to hold. Moreover, the two other mechanisms, while contradictory at first glance, might actually be complementary. European institutions might well exert some identity pull toward European élites and citizens, while strong identification with the EU might increase the support for and the legitimacy of the EU. This has important repercussions for the two puzzles of European integration to which I will now turn.

## THE DOUBLE PUZZLE OF EUROPEAN INTEGRATION

There are two puzzles in the European integration process from a neofunctionalist viewpoint that require further exploration:

1   What explains the continuing balance in the institutional make-up of the EU between intergovernmental and supranational institutions that continues to persist all the way up to the Constitutional Treaty?

2 Why are external aspects of European security policy still not integrated, while its internal aspects have moved much further along toward communitarization?

## Supranationalism versus intergovernmentalism

As to the first question, the 'expansive logic of sector integration' (Haas 1958: ch. 8) and its 'spill-over' effects explain to a surprisingly large degree why ever more policy sectors have become integrated and communitarized during the European integration process. To that extent, there is no need to discard neofunctionalism. Yet, if we follow the logic of Haas's arguments, we would probably have expected that the power of EU supranational institutions such as the Commission, the European Parliament, and the European Court of Justice would constantly increase in parallel to sector integration at the expense of intergovernmental institutions such as the European Council and the Council of Ministers. While the transition to qualified majority voting (QMV) implies a loss of veto power for individual member states, it affects the balance between the various institutions only indirectly. One could argue, for example, that the agenda-setting power of the Commission is strengthened under QMV, because it need not fear vetoes by individual member states.[7] But we can see that, over the past almost twenty years since the Single European Act, those who would have predicted that the Commission would become some sort of European government have been proved wrong. From Maastricht via Amsterdam and Nice all the way to the Constitutional Treaty, the balance of power between particularly the Council and the Commission has reached a rather stable equilibrium, even though the 'expansive logic of sector integration' and communitarization continued steadily to run its course. How can we explain this situation?

The first-cut answer pertains, of course, to the intergovernmental logic of treaty negotiations in the EU (Moravcsik 1998). Altering the balance of power between the EU institutions concerns constitutional issues which are the prerogative of the member states as 'masters of the treaties.' Moreover, these are among the most contested questions in the union, because they relate to the *'finalité politique'* of the EU, a debate which has recently gained momentum again following German foreign minister Joschka Fischer's speech at Humboldt University in 2000 (Joerges *et al.* 2000). Since the member states cannot agree on whether the EU should remain a fundamentally intergovernmental institution or whether it should move in the direction of a federal state, the continuous stalemate between the Commission and the Council is exactly what one would expect.

What, however, explains the rather stable preferences of the EU member states when it comes to such thorny constitutional questions? It is here that both neofunctionalism and its main competitor, liberal intergovernmentalism, come to a screeching halt in their explanatory power. For both neofunctionalism and liberal intergovernmentalism take economic interdependence as the starting condition for explaining member state preferences. They just assume different causal mechanisms as to how sectorial preferences translate into integration outcomes (see Haas 2001: 30, fn. 10, on this point). The two integration theories might be able to explain the variation between communitarized versus non-communitarized sectors (but see below). But they do not really address the question whether communitarization works via instituting QMV in the Council or via strengthening the powers of the Commission or via a combination of both. Ultimately, of course, liberal intergovernmentalism predicts that constitutional powers will remain with the member states, while neofunctionalism would expect an ever-increasing role for supranational institutions. But still, neither approach can explain the constitutional preferences of the member states.

A focus on collective identities might help in this context. Why is it that federal member states consistently favor federal solutions for the institutional make-up of the EU, while unitary member states usually prefer strengthening the intergovernmental pillar (see Koenig-Archibugi 2004)? As Markus Jachten-fuchs has demonstrated in detail, there is a clear correlation between a member state's constitutional tradition and its preferences for institutional solutions at the EU level (Jachtenfuchs 2002). Federally organized member states which are used to sharing sovereignty among the various levels of territorial governance are more than willing to give up sovereignty when it comes to the EU. The Federal Republic of Germany is perhaps the most striking example in this context. Its co-operative federalism is based on the principle of shared sover-eignty between the federal level and the *Länder* (Börzel 2002). For the past forty years, Germany has been more than willing to give up national sovereignty in favor of strengthened European integration.

The United Kingdom, in contrast, represents a unitary state, in spite of all recent efforts at regional devolution. With the one exception of Margaret Thatcher's endorsement of QMV during the negotiations leading up to the Single European Act, British leaders have consistently rejected strengthening supranational institutions of the EU. The British dominant discourse – whether among the political élites or in the mass media – strongly emphasizes intergovernmentalism (Marcussen *et al.* 1999).

But how can we explain that a country's constitutional tradition and experi-ences are linked to its preferences for intergovernmentalism versus supranation-alism? Simon Bulmer and Peter Katzenstein have argued in this context that German experiences with a federal state are simply externalized on to the European level, since institutional isomorphism makes life so much easier for German policy-makers and bureaucrats to function within the Brussels frame-work (Bulmer 1997; Katzenstein 1997). If that were the case, Germany should have both more influence in the EU policy-making process and, as a result, a better compliance record with EU law than, say, Britain. Neither is true, of course. Britain's compliance with EU law and regulations puts it among the top EU member states, while Germany features somewhere in the middle (Börzel *et al.* 2003). I suggest that we have to unpack the notion of 'constitutional tradition' to get a handle on the question. A country's insti-tutional division of territorial powers (or lack thereof) is not just about formal constitutional questions. It also comes with a set of collective under-standings about what it means to be a 'federal' or 'unitary' state. That sover-eignty can be shared or divided, for example, is deeply ingrained in the German collective identity pertaining to their state. That sovereignty resides in one single place, namely in the Parliament, is equally deeply ingrained in British understandings about the nation-state. This explains to a large degree the difficulties which Britain has continuously faced in accepting the ceding of sovereignty rights to the EU. It also accounts for the ease with which Germany has been prepared to support supranationalism.

Of course, the German dominant élite discourse on Europe also helps in this context, while the opposite is the case regarding Britain. German collective élite identity has deeply embraced the notion of a 'European Germany' (Thomas Mann) so that Germanness cannot be understood without reference to Europe. In particular, modern Germany is identified with supporting Europe and European integration as the ultimate proof that the country has overcome its nationalist and militarist past (Nazi Germany as the European 'other;' see Engelmann-Martin 2002; Risse and Engelmann-Martin 2002; also Diez Medrano 2003). In contrast, British democracy does not need Europe for its own legitimation. Rather, 'Europe' constitutes the 'friendly Other' in the British dominant discourse as a result of which British leaders usually sit on the fence when it comes to institutional questions of the EU.

In sum, the diverging member state preferences for the EU's institutional design and its *finalité politique* can be largely explained on the basis of their constitutional traditions and collective identities. A similar argument can be made with regard to the second neofunctionalist puzzle, which concerns the lagging behind of European foreign and security policy.

## The puzzle of European foreign and security policy

Why has European foreign and security policy (CFSP/ESDP) not been com-munitarized yet, but remains the one and only dominantly intergovernmental pillar of the EU's policy-making structure even after the Constitutional Treaty will have entered into force? Early (neo)functionalist reasoning confined spill-over effects and the like to 'low politics,' while the 'high politics' of foreign and defense affairs was unlikely to be affected by these dynamics (see also Walter Mattli's contribution to this volume). Yet, the puzzle remains: It is unclear, for example, where the realms of 'low politics' end and those of 'high politics' begin. What about monetary sovereignty and the Maastricht Treaty's introduction of economic and monetary union (EMU) leading up to the euro, the single currency? One could make the (ex post) argument that the single market includ-ing the four freedoms somehow required a single currency as its logical exten-sion, i.e. that we can observe functional spill-over mechanisms into the 'high politics' of monetary sovereignty here.

Similar arguments can be made with regard to internal security and home affairs. Internal security certainly concerns 'high politics' insofar as it refers to a constitutive feature of the modern nation-state, namely its domestic sovereignty in terms of its monopoly over the use of force. If nation-states are prepared to give up domestic sovereignty in internal security affairs, why are they not prepared to do so when it comes to external security and defense? It is noteworthy in this context that the treaties of Maastricht pretty much put internal and external security on a similar footing with regard to European integration. Both the second and the third pillars firmly remained intergovernmental in the Maastricht Treaty. Since then, however, the speed increased with which justice and home affairs (JHA) including aspects of internal security became integrated and were moved toward QMV, while CFSP/ESDP remained in the intergovernmental camp. The Constitutional Treaty, should it ever enter into force, will remove the pillar structure of the treaties as a result of which most internal security questions will be subjected to QMV and co-decision procedures, while CFSP/ESDP remains the one EU policy area in which supranational procedures still do not apply. Once again, one could argue that neofunctionalist spill-over mechanisms explain the incremental integration of internal security questions into 'normal' EU decision-making procedures. The single market not only necessitated a single currency, but also the removal of internal borders leading up to the Schengen agreements. Once you remove internal border controls, however, internal security questions assume center-stage and must be integrated, too. At least, this is a plausible argument to explain why JHA have been subjected to the same mechanisms of incremental integration as other EU policy areas.[8]

Thus, the distinction between 'high' and 'low' politics does not help in explaining the puzzle as to why foreign and defense affairs remain the odd one out in European integration. European integration has affected too many questions of 'high politics' in the meantime, including core features of the modern nation-state such as monetary sovereignty and internal security.

International relations theory presents a ready-made explanation for the puzzle, of course: Realism – from Morgenthau to Waltz (Morgenthau 1948; Waltz 1979) – tells us that states are extremely unlikely to give up external sovereignty and the ultimate decision over war and peace. When the survival of the nation-state is at stake as in questions of war and peace, states do not share or pool sovereignty. There are two problems with this argument, though, which sounds plausible at first sight. First, realism itself is indeterminate in these questions. At least, one can distinguish a version emphasizing that states are primarily 'autonomy-seeking' from a variant of realism which focuses on 'influence-seeking' behavior (on these distinctions, see Baumann et al. 2001). The refusal to extend QMV to decisions over war and peace would be consistent with the realist argument that states are likely to preserve as much autonomy as possible.[9] As to the 'influence-seeking' version of realism, however, things appear to be more complicated. If states seek to increase their power and influence in international politics, then the unwillingness of EU member states to give up external sovereignty in foreign and security affairs is outright self-defeating. The less Europe speaks with one voice in world politics, the less

EU member states are able to influence outcomes. The European divisions over the Iraq War only serve to highlight this point. Europe remains divided, while the US rules. Moreover, and whatever the version of realism one adheres to, balancing is to be expected as the standard behavior of nation-states. Balancing in a one-superpower world, however, requires pooling resources and building alliances. From this perspective, one would expect the EU to get its act together in foreign and security affairs in order to build a counterweight to US power. Yet, for all practical purposes, such European posturing seems to remain (French) wishful thinking for the time being.

Second, it is wrong that European states are not prepared to give up sovereignty in the realm of security and defense. Most EU member states are also members of the North Atlantic Treaty Organization (NATO) alliance. While NATO is an intergovernmental organization built on the consensus rule when it comes to decision-making, it features a completely integrated military structure. Once decisions have been made with regard to war and peace, German and other troops of NATO members are prepared to die under the command of US, British, or French generals. In the post-Cold War environment, this is no longer hypothetical, but routinely the case in Bosnia, Afghanistan, and elsewhere. Moreover, and perhaps more important, there is no agreement among EU member states that giving up sovereignty in the realm of foreign and defense affairs constitutes a bad idea. Rather, roughly two-thirds of the current EU member states – let alone their populations – would be more than willing to supranationalize and to communitarize external security and national defense. Thus, realism only seems to apply to *some* countries such as the UK. To put it differently: If we want to account for the puzzle of European foreign and security policy, we must explain the variation among EU member states with regard to their preparedness to communitarize defense affairs.

We might be able to solve the puzzle of why CFSP/ESDP has not (yet) been communitarized if we do not conceptualize national sovereignty as a quasi-objective reality, but as an inter-subjective social construction. National sovereignty is a social construct that is deeply embedded in the collective identity of a nation-state (see e.g. Biersteker 2002; Biersteker and Weber 1996). Interestingly enough in this context, the only available empirical study that seeks to explain the variation in the propensity of EU members to give up sovereignty in foreign and defense affairs concludes that, once again, federal states are much more likely to prefer communitarization of external security and defense policies than unitary states (Koenig-Archibugi 2004; see also Hooghe 2001 on a related point). The same member states that prefer supranationalism over intergovernmentalism in general are also prepared to supranationalize foreign and defense policies. What is less clear, though, are the causal mechanisms linking territorial structures to preferences for a common European foreign and defense policy. I suggest that the social constructions and collective understandings that come with federalism might be key. As argued above, countries whose élites and citizens are used to the notion that sovereignty can be divided and/or shared between various levels of governance are also more prepared to include supranational levels of governance in these understandings. Once one is prepared to accept supranationalism over intergovernmentalism in general, this might also extend into questions of war and peace. Borrowing from neofunctionalism, one could call this 'ideational spill-over.'

There is one further corollary on this issue. Those EU member states (such as Germany) who support a communitarized foreign and security policy are also those member states with mostly multilateral and co-operative foreign and security policies. They do not prefer a militarized European foreign and defense policy, but Europe as a 'civilian power' (on this concept, see Duchêne 1972; Maull 1990, among others). While a 'civilian power' does not refuse to use military force under exceptional circumstances, the emphasis is clearly on co-operative security policy, multilateralism, and the rule of (international) law. The new European Security Strategy exemplifies the foreign policy outlook of a civilian power (European Council 2003). In contrast, the UK and France, which are both rather centralized states and, given their traditions as colonial powers, have been more than willing to use military force if need be in the past, have also been reluctant to give up sovereignty concerning questions of war and peace. This leads me to speculate that federal states and civilian powers are more likely to support the communitarization of foreign and defense affairs, because they are more prepared to share sovereignty anyway, on the one hand, but also prefer co-operative and multilateral foreign policies over unilateralism, on the other hand.

## CONCLUSIONS

I have argued in this article that Ernst B. Haas was right when he talked in *The Uniting of Europe* about 'multiple loyalties' and identified various socialization mechanisms leading to European identity which combined the two logics of consequentialism and of appropriateness. One just needs to remember that this book was published in 1958, i.e. long *before* European integration had reached a stage when one could reasonably expect such socialization processes to occur. Unfortunately, Haas and his followers in European integration studies quickly gave up studying socialization processes and started intellectual fist-fights between neofunctionalism and (liberal) intergovernmentalism. It was only during the 1990s that rigorous empirical research began taking up the challenge of studying collective identity-building processes surrounding European integration. This research quickly debunked the idea that European identity was only possible by overcoming national identities, but confirmed what Ernst B. Haas already knew in 1958, namely, that transferring loyalty to Europe and the EU is possible without giving up one's national (or regional or local or gender) identities (see Herrmann *et al.* 2004).

As to the various socialization mechanisms identified by Haas, research has only started identifying the various causal pathways (see e.g. Checkel, forthcoming a). Preliminary results seem to challenge the assumption, though, held by Ernst

B. Haas and other soft rationalists, that the transfer of loyalties on to the European level simply followed from the material benefits received through European integration. If this were the case, farmers should be the most ardent supporters of the EU, throwing their tomatoes at Euro-sceptics rather than at bureaucrats in Brussels. There simply seems to be little spill-over from the material into the ideational realms.

At the same time, there is some evidence suggesting that socialization into European identity works not so much through transnational processes or through exposure to European institutions, but on the national levels in a process whereby Europeanness or 'becoming European' is gradually being embedded in understandings of national identities. The 'marble cake' model of European identity which I outlined above tries to conceptualize this process. This also suggests that the compatibility between European identity and national identities varies by country in a similar way as national constitutional traditions resonate with European integration to rather different degrees.

This latter reasoning might also shed light on the double puzzle of European integration, i.e. the persistent balance in the EU's constitution-building between supranational and intergovernmental institutions, on the one hand, and the lagging behind of foreign/defense affairs in European integration, on the other. If national processes and collective understandings are crucial to understanding the Europeanization of national identities, this will lead to uneven and varied degrees to which Europe can be embedded in collective identities. As argued above, federal states with respective constitutional traditions change their collective understandings to include Europe and orientations toward supranationalism more easily than unitary and centralized states.

If I am correct, we can speculate about the future of European integration: It is more than likely that foreign and defense affairs will follow other policy areas in gradually moving toward QMV and the like, albeit more slowly. Yet, the institutional balance between supranational and intergovernmental elements in the treaties will persist given the fundamental disagreements over the future of the EU among the member states and their populations which are deeply embedded in their own national and European identities.

**Address for correspondence:** Thomas Risse, Center for Transatlantic Foreign and Security Policy, Otto Suhr Institute of Political Science, Freie Universität Berlin, Ihnestr. 22, 14195 Berlin, Germany. Tel: +49 (0) 30 838 55527. Fax: +49 (0) 30 838 54160. email: risse@zedat.fu-berlin.de

## NOTES

1  I thank Tanja A. Börzel and an anonymous reviewer for critical comments and, above all, for turning around this article within three days!
2  Incidentally, if people want to understand Emanuel Adler's middle-ground theorizing about social constructivism and his work on social learning and cognitive evolution, they ought to read Ernst B. Haas, who was Adler's mentor, first.

3  Ernst B. Haas also contributed to the now famous constructivist mantra of the mutual constitutiveness of agency and structure. Just read *Beyond the Nation-State's* treatment of and attempt to reconcile functionalism and system theory (Haas 1964: 78–81).
4  I thank Tanja Börzel for alerting me to this point.
5  Haas completely acknowledged the common ground between neofunctionalism and intergovernmentalism and then wondered why Moravcsik in particular 'makes such extraordinary efforts to distinguish his work from these sources' (Haas 2001: 30, note 10).
6  A third concept of multiple identities pertains to cross-cutting loyalties. While I might strongly identify with my gender *and* with Europe, others who also identify with their gender might not identify with Europe at all (and vice versa).
7  I thank the anonymous reviewer for alerting me to this point.
8  Of course, one can also pinpoint external events and shocks such as September 11, 2001, to explain why internal security questions have become more integrated over time. See Kleine (2003).
9  Never mind, however, that the same European nation-states that seem to be eager to preserve their sovereignty and autonomy in external affairs have been more than willing to give up sovereignty in many other issue-areas of political life which is completely inconsistent with this variant of realism.

## REFERENCES

Adler, E. (1997) 'Seizing the middle ground. Constructivism in world politics', *European Journal of International Relations* 3(3): 319–63.
Adler, E. (2002) 'Constructivism in international relations', in W. Carlsnaes, B. Simmons and T. Risse (eds), *Handbook of International Relations*, London: Sage, pp. 95–118.
Adler, E. and Barnett, M. (1998) 'Security communities in theoretical perspective', in E. Adler and M. Barnett (eds), *Security Communities*, Cambridge: Cambridge University Press, pp. 3–28.
Anderson, B. (1991) *Imagined Communities. Reflections on the Origin and Spread of Nationalism*, London: Verso.
Baumann, R., Rittberger, V. and Wagner, W. (2001) 'Neorealist foreign policy theory', in V. Rittberger (ed.), *German Foreign Policy Since Unification. Theories and Case Studies*, Manchester: Manchester University Press, pp. 37–67.
Biersteker, T.J. (2002) 'Forms of state, states of sovereignty: the changing meanings of state, sovereignty and territory in the theory and practice of international relations', in W. Carlsnaes, B. Simmons and T. Risse (eds), *Handbook of International Relations*, London: Sage, pp. 157–76.
Biersteker, T.J. and Weber, C. (eds) (1996) *State Sovereignty as Social Construct*, Cambridge: Cambridge University Press.
Börzel, T.A. (2002) *States and Regions in Europe. Institutional Adaptation in Germany and Spain*, Cambridge: Cambridge University Press.
Börzel, T.A. (2005) 'Mind the gap! European integration between level and scope', *Journal of European Public Policy* 12(2): 217–36.
Börzel, T.A., Hofmann, T. and Sprungk, C. (2003) 'Einhaltung von Recht jenseits des Nationalstaats. Zur Implementationslogik marktkorrigierender Regelungen in der EU', *Zeitschrift für Internationale Beziehungen* 10(2): 247–86.
Bulmer, S. (1997) 'Shaping the rules? The constitutive politics of the European Union and German power', in P.J. Katzenstein (ed.), *Tamed Power. Germany in Europe*, Ithaca, NY: Cornell University Press, pp. 49–79.

Caporaso, J.A. and Jupille, J. (2001) 'The Europeanization of gender equality policy and domestic structural change', in M. Green Cowles, J.A. Caporaso and T. Risse (eds), *Transforming Europe. Europeanization and Domestic Change*, Ithaca, NY: Cornell University Press, pp. 21–43.

Carey, S. (2002) 'Undivided loyalties. Is national identity an obstacle to European integration?', *European Union Politics* 3(4): 387–413.

Castano, E. (2004) 'European identity: a social-psychological perspective', in R.K. Herrmann, T. Risse and M. Brewer (eds), *Transnational Identities. Becoming European in the EU*, Lanham, MD: Rowman & Littlefield, pp. 40–58.

Checkel, J.T. (ed.) (forthcoming a) *International Institutions and Socialization in Europe*. Special Issue of *International Organization*, Cambridge: Cambridge University Press.

Checkel, J.T. (forthcoming b) 'International institutions and socialization in Europe: introduction and framework', *International Organization*.

Citrin, J. and Sides, J. (2004) 'More than nationals: how identity choice matters in the new Europe', in R.K. Herrmann, T. Risse and M. Brewer (eds), *Transnational Identities. Becoming European in the EU*, Lanham, MD: Rowman & Littlefield, pp. 161–85.

Deutsch, K.W. *et al.* (1957) *Political Community and the North Atlantic Area: International Organization in the Light of Historical Experience*, Princeton, NJ: Princeton University Press.

Diez Medrano, J. (2003) *Framing Europe: Attitudes toward European Integration in Germany, Spain, and the United Kingdom*, Princeton, NJ: Princeton University Press.

Duchêne, F. (1972) 'Europe in world peace', in R. Mayne (ed.), *Europe Tomorrow*, London: Fontana/Collins, pp. 32–49.

Easton, D. (1965) *A Systems Analysis of Political Life*, New York: Wiley & Sons.

Engelmann-Martin, D. (2002) 'Identity, norms and German foreign policy: the social construction of Ostpolitik and European monetary union'. Ph.D. dissertation, Department of Social and Political Sciences, European University Institute, Florence.

European Council (2003) 'A secure Europe in a better world – European Security Strategy', Brussels: European Institute for Security Studies.

Guetzkow, H. (1955) *Multiple Loyalties: Theoretical Approach to a Problem in International Organization*, Princeton, NJ: Center for Research on World Political Institutions.

Haas, E.B. (1958) *The Uniting of Europe: Political, Social, and Economic Forces 1950–57*, Stanford, CA: Stanford University Press.

Haas, E.B. (1964) *Beyond the Nation-State. Functionalism and International Organization*, Stanford, CA: Stanford University Press.

Haas, E.B. (1970) 'The study of regional integration: reflections on the joy and anguish of pretheorizing', *International Organization* 24(4): 607–46.

Haas, E.B. (1990) *When Knowledge Is Power*, Berkeley, CA: University of California Press.

Haas, E.B. (2000) 'Interview', October 30th, Berkeley.

Haas, E.B. (2001) 'Does constructivism subsume neo-functionalism?', in T. Christiansen, K.E. Jørgensen, and A. Wiener (eds), *The Social Construction of Europe*, London: Sage, pp. 22–31.

Haas, E.B. and Haas, P.M. (2002) 'Pragmatic constructivism and the study of international institutions', *Millennium* 31(3): 573–601.

Herrmann, R.K., Risse, T. and Brewer, M. (eds) (2004) *Transnational Identities. Becoming European in the EU*, Lanham, MD: Rowman & Littlefield.

Hooghe, L. (2001) *The European Commission and the Integration of Europe. Images of Governance, Themes in European Governance*, Cambridge: Cambridge University Press.

Hooghe, L. (forthcoming) 'Many roads lead to international norms, but few via international socialization. A case study of the European Commission', *International Organization*.

Hooghe, L. and Marks, G. (2001) *Multi-Level Governance and European Integration*, Lanham, MD: Rowman & Littlefield.

Hooghe, L. and Marks, G. (2004) 'Does identity of economic rationality drive public opinion on European integration?', *PSOnline www.apsanet.org* (July): 1–5.

Jachtenfuchs, M. (2002) *Die Konstruktion Europas. Verfassungsideen und institutionelle Entwicklung, Weltpolitik im 21. Jahrhundert*, Baden-Baden: Nomos.

Jachtenfuchs, M. and Kohler-Koch, B. (eds) (2003) *Europäische Integration, 2. Auflage*, Opladen: Leske & Budrich.

Joerges, C., Mény, Y. and Weiler, J.H.H. (2000) *What Kind of Constitution for What Kind of Polity?*, Florence: The Robert Schuman Centre for Advanced Studies, European University Institute.

Katzenstein, P.J. (ed.) (1997) *Tamed Power. Germany in Europe*, Ithaca, NY: Cornell University Press.

Kleine, M. (2003) 'Die Reaktion der Europäischen Union auf die Terrorangriffe vom 11. September 2001 – Zu Kooperation und Nicht-Kooperation in der inneren und äußeren Sicherheit'. Diploma thesis, Otto Suhr Institut für Politikwissenschaft, Freie Universität Berlin.

Koenig-Archibugi, M. (2004) 'Explaining government preferences for institutional change in EU foreign and security policy', *International Organization* 54(1): 137–74.

Laffan, B. (2004) 'The European Union and its institutions as "identity builders"', in R.K. Herrmann, T. Risse and M. Brewer (eds), *Transnational Identities. Becoming European in the EU*, Lanham, MD: Rowman & Littlefield, pp. 75–96.

Lewis, J. (1998a) 'Constructing interests: the Committee of Permanent Representatives and decision-making in the European Union'. Ph.D. dissertation, Department of Political Science, University of Wisconsin-Madison, Madison, WI.

Lewis, J. (1998b) 'Wearing a Janus-face: the Permanent Representatives of the European Union'. Paper presented at the 11th International Conference of Europeanists, at Baltimore, MD.

Lewis, J. (forthcoming) 'Nesting identities in Brussels: socialization and everyday decisionmaking in the European Union', *International Organization*.

Liebert, U. and Sifft, S. (2003) *Gendering Europeanisation*, Brussels: P.I.E.–Peter Lang.

March, J.G. and Olsen, J.P. (1989) *Rediscovering Institutions*, New York: The Free Press.

March, J.G. and Olsen, J.P. (1998) 'The institutional dynamics of international political orders', *International Organization* 52(4): 943–69.

Marcussen, M., Risse, T., Engelmann-Martin, D., Knopf, H.J. and Roscher, K. (1999) 'Constructing Europe? The evolution of French, British and German nation state identities', *Journal of European Public Policy* 6(4): 614–33.

Mattli, W. (2005) 'Ernst Haas's evolving thinking on comparative regional integration: of virtues and infelicities', *Journal of European Public Policy* 12(2): 327–48.

Maull, H.W. (1990) 'Germany and Japan: the new civilian powers', *Foreign Affairs* 69(5): 91–106.

Moravcsik, A. (1998) *The Choice for Europe: Social Purpose and State Power From Messina to Maastricht*, Ithaca, NY: Cornell University Press.

Morgenthau, H.J. (1948) *Politics Among Nations*, brief edition, 1993, New York: McGraw Hill.

Nelson, B.F. and Guth, J. (2000) 'Exploring the gender gap: women, men, and public attitudes toward European integration', *European Union Politics* 1(3): 191–217.

Parsons, C. (2002) 'Showing ideas as causes: the origins of the European Union', *International Organization* 56(1): 47–84.

Parsons, C. (2003) *A Certain Idea of Europe*, Ithaca, NY: Cornell University Press.

Risse, T. (2003) 'The Euro between national and European identity', *Journal of European Public Policy* 10(4): 487–505.

Risse, T. and Engelmann-Martin, D. (2002) 'Identity politics and European integration: the case of Germany', in A. Pagden (ed.), *The Idea of Europe. From Antiquity to the European Union*, Cambridge: Cambridge University Press, pp. 287–316.

Ruggie, J.G., Katzenstein, P.J., Keohane, R.O. and Schmitter, P.C. (2005) 'Transformations in world politics: the intellectual contributions of Ernst B. Haas', *Annual Review of Political Science* 8 (forthcoming).

Spence, J.M. (1998) 'The European Union. "A view from the top" – top decision makers and the European Union', Wavre: EOS Gallup Europe.

Waltz, K. (1979) *Theory of International Politics*, Reading, MA: Addison-Wesley.

# Rethinking law in neofunctionalist theory

Gráinne de Búrca

## 1. LAW AND POLITICS IN EU STUDIES

The process of European integration is one which has been studied with great interest and intensity by scholars of law and of politics alike. Yet while the relationship between law and politics generally is a subject of enduring interest for political and legal theorists and for other scholars within the two disciplines, the relationship between legal scholarship and political science scholarship in the particular context of European Union (EU) studies was slow to develop. True, the initial 'ships-passing-in-the-night' phase – during which the number of EU legal scholars whose work took the political context seriously into account and the number of political scientists studying the EU who paid attention to the role of law could probably have been counted on one hand[1] – is long past. Yet while the last decade in EU studies has seen the emergence of a substantial body of research by political scientists on the significance of law, and an expansion in the range of legal scholarship which is attentive to the political and social impact of law, the relationship has not yet matured.

For some, the notion of interdisciplinarity is impossible (Fish 1994); for others, it reflects the attempt by one discipline to colonize another (Balkin 1996). Rather than engage with these conundrums I will refer not to interdisciplinarity – in the sense of a genuine synthesis between disciplines – but instead simply to the use by scholars within one discipline of the insights, methodologies, approaches, questions or data produced by another. From this perspective, the field of EU studies – and European integration studies more particularly – has only in the last decade or so begun to produce research in which scholars from one of these two disciplines in question engage seriously with the work of the other. While the list of EU lawyers using insights from political science has grown, some of the most interesting work on European integration in recent years has been done by political scientists who are examining the distinctive role of law (Sandholtz and Stone Sweet 1998; Stone Sweet *et al.* 2001; Stone Sweet 2004; Cichowski 2002; Börzel and Cichowski 2003; Martinsen 2004; Nyikos 2003; Alter 2001; Conant 2002). In what sense, then, has the relationship between the disciplines not yet matured? Let me answer this question by turning to the topic which the editor of this special issue on the neofunctionalist theory of Ernst Haas asked me to address.

## 2. LAW AND NEOFUNCTIONALISM: THE STORY SO FAR

I was asked to provide a 'legal perspective' on the question which all contributors are addressing, namely what is the explanatory scope of Haas's neofunctionalist concepts and ideas, in view of the puzzling fact that EU member states have been willing to compromise their sovereignty significantly in certain core areas but not in others. The relevance of neofunctionalism for law is a subject which has received some attention in political science literature over the past dozen years. Prior to that, even though Ernst Haas himself had received his Ph.D. in public law and government and discussed the possibility of a theory of functional law derived from sociological jurisprudence in one of his most famous works (Haas 1964a: 40–7), significant references to the relevance of law and to legal actors in subsequent neofunctionalist analysis were few. However, from 1993 onwards, the well-known and influential analysis of Burley and Mattli (1993), later Mattli and Slaughter (1995, 1998) spawned an active debate between neofunctionalists, intergovernmentalists and others about the role of the European Court of Justice (ECJ) in the integration process (Garrett 1995; Garrett *et al.* 1998; Tsebelis and Garrett 2001; Alter 1998; Wincott 1995, 2002). Interesting and illuminating for many though their analysis was, however, the legal perspective which it brought to bear on neofunctionalism as a theory of European political integration was nonetheless a partial one. The point was succinctly put by one commentator who asked, borrowing from the opening line of Mattli and Slaughter's third intervention on the topic, 'Political science has discovered the ECJ. But has it discovered law?' (Armstrong 1998). It set out primarily to sketch a theory of 'legal integration' rather than a more general theory of the role of law in political integration. And it was less a theory of legal integration than a particular analysis, using neofunctionalist concepts, of the role of courts and of litigation in the creation of an EU legal system. The relevance of neofunctionalist theory for law, and in particular the question whether this particular account of how political integration occurs can shed light on the specific role of law within that process, remains to be more fully explored.

The 'legal neofunctionalism' scholarship of Mattli and Slaughter was, however, important in that it brought the role of legal actors in the integration process clearly into the framework of integration theory. It did so by pointing to the significance of some key rulings of the ECJ, by examining the way in which relationships of collaboration were gradually created between the ECJ and national courts, and by examining the way in which a range of legal actors connected to the litigation arena (litigants, practising lawyers and academic consultants in particular) was mobilized as a consequence of these rulings and relationships. Since neofunctionalism had been strongly criticized and indeed recharacterized by its originators many years earlier as a pre-theory, its use in this way to analyse dimensions of legal integration was an interesting and unexpected revival of Haas's work. What the authors did was to use a range of concepts from neofunctionalist theory in order to analyse certain aspects of the EU legal system. Adopting this approach, they identified the instrumental self-interest of actors as a motivating force for integrationist behaviour on the part of the ECJ judges (supposedly to increase their own authority and legitimacy), of national judges (to empower themselves *vis-à-vis* other national branches) and of litigants (to advance their interests); applying the 'spillover' concept *inter alia* to the expansion of ECJ doctrine (such as the move from a doctrine of 'direct effect' to one of 'supremacy') and to the acceptance by member states of the Court's rulings as precedents; and identifying the process of 'upgrading of common interests' in aspects of the ECJ's teleological method of interpretation. Neofunctionalism's proposition that integration would begin in functionally specific and technical areas was found by the authors to be supported by the fact that judicial and legal language is specialized and technical, thus enabling integration of the legal sphere to proceed without undue political obstruction or contestation. In short, they argued that 'the legal integration of the community corresponds remarkably closely to the original neofunctionalist model developed by Ernst Haas in the 1950s' (Burley and Mattli 1993: 43). Theirs was a novel analysis of the story of European legal/judicial integration, so familiar to EU lawyers, and yet rarely the subject of a convincing and coherent theoretical account.[2] But it was an analysis which left important questions concerning the significance of law, the place of law in neofunctionalist theory, and more generally the relevance of neofunctionalist theory for legal scholars, unanswered.

## 3. POLITICAL INTEGRATION THROUGH LAW?

Neofunctionalism was a theory of regional political integration, elaborated in particular as a way of accounting for and explaining European integration in the 1950s and early 1960s. Legal scholarship on European integration has largely focused on the role of law within that process. While this includes the way in which legal integration (including the integration of separate national legal systems, and the integration of different areas of substantive law across states) occurs, it goes beyond legal integration and includes the role of law in the process of political integration more generally. To put this in different terms, both the integration *of* law (legal integration) and integration *through* law (law in the process of political integration) are worthy subjects of study (Armstrong 1998), in the sense that law is 'both the object and the agent of integration' (Dehousse and Weiler 1990: 243). A broader legal perspective on neofunctionalist theory would include not only the question whether neofunctionalism can account for the way in which a European legal system has emerged, but also whether the theory accommodates a significant role for law in the political integration process.

The assumption that law does play a significant role in the integration process, and a role which generally furthers rather than hinders economic and political integration, is one which has been made by the large majority of the 'community' (Schepel and Wesseling 1997) of legal scholars writing on European integration (with some exceptions, e.g. Shaw 1996), even though, as political scientists have frequently pointed out, this assumption has usually been made without thorough methodological inquiry or solid evidential backing. Nonetheless, this question of the relationship between law and integration remains a central one for almost all legal scholars of European integration. The most significant body of legal scholarship to consider the role of law in the European integration process is generally referred to as the 'integration through law' school,[3] taking its title from a major comparative research project published in the 1980s on that topic (Cappelletti *et al.* 1986). A quotation from the first volume of the latter collection gives a sense of the research questions and hypotheses which animated that project:

> Integration is fundamentally a political process: whether to engage in it, its pace, shape, success and failure are largely determined by political actors and political will. But the law has a vital role to play in the process. It defines many of the political actors and the framework within which they operate, controlling and limiting their actions and relations and determining, at least partially, the effects and effectiveness of their acts. At the same time it performs a role in ordering social life, translating the highly visible political acts into more mundane daily applications and, through this implementation, it determines the implications of the political decisions. It is the role of the law in implementing the political decisions to integrate (and in some instances conditioning these decisions) that is the focus of this work.
>
> (Cappelletti *et al.* 1986: Book 1, Volume 1, Chapter 2)

The various assertions and hypotheses identified in this paragraph – i.e. that law defines the framework within which political actors work and even defines some of the actors; that law partly determines the impact and effectiveness of political acts, that it orders social life, and that in implementing political decisions to integrate, law tempers or conditions such decisions – remain amongst the most salient and interesting questions for legal scholars of European integration. Within the framework of these inquiries, political integration is the dependent variable and law, in its differing manifestations, an independent variable.

The absence of a coherent explanatory theory or methodological framework within legal scholarship for testing these various assertions and hypotheses is not an unusual weakness characterizing the field of European integration. The lack of an empirical methodology is a feature common to a great deal of legal scholarship. Unlike most of the social sciences, much of the academic discipline of law does not concern itself with explaining change. With the significant exception of the field of socio-legal research, a great deal of legal scholarship deals either with the exposition and analysis of legal doctrine (legal 'policy', legislation and case law alike), on the one hand, or with legal theory (debate about the fundamental nature of law), on the other, and even when a contextual approach is taken (i.e. when legal doctrine is deliberately considered in its economic, political and social context), it is unusual for this to be done in a self-consciously scientific way. Explanation of causal mechanisms and attempts to demonstrate the dynamics of change in a methodologically careful way tend to be left to the social scientists, and most legal scholarship contents itself with observation, assertion, speculation, prescription and critique. The disciplinary differences partly explain the immaturity of the relationship between law and political science scholarship on European integration. To the political scientist, legal scholarship often appears to be arid, technical, atheoretical (apart from the 'metatheoretical' branches of legal and constitutional theory), full of unstated or unproven assumptions, lacking empirical support, and seemingly disinterested in the actual dynamics of political and social change. To the lawyer, political science scholarship often appears to be obsessed with methodology, jargonistic, and – in particular when it engages with law – remarkably banal, in that pages are spent demonstrating a proposition which lawyers take to be axiomatic (such as that 'courts matter' or 'judges have some autonomy').

## 4. RELATING LEGAL INTEGRATION AND POLITICAL INTEGRATION

Legal scholarship on European integration, then, has assumed that law matters within the process of integration and in many instances that it has advanced integration, but an explanatory account or causal theory of this relationship has rarely been sketched or provided. Most of the political science scholarship, on the other hand, which has considered the role of law in European integration has either proceeded from neorealist premises and presented law as an essentially passive, functional tool of integration with courts as tightly constrained agents (Garrett, Kelemen, Schulz, Tsebelis) or – like the work of Burley and Mattli in applying neofunctionalist theory – it has taken a relatively narrow definition of law and a specific dimension of the process of integration – in focusing mainly on *legal* integration. That said, the definitional slipperiness and ambiguity of the independent variable within integration theory in general and within neofunctionalism in particular was recognized by Haas himself: 'Semantic confusion about "integration" must be limited even if it cannot be eliminated . . . I consider it a process for the creation of political communities defined in institutional and attitudinal terms' (Haas 1970: 610). For Haas, political integration, understood as the creation of a political community, was the proper subject of integration theory. He argued that the study and demonstration of *particular* aspects of the process or particular instances of spillover were not necessarily the same as predicting or demonstrating political integration (Haas 1970: 628). More specifically, he argued against the disaggregation of integration into social and economic components, claiming that 'political integration, if that is what we are concerned about, is more important than economic and social trends; these are important because we think that they are causally connected with political integration' (Haas 1970: 628, fn 31). Although he did not address the issue of legal integration in this context, the same argument can be made, i.e. that within integration theory, and within neofunctionalism in particular, legal integration is primarily important insofar as it is causally linked to political integration. Just as he considered economic and social integration to be earlier indicators along the path to political integration (Haas 1970: 634), legal integration could be appraised in the same way. This is not to say that the question of how 'European legal integration' occurred is not in itself an interesting or important one – not at all, but it is nevertheless only a part of the integration picture. And just as Haas was interested in understanding the precise causal mechanisms linking such other kinds of integration to the 'creation of a political community', so legal scholarship on European integration today is still confronted with this original and complex question.

Burley and Mattli in their original analysis explained their dependent variable, legal integration, as 'the gradual penetration of EC law into the domestic law of its member states' (1993: 43). They defined this to include not only 'formal penetration' – by which they meant the extent of the ECJ's development of doctrines of supremacy (the range of EU laws which are said to take precedence over national laws) and direct effect (the range of cases in which individuals can make claims in their national courts based on EU law) – but also 'substantive penetration', meaning 'the spilling over of community legal regulation from the narrowly economic domain into areas dealing with issues such as occupational health and safety, social welfare, education, and even political participation rights'. In other words, while much of their focus was on the articulation and spread of key legal doctrine by the ECJ, they were also interested in the way in which the application of ECJ legal doctrine had spread from narrower economic issues to a wider range of social and political issues. Further, they also referred to Haas's prediction of the process of indirect penetration of the political by the legal (Burley and Mattli 1993: 72–73). Nonetheless, most of their analysis concentrated on the relations which developed between the European court and national courts, and with other legal actors connected to the litigation context. More specifically, their analysis of legal integration looked essentially at courts and at judicial action rather than at the integration of law through other means, such as through the implementation of EU law by domestic legislators, through the action of administrative officials whose job it is to implement the law, or through the adaptation by relevant social actors of their behaviour to comply with legal norms. Further, the actual impact of EU law either within the domestic order, or at the national and supranational level, in conditioning the way in which political decisions are made and take effect was not the subject of their analysis. In a piece which they published five years later, however, following the extensive debate which their original analysis had triggered amongst political scientists about the autonomy or otherwise of the Court of Justice, the authors argued that 'the larger question of the relationship between the ECJ and the integration process as a whole would have required an evaluation of the actual impact of ECJ decisions in specific issue areas' (Mattli and Slaughter 1998: 184). Yet while rightly acknowledging the interesting and difficult larger question concerning the impact of law on the integration process, their later work nonetheless continued to envisage this as a function of the impact of the Court of Justice, rather than of law more generally.

## 5. DOES LAW MATTER WITHIN NEOFUNCTIONALIST THEORY?

One of the challenges, therefore, for scholars of European integration is to ascertain whether neofunctionalism, as an account of the dynamic of the political integration process, can provide a satisfactory explanation of the role of law within that process. Neofunctionalist theory, in particular through its core concepts of 'spillover' and 'upgrading of common interests', and through its focus on the mobilization of societal actors and the actions of national and supranational political and bureaucratic élites, sought to provide a theoretical account of the way in which European integration proceeded. Briefly put, Haas's neofunctionalism maintained that where the recognition of common, functional welfare-based needs in specific sectors led to a decision amongst states to integrate those sectors (such as in the case of the European Coal and Steel Community, which was the case study for his *The Uniting of Europe*), an ongoing process of deeper integration would be triggered as a consequence of the self-interested activities of both societal actors and supranational (and national) organs and élites, and furthered by a mechanism of spillover from one sector to another. Throughout the process – which was conceived as one of incremental change more than grand design – values and preferences would gradually be changed and redefined, common interests would be upgraded and loyalties would be transferred to the supranational level. In his early work, Haas's famous definition of integration focused on the transfer of political loyalties and expectations towards a new centre (1958: 16), but in his later work he revised this in favour of an emphasis on the transfer of authority and legitimacy (1970: 633).

In the original version of Haas's neofunctionalism, there is no explicit account of law's role, and even in its revised version, where the emphasis on the transfer of authority and legitimacy suggests the significance of law, there was no express consideration of its role or relevance. Yet despite the absence of any such account, neofunctionalism as a theory has nevertheless always had a particular resonance for lawyers, primarily because its central concept of spillover provides a useful metaphor for the expansionary tendencies of EU law.[4] Legal scholarship on European integration is full of accounts not only of the way in which the Court of Justice interpreted key provisions of the European Community (EC) treaties over time to cover situations which seemed far removed from their original application (for example, the application of free movement principles to the areas of tourism,[5] abortion,[6] sport,[7] education,[8] and health[9]) but also of the way in which EU legislative competences to harmonize national laws which affect the functioning of the internal market were gradually used by political actors to adopt a broad array of measures in fields such as environmental and consumer protection policies, long before the latter fields were officially designated by the member states within the treaties as areas of EU policy competence (Weatherill 1997; Scott 1998: ch. 1; Weiler 1999: ch. 2). In other words, a kind of spillover *within* EC law from what appeared to be confined issue areas into a whole range of others – not only as a result of judicial interpretation by the ECJ but also as a result of legislative activity by the relevant EU bodies, and more particularly as a result of the interaction between the two (Martinsen 2004) – could readily be identified, in a way that resonates with many of the hypotheses of neofunctionalism concerning policy interdependencies and the gradual upgrading of interests.

If one of the main critiques of neofunctionalism was its inability to predict when integration would or would not proceed, this failure to address the role of law within the integration process can be counted as a part of that critique, since arguably it meant the omission of a significant explanatory factor in the variable and complex course of integration. In focusing on the incremental nature of change, on the linkages and interdependencies between different policy fields and between different actors, and on the importance of supranational institutions, and in its prediction of the eventual emergence of a political community, neofunctionalism offered a theory which seemed to fit many of the assumptions and arguments of legal scholars concerning the role of law in the integration process. As evidenced in the quotation from the Cappelletti project above, legal scholars of European integration have long asserted that law defines the framework and context within which political and social actors operate, that it affects and constrains these actions and relations, that it determines in part the impact of political acts, and that it conditions and tempers those acts in translating them into everyday application. However, neither neofunctionalism nor indeed legal scholarship itself has offered a theory or hypothesis concerning the causal mechanisms by which law advances, influences or otherwise affects the process of integration.

## 6. CONCEPTIONS OF LAW WITHIN INTEGRATION THEORY

To offer such a hypothesis or theory of course presupposes a conception of what law is. Yet as one legal commentator has noted, the 'judicial politics' approach adopted within some political science analyses 'suggests a supreme disinterest in the epistemic foundations of law' (Chalmers 2000). Certainly in the case of European integration scholarship, many of the political science accounts which have so far addressed the role of law, in particular those accounts which are informed by rationalist premises, but also those such as Burley and Mattli's neofunctionalist account underpinned by a liberal model, express a broadly positivist understanding of law as a system of authoritative rules, and an instrumentalist view of courts acting as strategic players who sometimes exploit the indeterminacy of those rules to pursue particular interests or achieve particular ends. A non-positivist account of law as a normative social practice, on the other hand, including an understanding of courts as entities engaged in a legitimately and explicitly interpretative enterprise, is likely to yield a rather different account of its role in the integration process. Yet as recent contributions to the literature on international relations and European integration have cautioned (Christiansen *et al.* 1999; Jupille *et al.* 2003), a debate which merely sharpens the contrast between the theoretical premises and the epistemological and ontological commitments of rationalism, on the one hand, versus constructivism, on the other, is doomed to stalemate, and is unlikely to advance an understanding of the integration process very far. The same can be said of a debate which would merely sharpen the related contrast between positivist and non-positivist understandings of law, in particular as regards the nature and sources of law. Broadly speaking, positivist accounts of law generally present law as *posited* and as being identifiable by pedigree rather than content, while non-positivist accounts consider law to be constructed through social practices (including judicial interpretation) and they assert a relationship between the content of a norm and its character as law.

In an attempt to avoid such a stalemate, I want to suggest a number of ways in which law can be said to affect the process of political integration. The aim of setting these out is to disaggregate the different ways in which law may be said to influence the integration process, in order to broaden the discussion beyond the focus on courts and to render these modes of influence susceptible to further inquiry in more particular contexts. The first three are closely related, and have begun to be examined within institutionalist and constructivist analyses of European integration. None of the five categories, strictly speaking, is premised on a clear choice between positivist and non-positivist understandings, but the emphasis on the role of interpretation in category three, on the legitimacy of law in category four, and on the influence of legal norms on the views and behaviour of social actors (other than simply by providing them with opportunities or imposing constraints) in category five clearly draw on non-positivist assumptions.

*First*, law acts as an *enabling* force, empowering – and in certain instances aiming to compel – political actors to pursue certain ends or to pursue them by using particular means. In the EU a clear example of this is the way in which legal competences – the powers held by the various legislative and administrative organs – are framed in the EC Treaty. These legally defined competences purport to shape the way in which powers can be exercised, in both procedural and substantive terms. To take two examples, the EC has the power under the EC Treaty to regulate the internal market, and to regulate aspects of public health, but the political power to enact law in these respective fields is structured in different ways by the respective treaty provisions which govern them. Not only are the various actors – Commission, Council, Parliament, committees, etc. – specified, but also the process by which they must negotiate and draft the policy, and significant dimensions of the normative context and content too are regulated by the treaty basis.[10] To give further detail to the examples: an internal market harmonization measure which touches on an aspect of environmental protection must be adopted under Article 95 EC, which sets requirements including the use of the co-decision legislative procedure, qualified majority voting in the Council, and the setting of a 'high level' of environmental protection as its base. The litigation which took place around the use of Article 95 EC instead of other potential treaty bases for environmental action suggests that these requirements do 'bite' (Scott 1998: ch. 1).[11] An EU health policy measure must be adopted under Article 152 EC, which prescribes the use of the co-decision procedure and qualified majority voting in three fairly circumscribed issue areas, and specifically states that there can be no harmonization of the laws and policies of the member states in the general field of health protection. This latter provision played an important part in the long-running controversy over the tobacco advertising directive, which was eventually annulled by the ECJ for having been wrongly adopted as an 'internal market' measure under Article 95.[12] It is not the specific instance of litigation in this context which is in itself important, but rather the fact that the legal and constitutional parameters shaping the policy powers of the legislative bodies in all instances of this kind (and not only those which were the subject of litigation) were treated as meaningful by the Court.

*Secondly*, and relatedly, law acts as a *constraining* force, intended to prevent political actors from adopting certain kinds of actions or policies. The legal prohibition on harmonizing health measures discussed in the previous paragraph – which pertains also in the fields of culture and education under the relevant provisions of the EC Treaty – can be seen as an instance of this kind. A more vivid example of the constraints imposed on political action by law is the prohibition on violation of values which are said to be protected as fundamental legal or constitutional rights. Even before the drafting and proclamation in 2000 of the Charter of Fundamental Rights, so-called fundamental rights were said – both by the ECJ and by the member states and EU political bodies initially in a 1977 Joint Declaration and eventually in Article 6 of the Treaty on European Union – to be binding constraints. Legal rights and principles of this kind also in certain circumstances impose positive legal obligations to act on the political bodies, but for present purposes the limits that they are said to impose present an interesting example of the potential role of law in integration. The adaptation of the investigative and enforcement practices of the Commission in the field of competition policy in response to the requirement to respect the procedural rights of companies being investigated provides one instance. The recent controversy in the European Parliament – which has now chosen to refer the dispute to the ECJ, alleging in particular the violation of the right to privacy and data protection[13] – over the EU–US agreement on the transfer of air passenger data[14] provides another current high-profile example.

*Thirdly*, law *structures* the parameters within which its interlocutors operate – courts being amongst the most authoritative but legislators, executives, administrators and other social actors being also included – when they interpret its meaning in particular contexts. In other words, all of those who apply the law, who implement it and who are required to comply with it engage in an interpretative process when they consider the relevance of the norms to the particular context in which they are operating. Socio-legal research on the interaction between regulators and regulated (Ayres and Braithwaite 1992; Campbell and Picciotto 2002) or, within the burgeoning literature on Europeanization, studies which examine the adaptation by administrators to legal measures, and studies on compliance with EU law (Vervaele 1999; Börzel 2003) are examples of the attempt to appraise the impact of law in this respect. The most closely studied arena of interpretative practice of course is that of courts and judges, in which the judicial culture of reason-giving (to a greater or lesser extent, depending on the particular legal system) and the publication of judgments enable us to assess how and why particular legal provisions are construed and interpreted in particular contexts.

*Fourthly*, and most elusively for the purposes of empirical methodology, law has a powerfully symbolic dimension (in the EU context, see Dehousse 1998, Dehousse and Weiler 1990: esp. 244–5), an important aspect of which entails the invocation of a claim to legitimacy. In particular, law's function in translating political decisions into binding norms invariably carries with it an assertion – whether more or less convincing – as to the legitimate authority of those decisions. Given the significance which Haas attached in his definition of political integration to the transfer of authority and legitimacy, this dimension of law has obvious relevance for neofunctionalist theory. However intangible it may appear, law's symbolic dimension can be illustrated by reference to the current constitutional process. Even if – as certain political actors may still wish to assert – the constitutional text drafted by the Convention and agreed by the Intergovernmental Conference does not make any major changes to the substantive content of the existing treaties, the fact that this text is to be adopted and proclaimed as constitutional law, and more specifically as the 'EU Constitution', has symbolic impact.

*Fifthly*, law provides reasons for action[15] as well as incentives for action on the part of social actors, and in so doing it can also shape the preferences and influence the values of actors. It provides them with reasons to change and to adapt their behaviour in response to legal norms, whether because they believe in the particular values expressed by those norms, or because they respect the processes from which those norms have emerged, or simply because laws are norms which have particular social and cultural status. Law also sometimes provides social actors with incentives to bring pressure to bear for the implementation and practical realization of legal norms in particular contexts, including through the courts. This latter dimension has been a primary focus for political scientists studying the integration process who, drawing in some cases on earlier work by legal scholars (Rawlings 1993; Barnard 1995; recently Chalmers 2000), have examined how the behaviour of particular litigants or categories of litigant before national and European courts has helped to propel certain legal claims based on EU law forward (Cichowski 2002; Stone Sweet and Caporaso 1998; Stone Sweet 2004; Alter and Vargas 2000). It is clearly much more difficult to subject the former dimension – the fact that law provides reasons for adapting social behaviour – to empirical scrutiny, although it is a subject with which socio-legal scholars and sociologists – at least since Durkheim's characterization of laws as 'social facts' which are simply the visible external symbol of the moral phenomena of social solidarity – have long grappled.

Let us take this fifth claim about law's influence, and try to exemplify the argument briefly by focusing in particular on the claim that law provides reasons for change and can shape the preferences and conduct of actors. I want to suggest a possible example of how the existence and embedding of a legal norm may have influenced the way in which integration proceeded in particular areas of EU policy. The norm in question is that of non-discrimination, a principle of EC law for several decades, and an actual rule of law since the 1957 treaty in a number of specific issue areas such as equal pay for men and women, and equal treatment of nationals from different EU member states. Initially through the practice of the ECJ, the principle of non-discrimination, or equal treatment as it became known in its positive formulation, was stated by the Court to be of wider application and to be both a 'fundamental right' and a 'general principle of EC law' potentially applicable to any instance of arbitrarily differential treatment within the field of the EU's competence.[16] This was used by litigants over time to successfully challenge employment and social discrimination against transsexuals,[17] and it became a pervasive part of EU law discourse. However, not only was the legal principle, once articulated in general terms by the Court, strategically used by litigants to break new ground, but its influence can also be seen in the somewhat more surprising area – because domestically more sensitive and more closely controlled by member states under the terms of title IV of the EC Treaty – of justice and home affairs. In the field of immigration policy in particular, it is arguable that the unexpectedly liberal Tampere agenda set by the European Council in 1999, and the legislation which was subsequently proposed by the Commission on the subject of long-term resident third country nationals, can be explained in part by reference to the broad normative appeal of the notion of non-discrimination, and the way in which it had taken hold within EU law. The lead suggested by the European Council in its Tampere conclusions was then taken up by the Commission in formulating its proposals, and it used the concepts of non-discrimination and fundamental human rights actively in drafting the provisions of the two major pieces of legislation which were put forward.[18] The initial proposals of the Commission were subsequently watered down in the course of the discussion and ultimate adoption of the legislation by the justice and home affairs Council, but significant elements of the non-discrimination approach nonetheless remain.[19] Further, while the final text of the family reunification directive in particular was considerably weaker than the original proposal in terms of the rights and protections offered, the European Parliament on this basis has initiated a challenge to the legislation before the ECJ, arguing that its provisions violate fundamental human rights and the principle of non-discrimination.[20] In other words, while law itself cannot explain the initial decision of member states to transfer policy-making power in particular issue areas to the EU, legal norms and principles can perhaps help to explain why particular kinds of – sometimes unexpected – decisions are taken in particular fields and why integration in those fields proceeds over time in a specific direction.

## 7. A BROADER AGENDA FOR LAW AND INTEGRATION THEORY

The more general question remains to what extent neofunctionalism provides an explanatory framework within which the various possible dimensions of law's impact on the process of political integration can be situated and tested. I have suggested above that neofunctionalist theory, despite its lack of explicit engagement with law, has an instinctive resonance with the premises and assumptions of legal scholarship on the place of law in the integration process. Key concepts of neofunctionalism such as spillover, its explanation of the role of supranational and societal actors, and its very definition of integration sit comfortably with many of the arguments of legal scholarship about law and integration. If the original neofunctionalist theory is understood not as a predictive theory providing an explanatory account of change, but rather as a model of the integration process which describes how things work, then undoubtedly law can quite neatly be 'fitted' into the model. But it is more difficult to argue that neofunctionalist theory even in revised form provides an explanatory account of the various ways and circumstances in which law does and does not influence or advance the process of political integration.

More recent scholarship on European 'institutionalization' – a term which Haas himself suggested as a proxy variable for the notion of political integration (Haas 1970: 633) and which explicitly declares certain affinities with Haas's neofunctionalism – offers more promising avenues of research for exploring the relationship between law and integration, although using the language of 'supranational governance' rather than integration (Sandholtz and Stone

Sweet 1998; Stone Sweet *et al.* 2001; Stone Sweet 2004; Cichowski 2002; Börzel and Cichowski 2003, Martinsen 2004). While adjudication is again a major focus of much of this scholarship, it generally provides a more developed account than other theories of integration of the relationship between transnational activity, adjudication and 'legal rules' – a term used in this literature to capture different kinds of law, including legislation, treaties and judicial rulings – in the dynamic process of European institutionalization. The framework provided by this body of scholarship lends itself well to testing some of the suggestions made above about the ways in which law may affect the process of integration.

Law is a complex social phenomenon, and an understanding of its place in the process of European integration requires the kind of explanatory theory which political scientists – many of whom were inspired by Haas's neofunctionalist analysis – have striven to develop and which legal scholarship has rarely seriously addressed. However, it also requires both a broader and a more nuanced conception of law than much of the political science scholarship has been prepared to consider, whether for fear that it would render less parsimonious the explanatory theory developed, or simply because it is more difficult to subject to empirical investigation. Certainly the dominant focus within political science scholarship on *courts* is explicable in part by virtue of the apparent ease with which the output of courts can be identified and measured, although, as more recent scholarship has begun to acknowledge (Alter 2000; Conant 2002), the gap between judicial rulings and their impact, and the relationship between judicial output and policy response (whether at the European or national level), requires a more subtle, nuanced and temporally sensitive analytical framework if the impact of adjudication is to be fully understood. That being said, the work of socio-legal scholars who are attentive to the importance of empirical methodology and explanatory theory, on the one hand, and the evidence of a newer generation of political science scholars who are engaging more convincingly with law, on the other, give reason to hope that the relationship between legal and political science scholarship on European integration is finally beginning to mature.

**Address for correspondence:** Gráinne de Búrca, Law Department, European University Institute, Villa Schifanoia, Via Boccaccia 121, San Domenico di Fiesole, I-50133, Italy. email: Grainne.DeBurca@iue.it

## ACKNOWLEDGEMENTS

Thanks are due to Neil Walker, Tanja Börzel and the anonymous referee for helpful comments on an earlier draft.

## NOTES

1 The key obligatory references here are to legal scholars Joseph Weiler and Eric Stein, and to political science scholars Stuart Scheingold and Mary Volcansek.

2 For a somewhat sceptical comment on their analysis, see Schmitter (2003, n. 12).
3 For a classic example, see Hallstein (1972, particularly ch. 2).
4 Haas himself in 1964 referred to the fact that several of the member state governments concerned had 'faithfully complied with' the ruling of the ECJ in *Van Gend en Loos* against them as an example of political spillover (Haas 1964b).
5 Case 186/87, *Cowan* v. *Le Trésor Public* [1989] ECR 195.
6 C-159/90, *SPUC* v. *Grogan* [1991] ECR I-4685.
7 Case C-415/93, *URBSFA* v. *Bosman* [1995] ECR I-4921.
8 Case 293/83, *Gravier* v. *City of Liège* [1985] ECR 593.
9 Cases C-120/95 *Decker* [1998] ECR I-1831, C-158/96 *Kohll* v. *Union des Caisses de Maladie* [1998] ECR I-1931, C-368/98 *Vanbraekel* v. *ANMC* [2001] ECR I-5363, C-157/99 *Geraets-Smits* v. *Stichting Ziekenfonds, Peerbooms* v. *Stichting CZ Groep Zorgverzekeringen* [2001] ECR I-5473 and C-385/99 *Müller-Fauré* [2003] ECR I-4509.
10 For an analysis of how the differing legal bases of internal market regulation and environmental regulation shaped governance in the field of waste transfer, see Armstrong and Bulmer (1998: ch. 8).
11 The fact that social actors and interest groups see the choice of legal basis as highly significant is evidenced in a recent memorandum of Greenpeace calling for a change in the legal basis for an environmental measure from Article 95 (internal market) to Article 175 (environment): http://eu.greenpeace.org/downloads/climate/PaperWithKeyImprovementsRegulation.pdf (last visited 21 September 2004).
12 Case C-376/98, *Germany* v. *Parliament and Council* [2000] ECR I-8419.
13 Case C-317/04, *Parliament* v. *Council*, pending.
14 See the Report of the Parliament's Committee on Citizens' Freedoms and Rights, Justice and Home Affairs, 30 March 2004, http://www.europarl.eu.int/meetdocs/committees/libe/20040405/530949en.pdf
15 There is a large and rich jurisprudential (legal-philosophical) literature on law's normativity. For a recent account arguing for a third and more temporally sensitive dimension of law's normativity, in addition to *nomos* and *thesmos* (reason and command), see Postema (2004: 207).
16 For a thorough treatment of how the legal principle of equal treatment evolved and was expanded over time in EC law, see More (1999).
17 C-13/94, *P* v. *S and Cornwall County Council* [1996] ECR I-2143 and C-117/01, *K* v. *NHS Pensions Agency*, 7 January 2004. The attempt to extend the principle to the issue of discrimination on grounds of sexual orientation failed because the ECJ deemed that issue to lie outside the EU's field of competence. For a critique of the latter, see Armstrong (1998).
18 See COM (2001) 127 and COM (1999) 638.
19 Directive 2003/86 [2003] OJ L 251/12 on family reunion, and Directive 2003/109 [2004] OJ L 16/44 on long-term residents.
20 Case C-540/03, *Parliament* v. *Council*, pending.

## REFERENCES

Alter, K.J. (1998) 'Who are the "masters of the Treaty"?: European governments and the European Court of Justice', *International Organization* 52(1): 121–47.
Alter, K.J. (2000) 'The European Union's legal system and domestic policy: spillover or backlash?', *International Organization* 54(1): 489–518.
Alter, K.J. (2001) *Establishing the Supremacy of European Law*, Oxford: Oxford University Press.

Alter, K.J. and Vargas, J. (2000) 'Explaining variation in the use of European litiga-
tion strategies: European Community law and British gender equality policy',
*Comparative Political Studies* 33(4): 452–82.
Armstrong, K.A. (1998) 'Legal integration: theorizing the legal dimension of European
integration', *Journal of Common Market Studies* 36(2): 155–74.
Armstrong, K.A. and Bulmer, S. (1998) *The Governance of the Single European Market*,
Manchester: Manchester University Press.
Ayres, I. and Braithwaite, J. (1992) *Responsive Regulation*, Oxford: Oxford University Press.
Balkin, J. (1996) 'Interdisciplinarity as colonization', *Washington & Lee Law Review* 53:
949–70.
Barnard, C. (1995) 'A European litigation strategy: the case of the Equal Opportunities
Commission', in J. Shaw and G. More (eds), *New Legal Dynamics of European
Union*, Oxford: Clarendon Press, pp. 253–72.
Börzel, T.A. (2003) *Environmental Leaders and Laggards: Why There Is (Not) a Southern
Problem*, London: Ashgate.
Börzel, T.A. and Cichowski, R. (eds) (2003) *The State of the European Union, Volume 6:
Law Politics and Society*, Oxford: Oxford University Press.
Burley, A. and Mattli, W. (1993) 'Europe before the Court: a political theory of legal
integration', *International Organization* 47(1): 41–77.
Campbell, D. and Picciotto, S. (eds) (2002) *New Directions in Regulatory Theory*,
Special Issue of the *Journal of Law and Society* 29(1).
Cappelletti, M., Seccombe, M. and Weiler, J. (1986) *Integration Through Law*, Berlin:
Walter de Gruyter.
Chalmers, D. (2000) 'The much ado about judicial politics in the United Kingdom: a
statistical analysis of reported decisions of United Kingdom courts invoking EU law
1973–1998', *Jean Monnet Paper* 1/2000.
Christiansen, T., Jørgensen, K.E. and Wiener, A. (1999) 'The social construction of
Europe', in T. Christiansen, K.E. Jørgensen and A. Wiener (eds), *The Social Construc-
tion of Europe*, special issue of the *Journal of European Public Policy* 6(4): 528–44.
Cichowski, R. (2002) 'Litigation, mobilization and governance: the European Court
and transnational activists', Ph.D. dissertation, Center for the Study of Democracy,
University of California-Irvine.
Conant, L. (2002) *Justice Contained*, Ithaca: Cornell University Press.
Dehousse, R. (1998) *The European Court of Justice*, Basingstoke: Macmillan.
Dehousse, R. and Weiler, J. (1990) 'The legal dimension', in W. Wallace (ed.),
*The Dynamics of European Integration*, London: Pinter, pp. 242–60.
Fish, S. (1994) 'Being interdisciplinary is so very hard to do', in S. Fish (ed.), *There's No
Such Thing as Free Speech, and It's a Good Thing, Too*, New York: Oxford University
Press, pp. 231–42.
Garrett, G. (1995) 'The politics of legal integration in the European Union', *Inter-
national Organization* 49(1): 171–81.
Garrett, G., Keleman, R.D. and Schulz, H. (1998) 'The European Court of Justice,
national governments and legal integration in the European Union', *International
Organization* 52(1): 149–76.
Haas, E.B. (1958) *The Uniting of Europe*, London: Stevens & Sons.
Haas, E.B. (1964a) *Beyond the Nation State: Functionalism and International Organi-
zation*, Stanford: Stanford University Press.
Haas, E.B. (1964b) 'Technocracy, pluralism and the new Europe', in S.B. Graubard
(ed.), *A New Europe*, Boston: Beacon, pp. 62–88.
Haas, E.B. (1970) 'The study of regional integration: reflections on the joy and anguish
of pre-theorizing', *International Organization* 24(4): 607–46.
Hallstein, W. (1972) *Europe in the Making*, London: Allen & Unwin. (Original publication in German, Duesseldorf, 1969.)

Jupille, J., Caporaso, J. and Checkel, J. (2003) 'Integrating institutions: rationalism, constructivism and the study of the European Union', *Comparative Political Studies* 36(1–2): 7–40.

Martinsen, D. (2004) 'European institutionalization of social security rights: a two-layered process of integration'. Ph.D. dissertation, Florence: European University Institute.

Mattli, W. and Slaughter, A. (1995) 'Law and politics in the European Union: a reply to Garrett', *International Organization* 49(1): 183–90.

Mattli, W. and Slaughter, A. (1998) 'Revisiting the European Court of Justice', *International Organization* 52(1): 177–209.

More, G. (1999) 'The principle of equal treatment: from market unifier to fundamental right', in P. Craig and G. de Búrca (eds), *The Evolution of EU Law*, Oxford: Oxford University Press.

Nyikos, S. (2003) 'The European Court of Justice and the national courts: strategic interaction within the EU judicial process', at: http://law.wustl.edu/igls/Conconfpapers/Nyikos.pdf.

Postema, G. (2004) 'Melody and law's mindfulness of time', *Ratio Juris* 17(2): 203–26.

Rawlings, R. (1993) 'The Eurolaw game: some deductions from a saga', *Journal of Law and Society* 20(3): 309–40.

Sandholtz, W. and Stone Sweet, A. (1998) *European Integration and Supranational Governance*, Oxford and New York: Oxford University Press.

Schepel, H. and Wesseling, R. (1997) 'The legal community: lawyers, officials and clerks in the writing of Europe', *European Law Journal* 3(2): 165–88.

Schmitter, P. (2003) 'Neo-neofunctionalism', in A. Wiener and T. Diez (eds), *European Integration Theory*, Oxford and New York: Oxford University Press, pp. 72–73.

Scott, J. (1998) *EC Environmental Law*, New York: Longman.

Shaw, J. (1996) 'European Union legal studies in crisis? Towards a new dynamic', *Oxford Journal of Legal Studies* 16: 231–53.

Stone Sweet, A. (2004) *The Judicial Construction of Europe*, Oxford and New York: Oxford University Press.

Stone Sweet, A. and Caporaso, J. (1998) 'From free trade to supranational polity: the European Court and integration', in W. Sandholtz and A. Stone Sweet (eds), *European Integration and Supranational Governance*. Oxford and New York: Oxford University Press.

Stone Sweet, A., Sandholtz, W. and Fligstein, N. (2001) *The Institutionalization of Europe*, Oxford and New York: Oxford University Press.

Tsebelis, G. and Garrett, G. (2001) 'The institutional foundations of intergovernmentalism and supranationalism in the European Union', *International Organization* 55(2): 357–90.

Vervaele, J. (ed.) (1999) *Compliance and Enforcement of European Community Law*, The Hague and Boston: Kluwer Law International.

Weatherill, S. (1997) *EC Consumer Law and Policy*, London: Longman.

Weiler, J. (1999) 'The transformation of Europe', in J. Weiler (ed.), *The Constitution of Europe: Do the New Clothes have an Emperor? and Other Essays on European Integration*, Cambridge: Cambridge University Press.

Wincott, D. (1995) 'The role of law or the rule of the Court of Justice? An "institutional" account of judicial politics in the European Community', *Journal of European Public Policy* 2(4): 583–602.

Wincott, D. (2002) 'A community of law? "European" law and judicial politics: the Court of Justice and beyond', *Government and Opposition* 35(1): 3–26.

# Ernst Haas's evolving thinking on comparative regional integration: of virtues and infelicities

Walter Mattli

## 1. INTRODUCTION

Comparative regional integration has emerged over the last decade as an exciting area of research. Regional integration frequently comes in waves but the various cases of integration pertaining to a given wave tend to show puzzling differences and variations to which a growing number of scholars have been turning their attention. Differences are many. Some integration schemes confer significant authority to supranational agencies, encourage the use of qualified or simple majority in joint decision-making, and make provisions for strong dispute settlement procedures, powerful enforcement tools, as well as extensive common monitoring. Other schemes are strictly intergovernmental in character and shy away from any institutional elements that weaken or undermine national sovereignty. This has prompted some scholars to search for sets of conditions that favour the formation of either supranational arrangements or intergovernmental regional projects (Laursen 2003; Atkinson 1999; Mansfield and Milner 1997; Grieco 1997; Yarbrough and Yarbrough 1997; Fawcett and

Hurrell 1995). Other scholars have been seeking to explain striking differences in the targets and contents of regional laws (Dubal 2001; Abbott 2000; Stevis and Mumme 2000; Galperin 1999; Steinberg 1997; Milner 1997; Hoekman and Sauvé 1994) or the varying types of regional legal systems, from detailed, comprehensive, and intrusive systems of laws to approaches characterized by legal minimalism, laissez-faire and deregulation (Duina 2004; Duina, forthcoming). Finally, a third group of scholars has been concerned with measuring and explaining the relative effectiveness and efficiency of issue-specific integration models (Teague 2003; Dubal 2001; Blum 2000) and, more generally, the varying pace and progress of integration schemes (Mattli 1999; Leucona 1999).

The field of comparative regional integration, however, is not new. In his early work Ernst Haas observed and studied integration not only in Europe but also in other parts of the world, such as Latin America, Africa, and the Arab world. The intensity of integration across regions varied enormously. The pace of implementation and concomitant socio-political and economic transformation was brisk and steady in Europe (at least through the mid-1960s) but mostly sluggish and halting elsewhere.

Haas's work on Europe has been immensely influential, so much so that the study of European integration is practically synonymous with Haas and his intellectual legacy (Burley and Mattli 1993; Mattli and Slaughter 1998; Pierson 1996; Sandholtz and Stone Sweet 1998; Stone Sweet 2004). His name, however, does not figure prominently in recent studies of comparative regional integration. In part, this is an oversight and thus unfortunate since several of his insights travel well and are quite relevant to present-day debates. But it also is, in part, Haas's own fault. While his early work on European integration is of unmatched brilliance and depth, some of Haas's later theorizing suffers from a series of methodological infelicities that have detracted from his fundamental contributions to comparative regional integration.

The purpose of this article is to trace and assess the evolution of Haas's thinking on integration with special focus on regions outside Europe. Section 2 reviews the basic model of integration; section 3 evaluates the revised neofunctionalist model; section 4 assesses the usefulness and power of the revised model as applied to Latin American integration of the 1960s; and section 5 concludes.

## 2. THE BASIC MODEL: EXPLAINING VARIATION IN INTENSITY OF INTEGRATION

The signing of an integration treaty does not establish integration. It only signifies a promise by the leaders of several states to engage in a particular course of action over a period of time towards the aim of tying the economies of their countries closer together. True integration is achieved through the implementation of this promise, which entails a lengthy process of establishing common rules, regulations, and policies. It is these rules, regulations, and policies, based either on specific treaty provisions or derived over time from the general principles and objectives written into integration treaties, which translate the aspiration for regional prosperity into reality. Treaty implementation, however, is a slow and arduous process laden with conflict.

## The explanandum

Successful integration, according to the early Haas, has several measures, manifestations, 'indicators' or 'symptoms' (Haas 1961). Besides an increase in frequency of intra-regional transactions relative to interregional ones, they include marked changes in (1) the conflict resolution mode, and (2) people's emotive attachment, identification, as well as expectations and outlook.

'Conflict resolution,' Haas noted, 'is a particularly interesting *indicator* for judging progress along the path of integration' (Haas 1961: 367; emphasis added). In a successfully integrating economy and polity, compromise and accommodation occurs on the basis of upgrading the common interest rather than accommodation by 'splitting the difference' or based on the minimum common denominator.[1] By redefining their conflict so as to work out solutions at a higher level, the parties not only ensure peaceful change but also create conditions conducive to the maximization of the spill-over effects of earlier integration steps.[2]

Another main indicator of progress is, as famously put by Haas, the extent to which 'political actors are persuaded to shift their loyalties, expectations, and political activities toward a new and larger centre, whose institutions possess or demand jurisdiction over the pre-existing national states' (Haas 1961: 366–7; Haas 1958: 5). In regions where actors' main emotive attachment and political activities remain centred on the nation-state, integration lies mostly dormant.

In sum, successful integration shows evidence of increased frequency of intra-regional transactions, actor adaptation to a new process of mutual accommodation, shifting loyalties and expectations, as well as gradual acceptance of supranationalism as the rightful and legitimate place of authority. Failing or stagnating integration will be characterized by a mode of inter-state interaction that follows the hallowed precepts of traditional inter-state diplomacy, placing a high and non-negotiable premium on national sovereignty.

## The original explanatory variables

What are the factors that account for the varying intensity and fortunes of integration schemes? Haas's original model identified three sets of internally coherent factors summarized as (1) social and political pluralism, (2) symmetrical regional heterogeneity, and (3) bureaucratized decision-making coupled with supranational agency. The content of each of these factors or explanatory variables can be high or low – a high value favouring integration, a low value rendering the likelihood of success more elusive.

(1) High social and political pluralism describes a situation of full mobilization of all segments of society via strong interest groups and political

parties, and leadership by élites competing for political survival and dominance under rules of constitutional democracy accepted by leaders and followers alike (Haas 1958, 1964, 2001: 29–31). Such pluralism is more likely to prevail in highly industrialized economies. Haas hypothesized that integration would proceed most rapidly when it responded to socio-economic demands emanating from a pluralistic industrial-urban environment. 'Because the modern "industrial-political" actor fears that his way of life cannot be safeguarded without structural adaptation, he turns to integration; but by the same token, political actors who are neither industrial, nor urban, nor modern in their outlook usually do not favour this kind of adaptation, for they seek refuge instead in national exclusiveness' (Haas 1961: 375; Haas 1968a).

(2) Symmetrical regional heterogeneity is said to be high if two conditions hold: first, each country within a region seeking closer economic ties is fragmented along similar lines of pluralism (and thus is internally homogeneous) and, second, each class, political party, or interest group has counterparts in other countries with which it can pursue common cause. Cross-national linkages, in turn, foster similarity in feelings, expectations, and outlook. Haas concluded that parallel pluralistic socio-political structures in a region are thus 'of far greater importance in explaining . . . integration['s] . . . success than is any argument stressing linguistic, cultural or religious unity' (Haas 1967: 319–20).

(3) Finally, Haas posited that highly bureaucratized decision-making renders interactions among civil services engaged in policy co-ordination easier and more productive. Further, to the extent that integration treaties allowed for supranational agency, national negotiators could rely on experts above the state to 'construct patterns of mutual concessions from various policy contexts' (Haas 1968b: 152) and serve as mediators or a repository of technical information. It is through these services that 'supranational bodies . . . readily lend themselves to accommodation on the basis of upgrading common interests' (Haas 1961: 377). They thereby tend to upgrade their own powers at the expense of the member governments.

The behavioural assumptions underpinning these sets of hypotheses are nicely summarized in a memorable passage of Haas's work on Europe: 'The "good Europeans" are not the main creators of the . . . community; the process of community formation is dominated by nationally constituted groups with specific interests and aims, willing, and able to adjust their aspirations by turning to supranational means when this course appears profitable' (Haas 1958: xiv). Their selection of means is the result of calculation, but they may change their minds and preferences (interests) as a result of new beliefs, ideas and values that they come to embrace (Haas 2001: 25).[3] Supranational actors are likewise not immune to utilitarian thinking; they seek unremittingly to expand the mandate of their own institutions to have a more influential say in integration matters.[4] In other words, the groups driving the process of integration are rational maximizers of their narrow self-interest;[5] they hail from the world of business, politics, and science, and their actions or beliefs need not be infused with pan-regional ideology or commitment

(Haas 1961: 377). Deeper integration is the intended as well as unintended consequence of their self-serving actions (Haas 1967: 325).

The effort Haas put into 'testing' his hypotheses was uneven. Clearly, Haas was first and foremost interested in understanding European integration; but as early as 1961 he began pondering the generality of his analytical framework. Europe scored high on all key explanatory variables, leaving Haas quite optimistic about the fortunes of the European Community (EC) Six. Not so, however, most other regional schemes; they received low values on most variables, though the testing was done in a rather cursory and unsystematic fashion. In the Arab world, for example, he found few cross-cutting ideological or economic links.

> Each modernizing elite in power ... acts and thinks only in the context of its state; each traditional-feudal oligarchical elite is intent on preserving its position and rejects cooperation ... They 'integrate' in meeting jointly experienced threats from outside the region; they cannot meaningfully work together on normally integrative tasks because they experience no common needs.
>
> (Haas 1961: 380–1)

Similar conclusions applied to most other cases.

These findings did not falsify the original neofunctional model but Haas remained guarded against sweeping statements of general validity or applicability of his framework.

> It is by no means clear that slightly different functional pursuits, responding to a different set of converging interests, may not also yield integration ... [I]f regional integration ... go[es] forward in these areas [outside Europe], it will obey impulses peculiar to them and thus fail to demonstrate any *universal 'law of integration'* deduced from the European example.
>
> (Haas 1961: 389; emphasis added)

Haas thought it possible, for example, that regional unity in Latin America be fathered in defence against the 'export prowess and possible protectionism of a United Europe' (Haas 1961: 382). In contrast, he insisted that such external factors were analytically irrelevant in European integration.[6]

In the end, integration outside Europe did not go forward: neither the Latin American Free Trade Association, the Arab League nor any of the many African integration schemes made much – if any – progress (Mattli 1999). This would suggest that Haas's basic model was analytically more robust than he was willing to entertain. In the early 1960s, however, the jury was still out, and Haas felt compelled to 'update' and 'improve' his analytical framework to accommodate unexpected new events and developments.

## 3. REVISITING THE ORIGINAL MODEL: THE ELUSIVE MISSING EXPLANATORY VARIABLE

One such new unexpected 'event' was Charles de Gaulle. He returned to politics in 1958 when the French Republic was threatened with civil war over Algeria. As newly elected president he carried through important constitutional reforms and, in 1961, liquidated France's Algerian commitment. He then proceeded to dent the dream of those who envisaged a supranational EC. He wanted integration to be limited to political actions based on agreements between independent and sovereign states. His opposition to the supranational model of integration reached its climax in 1966 in the 'Luxembourg compromise' which instituted the right of any member state to veto decisions in the Council of Ministers.

De Gaulle constituted a major headache for neofunctionalists – among others. He simply failed to fit their original model. '[S]omething is missing in the exploration of the integrative process presented in *The Uniting of Europe* . . . De Gaulle has proved us wrong. But how wrong? Is the theory beyond rescue?' (Haas 1967: 327; Haas 1970: 630). Haas was quick to point out that few French groups and parties shared their president's anti-community feelings; they scorned the general's attempt to revive a nineteenth-century concept of sovereignty and great power thinking. Nevertheless, France was 'the deviant case' (Haas 1967: 319), pointing to a hole in the neofunctionalist whole. 'We neglected to build a theory of integration supple enough to take account of . . . disintegrative phenomena' (Haas 1967: 316). Haas now argued the case for an improved theory – a theory that would not only be able to explain the stops and starts of European integration but also more generally say something 'about the logic of functional integration among nations' (Haas 1967: 327; Haas 2000).

Acknowledging the persistence and actuality of nationalism, Haas sought to remedy his theory, first, by elucidating the relationship between the pace of integration, three central components of nationalism, and changing perceptions of the value of integration, and, second, by introducing a new central actor into the analytical framework, statesmen – the voices of high politics – and pondering how variations in the compatibility of their aims with those of non-governmental élites affect the progress of integration. In my view the link between the two analytical extensions is only weakly drawn, and neither one adds much explanatory power. Let me discuss each in turn.

### Integration and nationalism

Drawing on Stanley Hoffmann's work (1966: 867–9), Haas distinguished three aspects or dimensions of nationalism: (1) national ideology, (2) national consciousness, and (3) national situation. The first refers to an explicit doctrine of élites, suggesting positive values with respect to one's own nation and less positive ones for outsiders. National consciousness is the feeling of belonging, identity, and loyalty shared among people living under one government. Finally, national situation is a condition in time and space describing the power, freedom of manoeuvre, and rank of one's own nation *vis-à-vis* others (Haas 1967: 316–17).

Haas claimed that '[s]upranational integration becomes explicable . . . whenever a certain relationship between these three aspects of nationalism happens to exist' (Haas 1967: 317). In the immediate World War II period, the national situation of most European states was grim: nations once supremely self-confident and proud were on their knees, traumatized by the war experience, dejected in the face of utter devastation, and eclipsed from the world-stage. National consciousness reflected this picture of gloom, doom, and loss – as did the national ideologies of Europe's ruling élites. The desolate situation on the continent prompted a search for revolutionary ways of rebuilding and guaranteeing security, welfare, peace, and plenty. Europe's élites eventually agreed to pool resources and integrate their economies and polities step by step.

The plan succeeded beyond anyone's wildest dreams, generating high intra-regional trade and investment and spreading prosperity and stability. However, with Europe's economic fortunes restored, the relationship between the three ingredients of nationalism had changed, endangering the very source of success.

> As long as the benefits of the common market are more important in people's minds than the means used to achieve these benefits, [national] institutions and procedures can be sacrificed. The very success of the incremental method becomes self-defeating as important élites recognize that welfare can be safeguarded without a strong Commission and overt political unity.
>
> (Haas 1967: 331)[7]

In other words, economic recovery fundamentally altered the national situations in the various member states which, in turn, strengthened national consciousness across the EC – a trend that the original neofunctional model had failed to anticipate. 'The functional logic which leads from national frustration to economic unity, and eventually, to political unification presupposes that national consciousness is weak' (Haas 1967: 331).

What then exactly is missing from the original model of integration? What is the correctly specified model? The answer is not entirely clear. On the one hand, we learn that 'it is the change in national situation and consciousness in France which enabled de Gaulle ... to follow the pro-sovereignty policy now whereas he failed in the same attempt in 1950' (Haas 1967: 319). This suggests that changes in national situations and consciousness are necessary but not sufficient conditions for a slow-down in integration; the ultimate cause is de Gaulle, a *deus ex machina* that remains largely unexplained. On the other hand, Haas tells us that

> [t]he chief item in this lesson is the recognition that pragmatic interest politics, concerned with economic welfare, has its own built-in-limits ... Pragmatic interests ... are ephemeral ... [B]ecause they are weakly held they can be readily scrapped. And a political process which is built and projected from pragmatic interests is bound to be a frail process, susceptible to reversal. And so integration can once more develop into disintegration.
>
> (Haas 1967: 327–8; Haas 1970: 617)

The problem with this proposition is that it does not explain cross-national variation in the willingness to deepen integration. All member states were experiencing fantastic economic growth in the late 1950s and early 1960s, and most of them were quite willing to deepen integration. France's pragmatic interests militated against such deepening. But why not others' interests? It is not clear. Perhaps the answer lies in the second extension of the model.

## Bringing 'high politics' back

A central idea in *The Uniting of Europe* is that the crucial drive behind integration stems from the convergence of economic aims, embedded in the bureaucratic, pluralistic, and industrial life of modern society. 'The economic technician, the planner, the innovating industrialist, and trade unionist advanced the movement, not the politician, the scholar, the poet, the writer' (Haas 1968b: xix). This idea was strongly influenced by the writings of David Mitrany who viewed high politics as an obstacle to integration, prosperity, and lasting peace. Peace, Mitrany argued, 'is more likely to grow through doing things together in workshops and [the] marketplace than by signing pacts in chancelleries' (Mitrany 1966: 25; 1943). Effective co-operation cannot start from the political but from the low-key economic and technical planes. 'Any political scheme would start a disputation; any working arrangement would raise a hope and make for confidence and patience' (Mitrany 1966: 99). Gradual functional developments and quiet provision of common services will build the necessary foundations for closer political associations (Mitrany 1966: 67; Claude 1971: 378–91).

Haas fully accepted this view. The logic of neofunctional integration, he argued, could move forward only 'because key politicians ... had simply decided to leave the game of high politics' (Haas 1967: 323), passing on the initiative (and much of the work) to economic technicians and kindred spirits. In other words, the early version of neofunctionalism viewed statesmen, politicians, and governmental élites as playing a role best described as auxiliary or 'creatively responsive' (Harrison 1974: 80). As holders of the ultimate political power, they could accept, sidestep, ignore, or sabotage the decisions of technocrats. However, given heterogeneity of their interests in certain issue-areas, unilateral evasion or recalcitrance may prove unprofitable if it sets a precedent for others (Haas 1958: xiv). Thus political actors would either choose to or feel constrained to yield to the pressures of converging supranational and subnational interests.

Not so de Gaulle, alas. He showed that statesmen were still forces to be reckoned with, and Haas – duly impressed by the general's obstinacy and huffiness – brought the voices of high politics back into the analytical picture by assigning de Gaulle and his kind the 'rightful' place in his revised theory of integration. He hoped the move would better the theory's grasp of the vicissitudes of integration in Europe and also shed sharper light on schemes in other parts of the world, particularly Latin America.

In a clear break with Mitrany, Haas now considered it entirely possible that the process of integration spurred by the vision, energy, and force of great statesmen could be 'more productive of permanence than an indirect process fed by the slow fuel of economic expectations', and therefore that '[i]ntegrative decisions based on high politics' be 'more durable than decisions based on converging pragmatic expectations' (Haas 1967: 328). Analytically, statesmen no longer were shadowy figures on the backstage of integration; they were placed on the same footing with non-governmental élites. Varying fortunes of integration were now better explained in terms of varying degrees of compatibility of the aims of statesmen and these élites, as summarized in Figure 1.

Haas's revised theory suggests that the process of integration is most nearly automatic when both statesmen and élites hold converging incremental-economic objectives, as was implicitly assumed in the original neofunctionalist model. Integration is also likely to succeed when 'heroic statesmen-leader' (Haas 1967: 329) share a political commitment with major societal élites in favour of an ever-closer union. However, when the 'dramatic-political' objectives of a statesman opposed to deeper union are matched with incremental-economic élite preferences or clash with the 'dramatic-political' objectives of non-governmental élites favouring integration, integration will be either erratic and reversible or simply impossible. Similar difficulties arise when élites insist on 'dramatic-political' aims while statesmen espouse incremental-economic objectives.

In my view this is infelicitous theorizing; it raises more questions than it answers. The problem with the 2 × 2 matrix is that 'aims' says little explicitly about substance, content, or desired finality of integration; instead, it seems to refer more to style and method of integration. What really matters, however, is whether the key actors share a strong commitment to deeper integration or not – whatever the method. Bismarck and Cavour were both 'dramatic-political' pro-unionists; de Gaulle was 'dramatic-politically' opposed to supranationalism. Not the style or method mattered (it was identical) but the preferences over content and finality. Further, to state that

## Aims of non-governmental élites

| | | DRAMATIC-POLITICAL | INCREMENTAL-ECONOMIC |
|---|---|---|---|
| Aims of statesmen | DRAMATIC-POLITICAL | INTEGRATION EITHER DIRECT AND SMOOTH; OR IMPOSSIBLE | INTEGRATION ERRATIC AND REVERSIBLE |
| | INCREMENTAL-ECONOMIC | INTEGRATION ERRATIC AND REVERSIBLE | INTEGRATION GRADUAL BUT AUTOMATIC |

*Figure 1* Varying fortunes of integration
Source: Haas 1967: 329; Haas 1968b: xxv.

integration will stall or be erratic 'if the statesman's commitment is to national grandeur and the élites' to economic gradualism' (Haas 1967: 329) amounts to little more than a re-statement in conceptual language of a well-known historical fact. Is the question not: what explains de Gaulle's stance on Europe and why was he able to slow down the process of integration? The $2 \times 2$ matrix simply reflects de Gaulle and other facts (real and potential); it does not explain them. Also, what if a 'heroic statesman-leader' with a pro-integrationist agenda faces societal élites 'dramatic-politically' opposed to integration? Will his heroic and leadership qualities succeed in defeating the opposition? The more general point is that concepts are poorly defined − if defined at all − making it difficult to gauge their exact explanatory meaning and power. Finally, pre-cisely how do these concepts relate to the first extension of the neofunctionalist model pertaining to nationalism, pragmatism, and cost–benefit calculus? De Gaulle, a 'heroic statesman-leader', felt that the price of deeper integration in terms of forgone national sovereignty was too steep to pay. Most French élites disagreed with him. Why? Was it because of differences in information, percep-tion, rationality, foresight, pragmatism, selfishness, or nationalistic feelings? The revised neofunctionalist analysis does not reach deep enough to provide clear and compelling answers.

## 4. LATIN AMERICAN INTEGRATION AND REVISED NEOFUNCTIONALISM

Let us now examine the usefulness and power of Haas's revised model in the context of Latin American integration. Can the varying fates of integration schemes be traced to the key explanatory variables proposed by Haas? The first subsection reviews historical facts, identifying the main integration schemes of the 1960s and describing their progress. The second subsection pre-sents Haas's analysis and offers a critique.

### Integration schemes and their fates

Initiatives for regional integration in Latin America have been triggered in large part by external shocks that threatened to inflict severe damage on the econ-omies of the region. One such external event was the creation of the EC. The EC's common external tariff and protectionist agricultural policy sent shock-waves through Latin America, a continent that depended heavily on free access to the markets of industrialist countries for its primary commodity exports. Another discriminating feature was the EC's extension of the preferen-tial arrangements of individual colonial powers to the whole Community. As a result, the dependent territories of France, Belgium, Italy, and the Netherlands in Africa and Asia had preferential market access to all the member states of the Community after 1958 (Dell 1963: 187). Thus, for example, cocoa and coffee exported from the French colonies in Africa were admitted duty free to the entire common market after the creation of the EC, while cocoa supplied by Honduras or coffee supplied by Brazil now faced a uniform external tariff.

This threat of trade diversion caught Latin America at a particularly inopportune moment. Latin America's trade gap with industrialized countries had been rapidly widening and its terms of trade deteriorating.[8] Furthermore, the average annual growth rate of Latin American Free Trade Association (LAFTA) economies had fallen from approximately 5 per cent between 1950 and 1955 to only 1.7 per cent between 1956 and 1959. The President of Uruguay captured the general sense of panic well when he noted that 'the formation of a European Common Market ... constitutes a state of near-war against Latin American exports. Therefore, we must reply to one integration with another one, to one increase of acquisitive power by internal enrichment by another, to inter-European cooperation by inter-Latin American cooperation.'[9] Successful economic integration, it was hoped, would improve Latin America's bargaining power and thus raise the price of its exports.[10] It would also contribute to import substitution industrialization at the regional level by forcing national economies to specialize within the framework of the expanded and protected regional market (Wionczek 1970).[11]

A first Latin American response to the European common market was the creation of LAFTA. It was established by the Treaty of Montevideo, which was signed in February 1960 by Argentina, Brazil, Chile, Mexico, Paraguay, Peru and Uruguay. Ecuador and Colombia joined LAFTA in 1961, Venezuela in 1966 and Bolivia in 1967. The signatory governments expressed their determination 'to establish, gradually and progressively, a Latin American common market' and 'to pool their efforts to achieve the progressive complementarity and integration of their economies on the basis of an effective reciprocity of benefits'.[12] In pursuit of these goals, the Treaty provided for the establishment of a free trade area. Tariff reductions were to be effected according to two schedules. The Common Schedule listed products whose tariff rates were to be eliminated by 1973. The National Schedules, on the other hand, included products on which individual member states granted concessions in annual bilateral negotiation sessions. The Treaty permitted temporary trade restrictions in case of payment imbalances or if import competition damaged an industry of strategic importance to a member's economy. Special provisions were made to assist the development of the more backward members of the Association. The LAFTA agreement also encouraged closer co-ordination of industrial policies.[13]

The implementation of the Treaty provisions, however, was arduous and remained unfinished. Chile's President, Eduardo Frei, complained in early 1965: 'The advance towards economic integration has become slow and cumbersome. The possibilities of making further headway ... seem to be exhausted.'[14] Trade expansion failed to materialize: while average share of intra-regional trade in total trade of LAFTA countries was 8.7 per cent from 1952 to 1960, the average from 1961 through 1964 was only 7.9 per cent, despite a slight increase in total trade from 1960. Intra-regional trade ceased to grow in 1967 while extra-regional trade continued to boom. Attempts to revive the process of integration by creating a LAFTA Council of Ministers proved unsuccessful. Failure was publicly acknowledged at LAFTA's 1969 Annual Conference. The ensuing Caracas protocol postponed the deadline for free trade from 1973 to 1980, suspended the Common Schedule, and made only token reference to the idea of a common market. For all practical purposes, LAFTA was shelved (Wionczek 1970: 54–8; Wionczek 1968: 91–156; Griffin and French-Davis 1965; Balassa 1971). In 1980, LAFTA was replaced by the Latin American Integration Association (LAIA), a considerably more flexible trade liberalization arrangement that granted tariff preferences to only about 10 per cent of all goods traded (OECD 1993: 59).

Besides LAFTA, there was another major integration scheme launched in the early 1960s, the Central American Common Market (CACM). It was established by the Treaty of Managua signed in December 1960 by El Salvador, Guatemala, Honduras and Nicaragua.[15] Costa Rica joined CACM in 1963. The Treaty provided for immediate free trade in all products originating in the region except for those listed. Trade in the excluded products, which comprised approximately 50 per cent of intra-regional trade, was to be freed by 1966. The signatories also agreed to adopt a common external tariff (without specifying a deadline), establish a Central American Bank for Economic Integration to serve 'as an instrument for the financing and promotion of . . . regionally balanced . . . economic growth', and 'ensure as soon as possible a reasonable equalization of the relevant laws and regulations in force . . . [with a] view to establishing uniform tax incentives [towards] . . . industrial development'.[16]

CACM was triggered, like LAFTA, by external events: fear of a protectionist common market in Europe and deteriorating terms of trade. Another event of importance was Fidel Castro's victorious revolution in Cuba. Schmitter notes that 'the pervasive fear of Castroide subversion after 1959 added a desperate sense of urgency, making élites much more willing to experiment with policy innovations' (Schmitter 1972: 18). Unlike LAFTA, CACM proved highly successful during its first decade (Hansen 1967; Cochrane 1969; Mohr 1972; Fagan 1970; Nye 1967; Wynia 1970). It quickly set up a Permanent Secretariat, directed by a Secretary-General, and other bodies including the Central American Economic Council, an Executive Council, the Central American Integration Bank, a Monetary Clearing House and an advisory Central American Monetary Council. By 1966, tariffs were removed on 94 per cent of intra-regional trade, and 80 per cent of extra-regional imports were covered by a common external tariff (OECD 1993: 56; Edwards and Savastano 1989). Intra-regional trade among CACM countries represented 5.9 per cent of total trade in 1958. In the span of only ten years, the number had increased to 24.2 per cent, a stunning 18.3 per cent leap. In the same period, the relative importance of CACM's two major trading partners declined. Trade with the United States decreased by 8.7 per cent, from 47.8 per cent to 39.1 per cent, in 1968, and trade with Europe fell from 29.8 per cent to 20.8 per cent. Equally significant was the change in the composition of intra-regional trade.

In the late 1950s, most trade was in food products and raw materials. A decade later, two-thirds of regional trade consisted of manufactured (mainly consumer) goods and chemicals (Wilford and Christou 1973).

CACM's success story came to an abrupt end when the El Salvadorean army attacked neighbouring Honduras on 14 July 1969. This attack cannot plausibly be attributed to the integration process but appears to be the result of other and more complex causes (Durham 1979).[17] The ensuing 'Soccer War' lasted only a hundred hours but left several thousand dead on both sides, turned 100,000 people into refugees, and destroyed half of El Salvador's oil refining and storage facilities. Attempts to renew economic integration in the following years were thwarted by lingering hostilities. The share of intra-regional trade in total trade of CACM countries represented only 11.9 per cent in 1988, a sharp decline from the 24.2 per cent twenty years earlier (Fuentes 1989).

## Haas's analysis of Latin American integration

Recall that Haas's original neofunctionalist model contained three key explanatory variables: (1) pluralistic and social structure, (2) symmetrical heterogeneity, and (3) bureaucratization of decision-making. The model assumed that states embarked on the road to integration not because of a clear common purpose but for individual national reasons. This framework, amended to reflect the causal power of three critical aspects of nationalism, 'remains valid and useful to others who would use common markets and economic interdependence as a means to promote political unity', Haas argued in the mid-1960s (Haas 1967: 321); and he insisted that his concern was 'not with the cultural uniqueness of this or that region but with investigating the generality of the integration process' (Haas and Schmitter 1964: 726).

LAFTA's halting pace came as no surprise to Haas; he had correctly predicted it in 1961 (Haas 1961). The factors on which he grounded his prediction were as follows: first, socio-political pluralism was not a given in most of Latin America where dominance of personalistic and familial ties, political authoritarianism, and various forms of socio-economic traditionalism stood in the way of general mobilization of large segments of society through interest groups and political parties. In short, '[t]he kind of pluralism most favorable to rapid integration exists only in spots and its consistency is far from reliable' (Haas and Schmitter 1964: 722).

Second, there existed no homogeneous structural relations among the countries and thus little regional symmetrical heterogeneity. For example, industrialists across the region tended to see their role in their respective societies differently from each other, and trade unionists in one country would or could not readily establish relationships with their counterparts elsewhere. Haas summed up the difference between Europe and Latin America as follows: 'Europe is divided by language and religion, but united by regionally similar social and economic conditions and institutions; Latin America is united merely by language and religion. For automatic integration this is not enough' (Haas 1967: 333).

Finally, decision-making in Latin America was highly politicized. The reason was that 'Latin America ha[d] not [yet] reached the end of ideology' (Haas 1967: 334). Slogans of socialism and capitalism, working class and aristocracy, the military and civilian, and church and state permeated daily political discourse. Dispassionate and pragmatic bureaucrats, the *tecnicos*, were few and far between. Group structure tended to be asymmetric, rendering it difficult for the *tecnicos* to constitute a homogenous class capable of engaging in 'symmetrical learning' through joint decision-making (Haas and Schmitter 1964: 731). In addition, bureaucrats tended to be linked to oligarchic groups, compromising their autonomy as decision-makers. The lack of any significant supranational agency in Latin American integration further limited the bureaucrats' manoeuvrability; that is, they could not count on natural allies at a higher level for mediation and technical assistance conducive to the upgrading of common interests.

In sum, incrementalism – which depends on institutionalized communication patterns between a wide range of societal groups and national élites, as well as recognized expertise of technicians and secure civil service status – could not spring from Latin American soil. However, this need not have precluded the possibility of successful integration, since Haas no longer considered incrementalism the only method of integration. Particular constellations of nationalism may override structural weaknesses in the region, as could 'high politics'. Let us examine each of these theoretical extensions as applied to Latin American integration.

Nationalism in the period from the 1940s to the 1960s evolved in Latin America differently from Europe. In Latin America, the 'curve of intensity' was rising steeply though from a low level whereas in Europe it precipitously declined from a very high level in the 1940s and gradually rose again in the 1950s to a new but lower level. But unlike in Europe, the national situation in Latin America was anything but rosy during most of the 1950s and early 1960s. There was rampant 'dissatisfaction with the present, resentment of the external world, and fear that the aspirations of Latin America will go unheeded and unaided' (Haas 1967: 332). Two elements of national ideologies seemed to converge: (1) the maturing of strong doctrinal identification with the existing states – 'making them nations, in effect, for the first time in their history' (Haas 1967: 333) – and (2) the identification with the regional approach to industrialization and modernization of Latin America. An indefinite continuation of convergence of these ideological strands, however, could not be assumed – as the de Gaulle episode had shown. Only a 'continuous series of frustrations at the national level [would]... keep the two national doctrines in harmony' (Haas 1967: 333; Haas and Schmitter 1964: 737). In other words, as long as regional initiatives were perceived as complementing (largely failing) national efforts, the price of integration was worth paying. Success at the national level, however, would strengthen national consciousness which, in turn, was likely to weaken the perceived need of integration (unless the link between prosperity and continuing integration was clear and obvious to all citizens – an assumption that Haas seemed to consider improbable).

Nationalism is a weak explanatory variable, however; and it does not appear to shed much light on the varying trends in Latin American integration. First, the variable is not based foremost on a set of positive objectives in Latin America but tends to take on a defensive or negative quality in the sense of heavily depending on the behaviour of outsiders (external threat and negative externalities → strengthened nationalism); and, second, it is posited ultimately to be inversely related to integration (integration → more regional trade → improved economic growth → strengthened national consciousness → rejection of deeper integration). The 'nationalism' variable thus seems better at explaining halting integration than success. But how do we then account for the highly successful first decade of CACM integration?

The theoretical answer must be 'High Politics'. 'Integration [in Latin America] ... proceed[s] – if it proceeds at all – in that section of our matrix in which statesmen and élites share a commitment to dramatic and heroic action' (Haas 1967: 334). Is the empirical record consistent with this proposition? The answer is not clear.

Haas classified the aims of non-governmental élites such as Raúl Prebisch, Felipe Herrera, Romulo Almeida, Victor Urquidi, José Antonio Mayobre and others closely associated with Economic Commission for Latin America (ECLA) as 'dramatic-political'. Regional integration, this group hoped, would endow Latin America with the means to make up for past time, gain strength and dignity *vis-à-vis* Europe and the United States, and assert itself in world politics (Haas 1967: 334–5). The 'dramatic-political' aims of these élites clearly were not enough to bring about integration. They needed to be complemented by equally grand political objectives and designs by charismatic leaders to have a fair chance at success. Governments (and many industrialists), however, showed little enthusiasm for regional initiatives.

> Each government is preoccupied with its own national development and with the problems it faces at home ... Political commitment of the kind which existed in Europe after 1945 has been absent at the highest levels of government. The politics of the ECLA Doctrine have not sufficed to create such a commitment.
>
> (Haas 1967: 336)

The answer to the question of why LAFTA integration failed thus boils down to simple lack of political will; and Haas's analysis implies that even if genuine political will had existed, the leaders would likely have failed because of unfavourable structural conditions. This still leaves us with two central unanswered questions: first, why did leaders lack political will given that the region was mired in economic malaise and remedies in the form of regional integration were loudly propagated by experts; and, second, what explains CACM's puzzling success during the 1960s?

None of the remaining theoretical ruminations by Haas (and Schmitter) prove particularly helpful in addressing these questions. We learn, for example, that a central new explanatory variable is the 'adaptability of the chief actors, governmental and private' (Haas and Schmitter 1964: 718). The argument in short is as follows: actors endowed with high adaptability are actors capable of successfully tackling challenges and resolving conflicts, thus fostering integration; actors not so endowed will bring integration to a halt. This proposition is pure tautology; it has no explanatory or predictive power. Simply recall that Haas (1961) considered 'whether and how conflicts are resolved' to be an indicator for judging progress along the path of integration, not an explanation of the process (see section 2 above).

We also learn that 'economic integration in the Latin American setting can obey the same dynamics as the European prototype only if certain *functional equivalents* can be discovered' (Haas 1967: 341; emphasis added). In other words, regions outside Europe may possess unique cultural or stylistic attributes (i.e. functional equivalents) that can do for these regions what the logic of a pluralistic-technocratic and post-nationalistic setting did for Europe (Haas and Schmitter 1964: 726; Haas 1967: 338–43).

What are these equivalents in Latin America? The list is rather haphazard, ranging from the factual to the contrived and normative, including a diffuse and particularistic style of decision-making – 'a culturally accepted admixture of family contacts, corruption, and special exemptions from theoretically general rules will furnish the lubricant for creating the new transnational ties which are essential for economic and political integration' (Haas and Schmitter 1964: 731); or an emphasis on complementarity and reciprocity – '[t]ranslated into political terms these concepts imply continuous bargaining, consistent measuring of gains and losses incurred by specific national firms and industries rather than by nations as a whole' (Haas and Schmitter 1964: 731). In short, functional equivalents are not alternative theories of integration. At best, they are untested hypotheses or extrapolations based on cursory readings of the facts; at worst, they are ad hoc statements, leaps of faith and speculations. Functional equivalents fail to shed light on the outstanding critical puzzles about integration; they leave us none the wiser.[18]

## 5. CONCLUSION

Some five years ago I was invited to give a seminar talk on legal aspects of European integration at the University of California at Berkeley. In the audience, which comprised mostly doctoral students and colleagues in international relations and comparative politics, sat an energetic senior gentleman who – with his mop of white hair and tanned face – cut a striking figure. During a lively discussion session, he intervened several times, brilliantly commenting on points of theory, complementing empirical observations with most interesting examples none of us had known, and at one point even reprimanding gently but nonetheless firmly a colleague for a faulty memory about a historical fact of nineteenth-century Europe. After the seminar, he came up to me and introduced himself: 'Hi, I'm Ernie Haas.' I was delighted, and we chatted for a while.

I can think of only half a dozen political scientists of the calibre of Ernie Haas. Not only was and remains he the most original and thorough thinker by far of European integration, he was also a man of extraordinary integrity and modesty. Reflecting on his work in 1970, he labelled neofunctionalism and rival approaches 'pretheories' for being 'lamentably unspecific and inconsistent as to the dependent variable' and '[un]clear with respect to the key independent variables' (Haas 1970: 613). More specifically, he criticized a 'tendency to mix [the dependent variable's] imputed characteristics with those of independent ... variables' giving rise to tautologies, as well as a 'tendency to add "fudge variables" whenever the standard ones do not seem to do the explanatory trick', a practice he readily admitted to have indulged in (Haas 1970: 630–1). 'This means that we ought to stop talking about "functional equivalents", ... "high politics" and similar mythical animals' (Haas 1970: 631; Haas 1976a, 1976b). A stunning admission – and excellent methodological advice. There is no shrill 'marketeering' in Haas's work but exemplary modesty and an untiring and uncompromising quest for scientific truth. What rarity, what beauty!

**Address for correspondence:** Walter Mattli, St John's College, Oxford University, Oxford OX1 3JP, UK. Tel: 01865 270841. Fax: 01865 277421. email: walter.mattli@st-johns.oxford.ac.uk

## NOTES

1  Haas noted quite clearly: '[A]ccommodation based on the minimum common denominator ... is *a symptom of the lack of integration rather than a cause*' (Haas 1961: 379 [emphasis added]). The implication is that Haas considered lowest-common-denominator intergovernmentalism a description rather than an explanation of failure.

2  Spill-over describes a situation where activities associated with sectors integrated initially affect neighbouring sectors not yet integrated, thereby becoming the focus of demands for more integration.

3  The view that interests, not directly ideas, determine actions but that 'world views, which were created by ideas, have very often acted as the switches and channeled the dynamics of interest' (Haas 2000: 11) is one closely held by Max Weber – whom Haas called 'the single most vital intellectual influence on my thinking' (Haas 2000: 11).

4  The introduction of an unambiguously utilitarian concept of interest politics that stands in sharp contrast to the notions of unselfishness or common good that pervade functionalist writing (see, for example, Mitrany 1966) is one of the lasting contributions of neofunctionalism.

5  Haas accepts a variant of soft rational choice ontology – an ontology that is not materialistic since values shape interests and values include many non-material elements (Haas 2001: 23). Agents in neofunctionalism are assumed to be acting consistently with their desires and beliefs but need not meet other conditions of rationality (such as absence of contradictions among beliefs, optimality in the search for solutions, perfect congruence between desires, beliefs, and actions). Since values differ, actor preferences will vary non-homogeneously, making only

'retrodiction [possible], not formal prediction of anything more specific than a range of possible outcomes' (Haas 2001: 30).

6  Haas noted, for example: 'It was not the fear of the Soviet Union nor the envy of the United States which did the job' (Haas 1967: 322).

7  This part of the analysis is concordant with my own view. I have argued that '[w]illingness [of political leaders to deepen integration] depends greatly on the payoff of integration to political leaders. If these leaders value political autonomy (absence of interference by supranational agents) and political power, they are unlikely to seek deep levels of integration as long as their economies are relatively prosperous. Why sacrifice national sovereignty and pay the price of membership in a regional group if the economy is growing relatively fast and voters are thus content? In other words, economically successful leaders are unlikely to pursue deeper integration because their expected marginal benefit from integration in terms of improved re-election chances (or simply in terms of greater likelihood of retaining political power) is minimal and thus not worth the cost of integration. This argument is consistent with the insight from the rent-seeking literature which stipulates that political leaders value independence and "bribe-money" from small and effectively organized groups that stand to heavily lose from integration. However, in times of economic difficulties, political leaders will be more concerned with securing their own survival and are thus likely to implement economic policies that enhance the overall efficiency of the economy; in other words, distributional considerations become of secondary importance, thus eliminating entrenched interest groups' resistance to integration' (Mattli 1999: 51).

8  The terms of trade of developing countries declined from 1950 to 1962 by 12 per cent; Latin America's terms of trade dropped 21 per cent in the same period, due in great part to adverse movements in coffee prices (Dell 1966: 9).

9  *The Observer* (London, 30 July 1961), p. 1; cited in Dell (1963: 210).

10  Some countries urged the formation of a Latin American economic bloc not only to face the European threat more effectively, but also to have greater leverage in dealings with the United States. Grunwald *et al.*, for example, noted: 'Very few Latin American leaders were ready to speak openly, but the feelings of many were echoed by Chile's President Eduardo Frei in 1964, when he called for the twenty poor and disunited [Latin American] nations [to] form a powerful and progressive union which can deal with the United States as an equal' (Grunwald *et al.* 1972: 8–9).

11  The idea of import substitution industrialization at the regional level was most forcefully propagated by Raúl Prebisch, the executive secretary of the United Nations Economic Commission for Latin America. Policies of import substitution at the national level had already been implemented after World War II in countries such as Argentina, Brazil and Chile (see Prebisch 1950).

12  The text of the Treaty of Montevideo is reprinted in Dell (1966: 228–56). Dell's book is an excellent early description and analysis of LAFTA. See also Wionczek 1966; Haas and Schmitter 1965; Gale 1969; Milenky 1973.

13  See the Treaty of Montevideo in Dell (1966: ch. sixteen).

14  Quoted from a letter by Frei dated 6 January 1965, addressed to Raúl Prebisch, José Antonio Mayobre, Felipe Herrera and Carlos Sanz de Santa María; reprinted in Dell (1966: 280).

15  The text of the Treaty can be found in Dell (1966: 256–69).

16  See chapters 7 and 8 of the Treaty of Managua.

17  According to William Durham, the critical issue leading to the hostilities was the presence in Honduras of some 300,000 Salvadorean immigrants. In June 1969, Honduras reversed its policy of tolerating the immigration and began expelling these Salvadoreans from their rural homesteads. The expulsions began shortly

before the soccer teams of the two countries met in the World Cup semi-final matches. With the defeat of the Honduran team in San Salvador in June 1969, many of the Honduran spectators were set upon and mauled by the crowd. The immediate reaction in Honduras was to step up the expulsion of Salvadorean immigrants. This prompted El Salvador to close its borders in the hope that such action would force Honduras to relocate the *campesinos*. This failed, however, and El Salvador launched its attack on Honduras to 'defend the human rights of their countrymen' (Durham 1979: 2 and 163–4).

18  What then may explain CACM's success in the 1960s? In *The Logic of Regional Integration* (Mattli 1999), I have argued that demand and supply conditions need to be satisfied in order for integration to succeed. First, the potential for economic gains from market exchange within a region must be significant. If there is little potential for gain, perhaps because regional economies lack complementarity or because the small size of the regional market does not offer important economies of scale, the process of integration will quickly peter out. However, the potential for gain may grow with the diffusion of new technologies. The supply conditions are conditions under which political leaders are willing and able to accommodate demands for regional institutions at each step of the integration process. Ability refers to co-ordination dilemmas in integration, leading to a key supply condition: the presence of a leading country in the region. Such a country serves as a focal point in the co-ordination of rules, regulations, and policies; it may also help to ease tensions that arise from the inequitable distribution of gains from integration, for example, through side-payments. Contested institutional leadership or the absence of leadership makes co-ordination games very difficult to resolve. I have argued that in the case of CACM institutional leadership was provided by the Americans. President Kennedy actively supported the scheme because it was thought to be an effective way of containing the spread of communism from Cuba; in addition, CACM offered new business opportunities for American firms (Mattli 1999: 151–2).

# REFERENCES

Abbott, F.M. (2000) 'NAFTA and the legalization of world politics: a case study', *International Organization* 54(3): 519–47.

Atkinson, G. (1999) 'Developing global institutions: lessons to be learned from regional integration experiences', *Journal of Economic Issues* 33(2): 335–49.

Balassa, B. (1971) 'Regional integration and trade liberalization in Latin America', *Journal of Common Market Studies* 10(1): 58–77.

Blum, J. (2000) 'The FTAA and the fast track to forgetting the environment: a comparison of the NAFTA and the MERCOSUR environmental models as examples for the hemisphere', *Texas International Law Journal* 35(3): 435–57.

Burley, A.-M. and Mattli, W. (1993) 'Europe before the Court: a political theory of legal integration', *International Organization* 47(1): 41–76.

Claude, I. (1971) *Swords into Plowshares*, 4th edn, New York: Random House.

Cochrane, J. (1969) *The Politics of Regional Integration: The Central American Case*, New Orleans: Tulane Studies in Political Science.

Dell, S. (1963) *Trade Blocs and Common Markets*, New York: Alfred Knopf.

Dell, S. (1966) *A Latin American Common Market?*, London: Oxford University Press.

Dubal, V. (2001) 'Why are some trade agreements "greener" than others?', *Earth Island Journal* 16(4): 44–7.

Duina, F. (2004) 'Regional market building as a social process: an analysis of cognitive strategies in NAFTA, the European Union and Mercosur', *Economy and Society* 33(3): 359–89.

Duina, F. (forthcoming) *Making Regional Markets: History, Politics, and Integration in Europe and the Americas.*

Durham, W. (1979) *Scarcity and Survival in Central America: Ecological Origins of the Soccer War*, Stanford: Stanford University Press.

Edwards, S. and Savastano, M. (1989) 'Latin America's intra-regional trade: evolution and future', in D. Greenaway, T. Hyclak and R. Thornton (eds), *Economic Aspects of Regional Trading Arrangements*, New York: Harvester Wheatsheaf, pp. 189–233.

Fagan, S. (1970) *Central American Economic Integration: The Politics of Unequal Benefits*, Research Series, no. 15, Berkeley: Institute of International Studies, University of California, Berkeley.

Fawcett, L. and Hurrell, A. (eds) (1995) *Regionalism in World Politics: Regional Organization and International Order*, Oxford: Oxford University Press.

Fuentes, J.A. (1989) *Desafíos de la Integración Centroamericana*, San José, Costa Rica: Instituto Centroamericano de Administratión Pública.

Gale, E. (1969) *Latin American Free Trade Association: Progress, Problems, Prospects*, Washington: Office of External Research, US Department of State.

Galperin, H. (1999) 'Cultural industries' policies in regional trade agreements: the cases of NAFTA, the European Union and Mercosur', *Media, Culture & Society* 21(5): 627–48.

Grieco, J. (1997) 'Systematic sources of variation in regional institutionalization in Western Europe, East Asia, and the Americas', in E. Mansfield and H. Milner (eds), *The Political Economy of Regionalism*, New York: Columbia University Press, pp. 164–87.

Griffin, K. and French-Davis, R. (1965) 'Customs unions and Latin American integration', *Journal of Common Market Studies* 4(1): 1–21.

Grunwald, J., Wionczek, M. and Carnoy, M. (1972) *Latin American Economic Integration and U.S. Policy*, Washington: The Brookings Institution.

Haas, E.B. (1958) *The Uniting of Europe: Political, Social, and Economic Forces 1950–1957*, Stanford: Stanford University Press.

Haas, E.B. (1961) 'International integration: the European and the universal process', *International Organization* 15(3): 366–92.

Haas, E.B. (1964) *Beyond the Nation State: Functionalism and International Organization*, Stanford: Stanford University Press.

Haas, E.B. (1967) '*The Uniting of Europe* and the uniting of Latin America', *Journal of Common Market Studies* 5(4): 315–43.

Haas, E.B. (1968a) 'Technocracy, pluralism, and the new Europe', in J. Nye (ed.), *International Regionalism*, Boston: Little Brown, pp. 62–88.

Haas, E.B. (1968b) *The Uniting of Europe: Political, Social, and Economic Forces 1950–1957*, 2nd edn, Stanford: Stanford University Press.

Haas, E.B. (1970) 'The study of regional integration: reflections on the joy and anguish of pretheorizing', *International Organization* 24(4): 607–46.

Haas, E.B. (1976a) *The Obsolescence of Regional Integration*, Berkeley: University of California Press.

Haas, E.B. (1976b) 'Turbulent fields and the theory of regional integration', *International Organization* 30(2): 173–212.

Haas, E.B. (2000) 'Conversation with history'; interview with Haas by Harry Kreisler, Institute of International Studies, University of California, Berkeley.

Haas, E.B. (2001) 'Does constructivism subsume neo-functionalism?', in T. Christiansen, K.E. Jørgensen and A. Wiener (eds), *The Social Construction of Europe*, London: Sage, pp. 22–31.

Haas, E.B. and Schmitter, P.C. (1964) 'Economics and differential patterns of political integration: projections about unity in Latin America', *International Organization* 18(4): 705–37.

Haas, E.B. and Schmitter, P.C. (1965) *The Politics of Economics in Latin American Regionalism*, Monograph Series in World Affairs, Denver: University of Denver Press.

Hansen, R. (1967) *Central America: Regional Integration and Economic Development*, Studies in Development Progress, no. 1, Washington: National Planning Association.

Harrison, R. (1974) *Europe in Question: Theories of Regional International Integration*, London: Allen & Unwin.

Hoekman, B. and Sauvé, J. (1994) 'Regional and multilateral liberalization of service markets: complements or substitutes?', *Journal of Common Market Studies* 32(3): 283–317.

Hoffmann, S. (1966) 'Obstinate or obsolete? The fate of the nation-state and the case of Western Europe', *Daedalus* 85(3): 865–921.

Laursen, F. (2003) *Comparative Regional Integration: Theoretical Perspective*, Aldershot: Ashgate.

Leucona, R. (1999) 'Economic integration: NAFTA and Mercosur: a comparative analysis', *International Journal on World Peace* 16(4): 27–52.

Mansfield, E. and Milner, H. (eds) (1997) *The Political Economy of Regionalism*, New York: Columbia University Press.

Mattli, W. (1999) *The Logic of Regional Integration: Europe and Beyond*, Cambridge: Cambridge University Press.

Mattli, W. and Slaughter, A.M. (1998) 'Revisiting the European Court of Justice', *International Organization* 52(1): 177–209.

Milenky, E. (1973) *The Politics of Regional Organization in Latin America: The Latin American Free Trade Association*, New York: Praeger.

Milner, H. (1997) 'Industries, governments, and regional trade blocs', in E. Mansfield and H. Milner (eds), *The Political Economy of Regionalism*, New York: Columbia University Press, pp. 77–106.

Mitrany, D. (1943) *A Working Peace System*, London: Royal Institute of International Affairs.

Mitrany, D. (1966) *A Working Peace*, Chicago: Quadrangle Books.

Mohr, A.F. (1972) *La Creación de un Mercado Común: Apuntes históricos sobre la experiencia de Centroamérica*, Buenos Aires: Instituto Para La Integración de América Latina.

Nye, J. (1967) 'Central American regional integration', *International Conciliation* (March): 1–66.

Organization for Economic Co-operation and Development (1993) *Regional Integration and Developing Countries*, Paris: OECD.

Pierson, P. (1996) 'The path to European integration: a historical institutional analysis', *Comparative Political Studies* 29(2): 123–63.

Prebisch, R. (1950) *The Economic Development of Latin America and Its Principal Problems*, New York: United Nations Economic Commission for Latin America.

Sandholtz, W. and Stone Sweet, A. (1998) *European Integration and Supranational Governance*, Oxford: Oxford University Press.

Schmitter, P.C. (1972) *Autonomy or Dependence as Regional Integration Outcomes: Central America*, Berkeley: Institute of International Studies, University of California, Berkeley.

Steinberg, R. (1997) 'Trade–environment negotiations in the EU, NAFTA, and WTO: regional trajectories of rule development', *The American Journal of International Law* 91(2): 231–67.

Stevis, D. and Mumme, S. (2000) 'Rules and politics in international integration: environmental regulation in NAFTA and the EU', *Environmental Politics* 9(4): 20–42.

Stone Sweet, A. (2004) *The Judicial Construction of Europe*, Oxford: Oxford University Press.

Teague, P. (2003) 'Labour standard-setting and regional trading blocs', *Employee Relations* 25: 428–52.

Wilford, W.T. and Christou, G. (1973) 'A sectoral analysis of disaggregated trade flows in the Central American common market, 1962–1970', *Journal of Common Market Studies* 12(2): 159–75.

Wionczek, M. (ed.) (1966) *Latin American Economic Integration*, New York: Praeger.

Wionczek, M. (1968) 'Latin American integration and United States economic policies', in R. Gregg (ed.), *International Organization in the Western Hemisphere*, Syracuse: Syracuse University Press, pp. 4–24.

Wionczek, M. (1970) 'The rise and the decline of Latin American economic integration', *Journal of Common Market Studies* 9(2): 49–66.

Wynia, G. (1970) 'Central American integration: the paradox of success', *International Organization* 24(2): 319–34.

Yarbrough, B.V. and Yarbrough, R.M. (1997) 'Dispute settlement in international trade: regionalism and procedural coordination', in E. Mansfield and H. Milner (eds), *The Political Economy of Regionalism*, New York: Columbia University Press, pp. 134–63.

# The European Constitutional Compromise and the neofunctionalist legacy

Andrew Moravcsik[1]

Over the past half-century the European Union (EU) has evolved until its policies and institutions are of a scope and significance without parallel among international organizations. Within Europe, tariffs, quotas, and most customs barriers have been all but eliminated. In regulatory areas such as environmental policy, competition, agricultural and industrial standardization policy, the EU is a dominant regional and global force. Similarly the EU is a *bone fide* superpower in the area of global trade. The European Court of Justice (ECJ) has established the supremacy of EU law, the right of individuals to file suits, and constitutional review for consistency with the Treaty of Rome, which is binding through the near-uniform acceptance of its decisions by domestic courts. Taken as a whole, its policies make Europe a 'quiet superpower' with power that matches or exceeds that of the US in almost every area except the deployment of high-intensity military force.[2] The powers of the directly elected European Parliament (EP) have steadily increased over the past decade. The European Commission enjoys exceptional autonomy among international secretariats. Under the aegis of the European Council, thousands of meetings among national officials, ministers and heads of state and government are held annually, resulting in hundreds of pieces of legislation.

Since the 1950s, this spectacular record of growth and achievement has led most analysts to treat the EU as an institution on an upward, if uneven, course for 'ever closer union.' For scholars, this sort of thinking is associated with neofunctionalist theory. The study of regional integration emerged in 1958, the very moment that the European Economic Community (EEC) was founded, with the publication of Ernst Haas's classic, *The Uniting of Europe*. Haas sought to develop a theory that explained why, once an initial commitment was made, forward momentum of integration was inevitable. In this he very explicitly sought to theorize the strategy being pursued at the time by Jean Monnet, often viewed as a 'founding father' or 'saint' of European integration.[3] Thus neofunctionalism remains a touchstone for scholarship and, albeit tacitly, for practical politics concerning the EU.

The neofunctionalist tendency to think of the EU as 'becoming' rather than 'being' remains at the heart of current debates on the future of the EU. Bitter battles between Europhiles and Euroskeptics grab headlines, seduce scholars and motivate politicians. Europhiles view the continued growth of the EU as desirable, even essential. Some go further, arguing that if integration ceases, the EU may collapse – colloquially known as the 'bicycle theory.' Euroskeptics, led by British and American conservatives, warn of the rise of a technocratic 'superstate' – a 'bureaucratic despotism' recalling the *ancien régime* in France and, in a few more extreme formulations, the Nazi dictatorship in Germany.[4] Their vehemence notwithstanding, battles between Europhiles and Euroskeptics disguise broad agreement that further centralization toward something akin to a federal state is the inevitable trajectory for Europe, whether European's want it or not, and that such a state-like governance system can legitimate itself only by becoming more democratic, that is, more accountable to direct popular majorities. It is on this basis that the recent draft constitution was negotiated, and it is on the basis of these same two claims, albeit a different evaluation of them, that Euroskeptics oppose its ratification. Most who speak of 'ever closer union' thus implicitly follow the footsteps of Haas and Monnet.[5]

In this paper I advance three claims. First, neofunctionalism is not a theory, in the modern sense, but a framework comprising a series of unrelated claims. Haas's bias toward 'ever closer union' meant that this framework was overambitious, one-sided and essentially unfalsifiable. It sought to explain long-term dynamic change without micro-foundational theories of static preferences, bargaining and institutional delegation – an effort that proved empirically and theoretically futile. For these reasons, it is generally not right or wrong to speak of neofunctionalism being true or false; it is simply meaningless.

Second, when specific elements of neofunctionalism are defined more precisely and tested more rigorously – something that occurred only within the past decade – they prove to be exceptional rather than central to an empirical understanding of European integration. The various theoretical claims underlying neofunctionalism, except for its stress on economic interests, identify anomalies.

Third, today neofunctionalism directs us to pose less fruitful questions about European integration than was once the case. The EU's current constitutional *status quo* appears stable and normatively attractive. Beyond incremental changes in policy, it is difficult to imagine functional pressures, institutional pressures, or normative concerns upsetting the stability of the basic constitutional equilibrium in Europe today. There is thus a tension between the optimistic rhetoric of 'ever closer union' – itself in part a legacy of Haasian neofunctionalism – what we might call a 'European Constitutional Compromise' (or, if you are British, 'European Constitutional Settlement'). While a bias in favor of 'ever closer union' continues to suffuse EU scholarship, distorting our understanding of European integration, empirical analysis of the broader importance of the EU in European politics, global affairs, and democratic theory might do better to begin by acknowledging the existence of this political equilibrium. Today the central debate in the EU is not about how to continue on the road to further integration, but about precisely where to stop – a debate for which neofunctionalism is ill-equipped.

## NEOFUNCTIONALISM AND THE FALLACIES OF GRAND THEORIZING

We begin with Ernst Haas. A useful point of departure is his classic monograph, *The Uniting of Europe*, in which Haas sets forth a neofunctionalist explanation of the evolution of the European Coal and Steel Community (ECSC) and the founding of the EEC. Following Monnet, Haas denies that regional integration, once it gets started, is either an enterprise conducted by European idealists for its own sake, an instrument of Cold War geopolitics, or a pragmatic response to exogenous economic challenges. Integration, he argues instead, is the inevitable, if indirect and unintended, consequence of previous decisions to centralize regional governance – though this teleology was later heavily qualified. Under specific circumstances, he theorizes more generally, economic pressure groups and supranational officials (like Monnet) assure that regional integration continues onward toward what the Treaty of Rome was to call 'ever closer union.' The neofunctionalist claim is that the essence of integration lies in the fact that this is not the result of conscious choice. Colloquially, it is not really about what it seems to be about. Entrepreneurs only exploit economic issues to achieve a broader end. This conclusion rested on two interrelated claims.

*(1) Integration progresses when organized economic interests pressure governments to manage economic interdependence to their advantage by centralizing policies and institutions.* Haas distinguished neofunctionalism from what were perceived in the 1950s as polar alternatives in explaining world politics: 'realism' and 'idealism.' He thus rejected the view that European integration was primarily about

the realization of a European ideal (a view called at the time 'federalism').[6] '"Good Europeans" are not the main creators of the regional community,' he maintained; instead 'major interest groups as well as politicians determine their support of, or opposition to, new central institutions and policies on the basis of a calculation of advantage.'[7] Haas similarly swept aside the traditional 'realist' view that European integration was primarily about military balancing against the USSR, the USA, or Germany.[8] Instead, Haas sought to apply elite pluralist interest group theory to the management of a modern economy.[9] Elite groups most intensely concerned with an issue, Haas asserts, have the greatest impact on national decision-making, which is why a majority, in the strict sense, is not required to make policy. In an era of 'the end of ideology,' in which forces like nationalism are anachronisms, 'not cultural unity but economic advantage proved to be an acceptable shared goal among the Six.'[10] Most analysts, as we shall see, now accept this pluralist and rationalist account of the EU's social foundations – but Haas's second claim is more controversial.

(2) Initial decisions to integrate economically create economic and political spill-overs – unintended or unwanted consequences of earlier decisions – which are the major force propelling regional integration further forward. Steps toward integration at any given time tend to generate unexpected pressures for further integration – a phenomenon Haas terms 'spillover.' Haas's decisive theoretical claim is that decisions in favour of integration cannot be explained as responses to exogenous shocks and trends (rising economic interdependence, heightened military threats, or trends in cultural socialization) per se but are instead endogenous to prior integration. In his words, 'The ECSC experience has spawned a theory of international integration by indirection, by trial and error, by miscalculation on the part of the actors desiring integration, by manipulation of elite social forces on the part of small groups of pragmatic administrators and politicians in the setting of a vague and permissive public opinion. "Functionalism" and "incrementalism" rather than "federalism" and "comprehensive planning" are the key terms.'[11] During the 1960s, Haas accounted for further EU developments by noting: 'The irony of [EEC developments in the 1960s] ... is that they had not all been planned or approved by governments in 1958.'[12] In sum, once initial decisions are taken, unintended feedback from those decisions becomes the primary force underlying integration.

Haas highlights two types of 'spillover.'[13] The first type, functional spillover, occurs when cooperation in certain sectors of the economy (or society) creates technocratic pressure for cooperation in adjoining sectors, thereby propelling integration forward. Haas elaborates his 'chief finding' that 'industrial sectors initially opposed to integration ... do change their attitudes and develop strong positive expectations if they feel that certain common problems can be more easily met by a federal authority.'[14] The second type, political spillover, occurs when ongoing cooperation in certain areas empowers supranational officials to act as informal political entrepreneurs in other areas. In order to manage complex technocratic issues more effectively, rational governments must delegate discretion to experts, judges and bureaucrats, thereby creating powerful new supranational actors with an interest in cooperation.[15] To the extent that these types of spillover propel integration forward, Haas concludes, 'the vision of Jean Monnet has been clearly justified by events.'[16]

Though it may seem disarmingly simple, neofunctionalism was at the time an uncommonly ambitious intellectual enterprise for three reasons.

First, neofunctionalism is *dynamic*. It seeks to explain not just static decision-making under stable political conditions, but dynamic political transformation over time. Haas invokes spillover not primarily to explain why societal groups or supranational entrepreneurs come to support decisions taken by states, or why each stage of integration provides a stable platform for the next. (Each of those claims could be part of any rationalist account.) Instead spillover is meant to explain how the response of societal groups and supranational entrepreneurs to initial integrative steps trigger entirely new and unexpected steps toward regional integration. It is not a theory of equilibrium, but of change.[17]

Second, neofunctionalism is, at least in its initial formulation, *parsimonious and predictive*. This is related to its ambition to explain integration as an endogenous consequence of earlier decisions, rather than as a response to exogenous forces, trends and shocks.[18] Once the basic condition of a number of interdependent developed market democracies is fulfilled, further integration stems from a dynamic of spillover divorced from any particular political or economic circumstances. Once initial decisions are taken, Haas maintained, spillover is automatic rather than contingent on specific external stimuli.[19] This is why Haas so confidently advances deterministic predictions, without only a parsimonious input of data: 'The progression from a politically-inspired common market to an economic union and finally to a political union among states is automatic,' he wrote. 'The inherent logic of the functional process in a setting such as Western Europe can push no other way.'[20] Haas sought a predictive theory – even at the expense of developing a complex and contingent explanatory account of causal mechanisms.[21]

Third, perhaps most important yet perhaps most neglected, neofunctionalism is *a comprehensive synthesis rather than a single theory*. Haas's overarching aspiration is totalizing. He does not seek to explain a particular aspect or to analyze a particular cause of integration, but to provide a single framework for analyzing integration as a whole. He grasps that a comprehensive theoretical understanding of institutionalized cooperation among advanced industrial democracies requires a series of disparate theoretical claims: societal preferences (beyond the initial founding) reflect pressures from pluralist economic interests, cooperation creates uniform incentives for institutionalization, supranational officials play a powerful role in interstate bargaining, unintended socioeconomic consequences are cumulative and self-reinforcing, and so on. Haas views these elements as mutually supportive links in an integrated ideal-type of the process of regional integration among capitalist democracies. Today we would call each of these building blocks by new names: 'endogenous' theories of foreign economic (trade, monetary or regulatory) policy, interstate bargaining theory (including theories of political entrepreneurship), theories of delegation to and compliance under international regimes, theories of historical institutionalist change that investigate the sources of institutional autonomy over time, and dynamic input-output theories that specify the conditions under which (or even just a controlled measurement of when) a trend in some economic activities impacts others. In the late 1950s, none of these theoretical building blocks existed, though over the next three decades, the more honest among the pioneers in each of these areas would credit Haas for providing pioneering inspiration.[22]

Haas's dynamic, predictive, totalizing ambition help make *The Uniting of Europe* a truly visionary work. Fifty years ago he glimpsed that there could be a distinctive political science of non-military international interdependence and governance, of which the process of European integration was the harbinger. Neofunctionalism was a dynamic, parsimonious theoretical synthesis to explain politics in this realm – a realm we now call 'international political economy' or 'global governance.' Haas also perceived that the essence of European integration lay in functional economic pressure, not federalist efforts to mobilize public opinion or realist efforts to mobilize the West against the Soviet Union. Yet the ambition of neofunctionalism was also a weakness, for it meant that Haas's formulation advanced ambitious claims before the concrete causal processes were theoretically understood. This rendered neofunctionalism a fragile research program, as we are about to see.

## The theoretical fragility of neofunctionalism

By the early 1970s it was evident even to its creators that neofunctionalism required fundamental revision. At one level – the one most commonly discussed – the failure of neofunctionalism was empirical.[23] European integration did not, as Haas had predicted, expand steadily but by stops and starts. President Charles de Gaulle launched a frontal attack on the EEC, and institutional deepening appeared to be at a standstill. Significant domestic conflict remained. Integration had focused not on areas of state intervention and planning, such as atomic energy and public transport, but on areas of market liberalization, such as tariff policy. It had not generated uniformly stronger centralized institutions but a curious hybrid still heavily dependent on unanimous consensus among governments – a trend Haas already glimpsed in 1958. Because these events seemed to disconfirm the simple conjecture of steady integration, they were universally viewed by Haas and others – incorrectly, in retrospect – as a 'refutation' or 'disconfirmation' of neofunctionalism. And governments did not always privilege regional over global multilateral cooperation. By the early 1970s, neofunctionalists introduced concepts like 'spillback', 'spill-around', 'building', 'retrench', 'muddle about', 'encapsulate' and 'stagnation' (alongside 'spillover') to designate possible outcomes.[24] These events seemed to disconfirm early, teleological variants of neofunctionalism.[25]

Yet the critical weaknesses of neofunctionalism were not empirical but theoretical. Scholars might, after all, have responded to apparent anomalies by further specifying and refining neofunctionalist arguments to generate more rigorous, nuanced and accurate explanations of variation in regional integration. Yet this failed to occur, at least until the 1990s. Instead, once the simple and under-specified teleology toward integration was abandoned, neofunctionalism appeared to lack conceptual resources to construct a positive theoretical response. Instead, neofunctionalists invoked various exogenous factors *ad hoc* to explain anomalies in neofunctionalist predictions: anachronistic concerns of high-politics and nationalism, basic ideological antipathy toward transfers of sovereignty, pressures to widen the EEC or expand global institutions like the General Agreement on Tariffs and Trade (GATT) at the expense of regional deepening.[26] These *ad hoc* factors were invoked as impediments to integration, thereby implicitly assuming what neofunctionalists might have reasonably been expected to prove, namely that endogenous spillover from previous decisions is the primary force in favor of regional integration. The relationship of these exogenous factors to core endogenous (neofunctionalist) dynamics was left unspecified. A quarter century of theoretical stagnation ensued.

This theoretical stagnation occurred not so much because the initial conjectures drawn from neofunctionalism were shown to be incorrect, but because neofunctionalism did not really constitute a properly specified theory susceptible to incremental improvement. The basic reasons are closely related to neofunctionalism's ambition. Neofunctionalism sought to construct a comprehensive *synthesis* without a reliable set of theoretical *elements*, to analyze *dynamic* change without a reliable account of *static* decision-making, to analyze *endogenous* causes without a reliable account of *exogenous* causes and, above all, to *predict* without a reliable *explanation*. These weaknesses are related, and at their common core lies a failure to provide rigorous, micro-foundationally grounded theories of national economic preference formation, interstate bargaining, and institutional delegation.

Neofunctionalism sought to construct a comprehensive *synthesis* without a reliable set of theoretical *elements*. Recall that neofunctionalism is a framework, not a theory. Its constituent theoretical building blocks – the claim that interests were economic, supranational entrepreneurs are influential, institutional delegation is open-ended, and so on – are not derived from common foundations. None implies the veracity of the others. Each is related to the others in a purely conjectural way. One could confirm the importance of pluralist producer interests, for example, without accepting hypotheses about the importance of supranational officials – as liberal intergovernmentalists would later do. In an influential critique, Donald Puchala invoked the metaphor of the blind men and the elephant: different theories explain different aspects of the (elephantine) integration process.[27] Neofunctionalism is only as valid as the individual theories that form the links in its chain of argument. And any test of the neofunctionalist framework as a whole against the track record of integration will be at best imprecise and at worst inherently inconclusive – particularly if, as we shall see is the case, the individual elements are underspecified. To refine and evaluate the neofunctionalist framework, it would have to be disaggregated.[28]

The difficulties were doubled insofar as neofunctionalism seeks to analyze *dynamic* change without a reliable account of *static* decision-making – to *predict* without *explaining*. The critical problem was that to derive dynamic prediction, static decisions must in turn be grounded in theories of political behavior that are general, actor-oriented and choice-theoretic. The fundamental weakness of neofunctionalism, Haas later admitted, lay in the lack of any general micro-foundational theory for analyzing various types of political choice.[29] Without this essential building blocks, any prediction from the approach – notably Haas's claim that further integration would follow automatically from previous decisions – could only be an indeterminate conjecture rather than a precise prediction. Feedback, Haas conceded in his later self-criticism, '*may* transform the system' but need not do so. Once neofunctionalism dropped the optimistic notion that integration was automatically self-reinforcing and would smoothly evolve along a smooth teleology to federal union without triggering fundamental distributive or ideological conflicts, it could say 'little about *basic causes*' of national demands for integration or interstate agreements to achieve it – so two leading neofunctionalists concluded. This is why the taxonomy of alternative outcomes consistent with the underlying theory arose: 'spillover,' 'spillback,' 'spill-around,' and 'encapsulation.' By 2004 Haas and others were arguing that there really was no difference between neofunctionalism and 'liberal intergovernmental-ist' theories, which stressed exogenous economic interests, interstate bargaining, and rational delegation – evidence of just how indeterminate neofunctionalism had become.[30]

Haas himself understood these weaknesses. In the early 1970s he proposed that 'the study of regional integration should be both included in and subordi-nated to the study of changing patterns of interdependence.'[31] Consistent with this auto-critique, Stanley Hoffmann, Robert Keohane, Joseph Nye, Henry Nau, and many others, eventually drew the conclusion that the European Com-munity (EC) should be viewed as an 'international regime' (a term Haas coined) designed to manage interdependence.[32] Such general theories of interdepen-dence highlighted the purposive choices of states and social actors rather than the unintended consequences of broad structural constraints.[33] For example, while neofunctionalists maintained that the pursuit of economic interest is the fundamental force underlying integration, they offered only a vague under-standing of precisely what those interests are, how conflicts among them are resolved, by what means they are translated into policy, and when they require political integration.[34]

The lack of rigor and precision in addressing these issues was particularly troubling in Haas's case, because neofunctionalism aspired to trace dynamic endogenous effects (incremental feedback, unintended consequences, and the resulting change over time) without a baseline theory of exogenous constraints (state economic interests, political constraints, and delegation) through which dynamic change must take place.[35] Theories that ignore the need for focused general theories, and instead treat regional integration as a *sui generis* phenom-enon, Haas argued in a self-critique over a decade after *The Uniting of Europe*, breed theoretical insularity and are little more than 'pre-theories.'[36] Certainly none was theorized so as (even in the abstract) to support predictions or explanations of *variation* in outcomes.

By the mid-1970s, these criticisms had inspired a degree of consensus concerning the proper theoretical direction forward. Unintended consequences and feedback, the initial core of neofunctionalism, should take a secondary role to the concrete beliefs, preferences and strategies of political actors – the analysis of which required explicit theories of interest group politics, interstate bargaining, and international institutions.[37] 'All political action is purposively linked with individual and group perception of interest,' Haas wrote, thus greater attention should be focused on 'the type of demands that are made, the variety of concessions ... exchanged, and the degree of delegation of authority to new central institutions.'[38] Hoffmann, Keohane, and even, if to a lesser degree, Haas himself proposed studying the EC as an international regime constructed through a series of purposive decisions by governments with varying preferences and power. Hoffmann proposed a synthetic approach that examined first 'the domestic priorities and foreign policy goals of the member states, then ... the impact of the environment [and] finally the institutional interplay between the states and the Community.'[39] When EU studies was revived in the late 1980s, Keohane and Hoffmann proposed that institutional spillover through delegation to international officials required a prior intergovernmental bargain among member states, thereby refocusing our attention on the exogenous determinants of major decisions – a school that developed a variant of historical institutionalist theory known as 'regime theory.'[40]

Yet until the 1990s, this advice was not taken. Much scholarship on European integration over the past two decades remains blissfully uninformed by the self-criticism of neofunctionalists – and by advances in international relations theory over the past thirty years.[41] From 1958 through the late 1980s, neofunctionalism was the only game in town. A few British writings on 'federalism' and some diplomatic history stressing geopolitical threats aside, neofunctionalism was regional integration theory, and regional integration theory was neofunctionalism. The persistence of neofunctionalism as a leading theoretical approach for explaining the EU, while the rest of international relations moved on toward more rigorous explanations, contributed to the theoretical insularity of EU studies. One result has been a persistent bias toward predictions of future trajectory of 'ever closer union.' Another has been the multiplication of conjectures about integration, without the concurrent generation of many reliable empirical conclusions about the relative importance of different forces that have made the EC what it is today.[42] With neofunctionalism remaining underspecified, and few alternative frameworks at hand, a rule of thumb emerged in research on the EC: Whenever integration stagnated, scholars criticized neofunctionalism; whenever integration progressed, they rediscovered it.[43]

Neofunctionalism's flaws became clearer in the late 1980s and early 1990s when a coherent alternative was proposed by historian Alan Milward and similarly inclined political scientists.[44] Their view rests on the premise that major steps toward regional integration result, as does global economic integration, from a three-step process: (a) national preferences develop in response to exogenous changes in the nature of issue-specific functional interdependence; (b) interstate negotiation proceeds on the basis of relative bargaining power; and (c) delegation to supranational institutions is designed to facilitate credible commitments. This view does not differ much from neofunctionalism in its broad assumption that states are (often) rational and instrumental, or in its assumption that modern states place a high value on interests linked to the provision of welfare and security for the citizens of an advanced industrial democracy. Yet liberal intergovernmentalism departs in assuming that the primary sources of economic integration are exogenous rather than endogenous, interstate bargaining reflects intentional state action on the basis of relative power rather than supranational entrepreneurship, and, unlike neofunctionalism, provides a clear theoretical starting point for explaining delegation to supranational institutions. This view, worked out in detail in the 1990s, is now often referred to as a 'liberal intergovernmentalist' (LI) account.[45]

The LI account rests on theories of political economy, bargaining and delegation that are now standard in international relations, and indeed political science, theory. In this view, the primary impetus for integration has been a series of exogenous functional challenges. These include intra-industry trade in the 1950s and 1960s, monetary fluctuations and capital mobility in the 1970s and 1980s, greater foreign direct investment and regulatory conflict in the 1980s, and the collapse of Communism in the 1990s. Governments negotiated agreements on this basis, with supranational officials playing an epiphenomenal role. And they delegated to international institutions in what was largely a rational and controlled way. This poses a serious empirical challenge to neofunctionalist claims – to which we now turn.


## The empirical fragility of neofunctionalism

We have seen that the theoretical essence of any 'grand theory' (multi-causal theoretical synthesis) lies in its elements, not in the synthesis itself. The central issue at stake between neofunctionalism and liberal intergovernmentalism is thus not which *framework* is correct, but the extent to which the *elements* of each are correct. Three questions are paramount: (1) To what extent do state preferences for integration reflect exogenous pressures (and intended policy consequences), or to what extent do they reflect unintended and unwanted consequences of past bargains? (2) To what extent are the negotiated deals among states a function of relative bargaining power or to what extent are they a function of the actions of supranational entrepreneurs? (3) To what extent do states delegate with the intention of creating credible commitments or to what extent are any subsequent constraints an unintended consequence of delegation? In each case, the subsequent empirical literature has strongly supported the LI account. Let us consider each question in turn.

*Are preferences exogenous or endogenous to integration?*
Most scholars of European integration now believe that Haas was correct that
the primary motive forces behind integration have been pluralistic pressures
from producer groups. To be sure, geopolitical ideology – specifically, the
German concern to re-establish its security, unity and autonomy after World
War II – has played an important role over a half century.[46] Yet, overall, the
substantive range of cooperation in the EU has reflected, above all, functional
pressure to manage the concrete, largely issue policy externalities resulting
from socioeconomic interdependence as filtered through interest group politics.[47] Major steps forward in the development of European institutions have
traditionally rested on 'grand projects' such as the customs union, common
agricultural policy, single market, single currency, or Eastern enlargement. In
each case, the pressure to manage substantive policies stemming from new
forms of regional interdependence motivated governments to make new
institutional commitments.

Yet the historiographical and social scientific consensus today is that the
primary causes of integration have been more exogenous than endogenous (to
previous integration). Consider, for example, the founding of the EEC in
1955–1958. In *The Uniting of Europe*, Haas's core empirical claim is that the
EEC should be understood as a form of 'spillover' from the ECSC – a position
he explicitly opposes to the view that exogenous shifts in national economic
interests supported cooperation. Thus Haas stresses that cooperation moved
forward in nuclear energy and transport plans, areas of sectoral integration
closely linked to coal and steel, and thus favored by Monnet. Yet this is
inconsistent with the historical record. Within a few years it became clear
that nuclear and transport integration were going nowhere, whereas the
common market – which Haas rightly views (as it was viewed at the time) as
something of a repudiation of Monnet's sectoral approach – was succeeding.[48]

Throughout, Haas neglects the more plausible alternative hypothesis that
integration reflected exogenous economic pressures derived from changes in
technology and markets.[49] He does consider for one paragraph (five pages
before the conclusion of his 527-page book) this alternative explanation, yet –
despite the fact he concedes that positions at the Messina conference were
precisely in keeping with underlying economic incentives – he dismisses such
an 'intergovernmental' explanation in a single sentence, without presenting
any evidence, in favour of an *ad hoc* social-psychological mechanism (namely
that governments cooperated because they felt a greater sense of 'engagement').[50] Haas also overrides evidence that, he acknowledges, demonstrates
that the institutional structure of the EEC was less centralized than that of
the preceding ECSC – an apparent anomaly for neofunctionalist thinking.
Instead of acknowledging the disconfirmation, he redefines 'supranational' to
include any forward movement toward integration, even where it *reduces*
central authority.[51]

This sort of testing is loose to the point of tautology: Continued integration confirms neofunctionalist theory, no matter what its form, rather than neofunctionalist

theory predicting a particular form of integration. Subsequent formulations of neo-functionalist theory grew even vaguer, seeking to incorporate any possible cause of forward movement in the EU. Consider, for example, Saeter's reformulation of neo-functionalism, later cited approvingly by Haas, that simply asserts (incorrectly) that no theory except neofunctionalism can explain change over time, so alternative theories need not be tested at all.[52] Today one sees the same form of argument with insufficiently theorized constructivist or neofunctionalist accounts, which often code any change in time in preferences as evidence confirming the theory.

The empirical evidence is far more supportive of Milward's and Moravcsik's claim that the EEC was founded in response to the epochal post-war shift in trade patterns from North–South commodity trade to North–North intra-industry trade – the bulk of which was complete well before EEC tariff reduction was complete. Whereas the EEC surely added to this level of North–North trade, it is not the underlying historical cause of the shift, nor is there any evidence that the increases in trade were unintended or undesired.[53] Overall, the evidence is overwhelming that European integration in this period deepened not because of economic spillover from prior integration, but on the basis of a convergence of interest, led in the initial period by enduring liberal interests in Germany and the Netherlands.[54] It is now widely accepted that governments perceived regional integration as an inevitable adaptation to economic tends – though some, including myself, have argued that certain institutional elements in the EU cannot fully be explained in this way.[55]

The more recent literature is littered with failed attempts to assert the importance of spillover – often within a 'historical institutionalist' or 'institutionalist' framework – as the central dynamic of European integration. Paul Pierson's theoretical work provided a useful micro-foundational account of this phenomenon, arguing that spillover was only likely to occur under rather specific circumstances, namely where policy consequences and future circumstances are uncertain, state preferences are unstable, or time horizons are short. Yet the historical record resists such an interpretation. Though the EC has moved toward greater trade liberalization and reestablished an element of monetary cooperation, the relative positions of governments have remained surprisingly stable over four decades. Germany and Britain favored industrial trade liberalization, while France is more skeptical. Since 1950, France has consistently advocated the creation of subsidized markets for surplus agricultural products, while Germany demands high prices, and Britain has opposed all agricultural cooperation. Views on regulatory harmonization have moved toward liberalization, but the configuration of national preferences continues to reflect per capita income and trading interests. Finally, the common assertion that various major decisions in EC history have had important unintended consequences due to changes in circumstances rests on a superficial reading of the historical record.[56]

Statesmen have been aware of long-term processes and when the EU has been socially and institutionally transformative, but more often than not this has been because statesmen deliberately designed it that way. Charles de Gaulle sought to exploit integration to modernize French industry; the German and French governments consistently argued in favor of integration as a means to banish conflict among European nations; France sought to exploit the EC to avoid the creation of a free trade association (FTA); and Helmut Schmidt employed the European monetary system (EMS) to discourage currency devaluation by neighboring countries. Despite the odd counterexample – importantly in recent times the reversal of German macroeconomic policy after reunification – monetary preferences have also remained remarkably stable, evolving only slowly in response to changing structural conditions. Where the outcomes of policies are uncertain, policy-makers have sometimes taken an ideological view toward the future of integration, but one itself based on a long time horizon.

Closer examination reveals that the major consequences were known to the negotiating governments, but often suppressed in public statements. One example must suffice. In a very influential line of theorizing, Fritz Scharpf has made much of the claim that overproduction and high subsidies were an unintended consequence of the common agricultural policy (CAP), into which governments are now trapped.[57] In fact it is clear that statesmen knew this would occur but rejected expert recommendations because lower subsidies were politically unpalatable, particularly in Germany.[58] Most cases of 'unintended consequences' simply cannot withstand historical scrutiny.

*What factors shape interstate bargaining outcomes?*
In *The Uniting of Europe*, Haas sought to argue that supranational political entrepreneurs like Monnet have propelled the system forward in ways unexpected, unwanted or unachievable by the leaders of national governments – thereby demonstrating the decisive importance of 'political spillover.' Like his approach to explaining preferences, Haas never provided a compelling account of why supranational officials enjoy an advantage over national officials in the provision of information, expertise, legitimacy, legal competence, or skill. True, the Commission and other supranational bodies, and even earlier Jean Monnet himself, often pressed for further integration, and integration often progressed. Yet the conjecture that entrepreneurs were therefore decisive is unwarranted.[59] The observation that entrepreneurial involvement is found around decisions to move integration forward is equally consistent with supranational entrepreneurs whose activities are futile, reactive, or redundant. Instead we need theories of informal integration – something Haas declined to provide and which has only been theorized more fully in the last few years.

Though when neofunctionalism was revived in the late 1980s, this was the first aspect to be picked up – with an extensive literature on Delors – few have attempted to specify and test rigorous theories of informal entrepreneurship in the EU, or anywhere else in international life.[60] Yet more rigorous theories of informal entrepreneurship can offer important insights into world politics. All such theories rest on the assumption that the power of an entrepreneur stems from informational asymmetries that work in the entrepreneur's favor. We must assume that information is costly and difficult to obtain, that the rationality of powerful state actors who can produce such information is severely bounded, and that supranational actors are privileged in the production of such information, such that a decisive asymmetry of information, legitimacy, or expertise results. The validity of this assumption is hardly obvious, given that nation-states are immediate stakeholders with a large incentive to manage negotiations intelligently, enormous financial and bureaucratic resources, considerable EU experience, and over the years political leaders of the caliber of Konrad Adenauer, François Mitterrand, and Tony Blair. The central theoretical task in the study of informal entrepreneurship is thus to specify the various conditions under which we might expect to observe such asymmetries in favor of supranational *vis-à-vis* state officials. Do supranational actors possess greater personal political skill? Greater legal or technical expertise? Greater legitimacy? A unique status as trusted mediators? A synoptic view of the whole unavailable to member state executives? Each of these lines of argument can be theorized. The empirical task is then to ascertain to what extent such informational asymmetries exist, under which theoretical circumstances they arise, and whether they are linked to major institutional innovations in European integration. Only then can we reject spurious correlations.

Empirical research conducted on this theoretical basis demonstrates that the existing neofunctionalist literature on the subject is quite misleading.[61] Most supposed examples belong to what Milward has satirically termed 'the hagiography of European saints.'[62] Consider, for example, Haas's own analysis of the period between the founding of the ECSC and the negotiation of the 1957 Treaty of Rome, which stresses the entrepreneurial role of convinced Europeans like Spaak and Monnet. Haas's account, we now know, is almost precisely the opposite of the historical record. Monnet himself, far from being a successful political entrepreneur, played a *counterproductive* role for most of this period. He stuck to the theory – also at the heart of Haas's neo-functionalism – that integration would stem from regulated and technolically sophisticated sectors of the economy like energy, nuclear and transport cooperation, rather than from market liberalization. He was thus so hostile to the customs union plan in 1955–56 that he begged Spaak, Beyen, and Konrad Adenauer persistently to kill it. Nor was Monnet to enjoy much success later. Even his best and most sympathetic biographer admits that he had little impact after 1950 – precisely the opposite prediction from that of Haas.[63] It is a mark of the tacit impact of neofunctionalist assumptions about the importance of entrepreneurship that neither the public discourse of the EU, nor scholarly studies of European integration, have taken note of these historical facts.

A broader analysis suggests that informal entrepreneurship by the Commission or Parliament has rarely been decisive.[64] Informational asymmetries are exceptional and only rarely have helped account for advances in European integration. Certain aspects of the single market initiative under Jacques Delors constitute nearly the only empirically verified case in which supranational entrepreneurship by the Commission or Parliament had a decisive impact on major interstate bargains beyond what member states themselves could and would have achieved – and even this case is limited in scope. In nearly all other important cases, even the strongest evidence suggests a secondary or even counterproductive impact for the Commission, Parliament and other central entrepreneurs.

Despite its weakness in explaining the origins of state preferences and inter-state bargaining outcomes, neofunctionalism retains a prominent role in theorizing about the EU.[65] One reason is that scholars tend to 'select on the dependent variable,' paying disproportionate attention to situations in which the evidence supports a neofunctional view.[66] One of these is in the study of the ECJ – a rare area in which neofunctional claims have consistently been validated empirically. Yet we should beware of generalizing to the EU as a whole, for two reasons. First, the ECJ, despite its importance, is hardly the only or most influential institution in shaping the trajectory of European integration. Second, the conditions under which European judges were able to wield unintended and important powers were quite singular. We learn from the ECJ literature that among the preconditions for such an evolution were the existence of autonomous domestic courts with an incentive to recognize the European law, an ECJ that favors further integration, the existence of many economically motivated litigants, and an ability to act without immediate response from the member states.[67]

Similar issues of selection bias weigh down the literature on the Commission, where disproportionate scholarly attention has been paid to a relatively small number of categories of policy-making in which the Commission has exploited unexpected autonomy to proactively promote integration within its 'everyday' legislative and regulatory functions. A handful of examples are constantly recycled: some environmental policy directives in the 1970s, telecommunications regulation under Article 90, some parliamentary actions in the mid-1990s, and gender equality. These are peripheral to the overall trend in EU policy-making, and often occurred under conditions predicted by LI theory. In many other cases, moreover, the Commission has failed in such efforts – an example being sustained Commission efforts to manipulate structural funding to force its priorities on member states (in Scotland and elsewhere). Obviously theories about endogenous causality, supranational entrepreneurship, and unintended spillovers offer important insights into European integration. Looking back over nearly a half-century, we can conclude that for those who study a subset of specific issues, neofunctionalist causal mechanisms may offer essential theoretical tools: yet such processes generally remain peripheral to the overall dynamics of European integration.

## BEYOND NEOFUNCTIONALISM: A EUROPEAN CONSTITUTIONAL COMPROMISE?

Perhaps the greatest weakness of neofunctionalism as a theory of regional integration concerns not its inability to explain the past, but its inability to illuminate the fundamental issues facing Europe today. Today the central issue of European integration is no longer the question of how to bring about 'ever closer union' – as the 1950s-style technocratic slogan embedded in the

Treaty of Rome put it. It is instead the question of how to fashion a constitutional order that assures 'unity in diversity' – the EU's more recent slogan. This issue can be restated in constitutional terms: How broad should the scope of EU activity, as opposed to nation-state activity, be?[68] And how is power and authority to be divided (or shared) among national and supranational levels, and among various supranational political institutions?[69] What is to be the relationship of these institutions to individual citizens, interest groups, and existing structures of political representation? These constitutional questions are of central normative and positive importance in the EU, underlying discussions of subsidiarity, constitutional structure, democratic legitimacy, and substantive policy.

Neofunctionalism offers a rather one-sided analysis of this problem, one that biases the result toward centralizing responses and thus renders itself less relevant to current concerns.[70] The assumption of neofunctionalism is that, unless atavistic nationalism and ethnocentrism intervene, the EU is destined to continue to integrate. Yet what is most striking about the last fifteen years of constitutional change in the EU is the conservative nature of the result. Voting weights and the structure of the Commission have been adjusted, the use of qualified majority voting and the prerogatives of the Parliament have been expanded at the expense of the Commission, and the EU has reinforced essentially intergovernmental cooperation (mostly outside the core 'first pillar' of EU institutions) in a number of areas, including immigration and foreign policy. Yet when all is said and done, the expansion in the EU's institutional prerogatives has been modest. Taken together, all the institutional changes aimed at deepening the EU undertaken since the Maastricht Treaty of 1992 have not had as much impact as the process of enlargement – and even the latter has not generated fundamental institutional change or a decisive expansion in the substantive scope of policy-making under the 'Community method.'

Perhaps, then, we are starting to glimpse what we might term a 'European Constitutional Compromise' (or, if one is British, a 'European Constitutional Settlement') – a stable endpoint of European integration in the medium term.[71] The EU appears indeed to have reached a plateau. It may expand geographically, reform institutionally, and deepen substantively, but all this will take place largely within existing contours of European constitutional structures.

Are current arrangements stable against both exogenous shocks and spillover? Is pressure for future progress, whether endogenous or exogenous, likely due to substantive, institutional or normative pressures? I argue below that new challenges to functional effectiveness, institutional stability, or normative legitimacy are unlikely to undermine the European Constitutional Compromise. Let us consider each dimension in turn, beginning with the substance of policy.

### The substantive dimension of the European Constitutional Compromise

Perhaps the most striking characteristic of the EU as a constitutional system is the limited substantive scope of its mandate. In 1988, Jacques Delors famously predicted that in ten years '80 percent of economic, and perhaps social and fiscal policy-making' applicable in Europe would be of EU origin.[72] This prediction has become a fundamental 'factoid' in discussions of the EU – often cited as 80 percent of lawmaking *in all issues* in Europe *already* comes from Brussels.[73] Yet recent academic studies demonstrate that the actual percentage of EU-based legislation is probably between 10 and 20 percent of national rule-making.[74] Given the basic structure of the EU constitutional order, this is hardly surprising.

Consider first the substantive limitations on EU policy-making. While there are important areas of centralized governance (monetary policy, anti-trust policy, and restrictions on internal tariffs and quotas) or joint decision-making by EU member states within common institutions (external trade policy, industrial standards, agricultural policy, various economic regulatory matters, certain rules regarding establishment, investment and service provision, and perhaps also basic human rights), these are hardly exhaustive.[75] Many areas are essentially untouched by direct EU policy-making, including taxation, fiscal policy, social welfare, health care, pensions, education, defense, active cultural policy, and most law and order. Moreover, none among the latter policies appears a promising candidate for communitarization. The single market has been declared complete, though incremental expansion continues. In other areas – defense policy, immigration and asylum, law and order, fiscal policy, social policy, even indirect tax harmonization, should it come to pass – EU policy plays a subordinate role. EU policy in these areas tends to proceed by unanimity, with a subordinate role, if any, for the Commission, Parliament and Court. Again selection bias disguises the truth. The limited substantive scope of the EU is obscured by the existing scholarly literature on the EU, which focuses, understandably, on areas of intense EU activity. There is, for example, a considerable literature on the expansion of EU activity in areas like immigration, social policy, and defense. Yet this is in certain respects mis-leading. Even in areas where there is considerable progress, it is quite limited. By 'selecting on the dependent variable' in this way, EU policy-making literature creates the impression of unbounded expansion of policy-making – whereas in fact we observe only limited forays into new areas.

Consider immigration policy.[76] Cooperation in this area consists largely of 'soft' norms for national policies, coordinated activity *vis-à-vis* third countries, the exchange of data, codification of existing international obligations, and administrative coordination of parallel national policies (such as the granting of visas and passports). This takes place with reduced norms or oversight by the Commission, Parliament or Court, while national governments retain near total discretion in setting rules, deciding individual cases, imposing overall controls on immigration, designing programs to encourage or inhibit immigration, and nearly all other discretionary aspects of status once in EU member states. There appears, moreover, to be little evidence of policy externalities that might give rise to pressures for a wholesale centralized harmonization of such decisions. Measured by the scope of meaningful policy discretion, EU immigration controls remain secondary to national ones.

Consider also social policy, which many consider to be the area of greatest promise in the EU. In recent years, EU social policy has inspired an enormous academic literature and considerable political attention, focusing primarily on the innovative 'open method of coordination' (OMC). EU member states are engaged in the OMC, which leads them to exchange information, benchmark policies, and evaluate results. Again, the academic literature is enthusiastic. Leading constitutional lawyers view this process as a striking formal innovation.[77] Leading policy analysts view it as a fundamental shift in the nature of regulation, if not modern state formation.[78] Leading political philosophers and social theorists view it as the central element in an emerging European identity.[79] Leading Socialists view it as the basis for balancing the 'neo-liberal' tendencies of the EU. Students of social policy view it as a promising road for future spillover and integration in a 'historical institutionalist' mode.[80]

Yet there is little evidence that any of this matters for policy outcomes.[81] Controlled empirical studies of the process of European social policy cooperation agree that its substantive results to date have been extremely modest, if present at all. There is some sketchy evidence that governments may have used the information exchange to help plan social reforms, but no solid evidence either of any impact on or policy learning with regard to substantive policy – though some studies point to the ways in which certain governments have improved their administrative procedures, perhaps in part as a result of OMC lessons.

More fundamentally for our concern here, little evidence suggests the existence, viewed from the perspective of the national governments, of underlying negative policy externalities that an EU social policy could plausibly mitigate. Studies of a potential 'race to the bottom' among European governments in social policy have produced little evidence that such problems are significant in the present or inevitable in the future.[82] As a constraint on social spending, almost all analysts agree that domestic demographic, fiscal and policy constraints weigh larger than regional interdependence or policy-making externalities. Moreover, given that the central issue facing European governments is how to consolidate and stabilize welfare systems, it is unclear that any European social policy – except a neo-liberal one – is justified. Finally, to the extent that there are policy externalities to social policy, there is no agreement on the distributional implications of such a policy. To take only the simplest aspect, how would a European social policy balance the claims of rich and poor countries? To be blunt, to what extent should European intervention in social policy aim to redistribute wealth toward a German worker and to what extent toward a Polish one?[83] This is why, although there is considerable discussion of social policy in Europe today, concrete progress and the range of realistic proposals are modest.

This is not to dismiss concerns about spillover entirely. Issues surely exist. Perhaps fiscal policy coordination among Euro countries, anti-terrorism policy, and the General Services Directive would be useful places to seek unintended or unwanted spillovers of significant size. Some other issues, most notably certain aspects of defense or immigration, might generate pressures strong enough to motivate governments to expand the scope of integration. Yet even in these areas, no serious analyst sees a medium-term prospect of centralizing policy in Brussels, and the major reason for this is the lack of functional pressure.

## The institutional dimension of the European Constitutional Compromise

The absence of opportunities for substantive expansion in EU policy-making on a scale required to alter its constitutional order is further assured by the institutional dimension of the European Constitutional Compromise. Institutional constraints on EU policy today go far beyond the fact that wealthier member states, notably Germany, are less willing than in the past to provide modest side-payments to facilitate interstate bargains.[84] Constraints are embedded in the very essence of the EU's constitutional order, which impose exceedingly tight limits on policy innovation – thereby rendering change through either everyday policy-making or constitutional revision quite unlikely. The EU, to a first approximation, does not tax, spend, implement or coerce and, in many areas, does not even hold a legal monopoly on public authority. This limits the issues it can possibly subsume, absent a unanimously approved redesign of its structure far more fundamental than anything contemplated at the recent constitutional convention.[85] In sum, the EU is not simply unwilling to act in new areas that require coercive, fiscal or human resources; it is constitutionally unable to do so, even as a result of unintended consequences.

We begin with the most basic.[86] The EU has no police, no army, no significant intelligence capacity – and no realistic prospect of obtaining any of these. Even if the most ambitious plans currently on the table in European defense were fully realized, the EU would manage only 2 percent of European North Atlantic Treaty Organization (NATO) forces – and these forces could be employed only for a narrow range of peace-keeping ('Petersburg') tasks. Any deployment can take place only with the consent of each home country – a 'coalition of the willing' approach that makes current efforts to create joint European military forces as intergovernmental commitments as consistent with NATO as with the EU. Fiscal constraints will mean some rationalization of defense procurement, yet the EU does not envisage thereby gaining control over military spending. Similarly, although the EU helps to coordinate efforts to combat international crime, the structure of national police, criminal justice, and punishment systems remains essentially unchanged – save for some information sharing.

The ability to tax, spend, and redistribute wealth is the pre-eminent activity of the modern state. Yet the EU does little of it. EU taxation is capped at about 1.3 percent of the combined gross national product (GNP) of its members and is substantially below that level now. It represents only about 2 percent of the public spending by European national and local governments (as compared to 70 percent of US public spending by the federal government). EU funds are transfers from national governments, not direct taxation; and their disbursement is directed to a small range of policies like the CAP, regional funds and development aid – leaving little room for discretionary spending by Brussels technocrats. (Efforts to develop such a capacity were cut back by member states.) Even in areas of EU fiscal activity, such as agriculture, most public funding remains national. France is the biggest CAP beneficiary, but national sources provide two-thirds of French farm spending – often enough to counteract EU influence where desired. None of this can change without the unanimous consent of the member states.

Of course, great power resides in the ability to oversee the implementation of detailed regulations, even if non-fiscal, but we must ask: Who implements most EU regulations? Not, in most cases, the Brussels bureaucracy. The EU's employees, who number less than 30,000 – of which 4,000–5,000 are real decision-makers – constitute a workforce no larger than that of a medium-sized European city. They number about *one-fortieth* of the non-military federal workforce in the US, a country noted for the small size of federal civilian employment. So the task of implementing EU regulations falls to national parliaments and officials. Thus, while it is hard for such governments to avoid compliance permanently, they can shade it to benefit this or that domestic group, and delay it for years.

The EU is thus condemned in perpetuity to be what one scholar terms a 'regulatory polity' – a system with instruments of regulation, but little fiscal discretion.[87] It is similarly condemned to delegate back to member states the implementation of its own regulations. Both aspects are critical because the most important issues that remain in the hands of national policy-makers – issues such as social welfare provision, health care, pensions, defense, education, and local infrastructural policy – all involve both discretionary taxation and fiscal capacity, as well as complex systems of bureaucratic monitoring and implementation.[88]

The only major exception to this rule concerns the actions of the ECJ, whose policy autonomy is in fact expanded by the constraints on EU decision-making. Still the ECJ is itself limited by political and legal constraints imposed by member states, as its recent, more cautious approach to certain problems suggests. In the scholarly literature, much has been made of this area of neofunctionalist policy-making in a sea of intergovernmental agreement – another example of the 'selection on the dependent variable' bias in the scholarly literature. Whereas this exception merits closer attention, it does not fundamentally alter the prognosis for the basic trajectory of the EU's institutional evolution.

## The normative dimension of the European Constitutional Compromise

There are those who argue that spillover will emerge not simply for reasons of substantive policy or because of delegation to autonomous centralized institutions, as neofunctionalists argued, but because the success of the EU has now provoked a crisis of legitimacy. In this view – perhaps closer to the classical 'federalism' of Spinelli and others than to Haasian neofunctionalism – the EU must democratize or decay.

It is not hard to see why the EU appears democratically illegitimate. Only one branch of the EU is directly elected: the EP. The EP is weaker than national counterparts, and its elections are decentralized, apathetic affairs, in which a small number of voters act on the basis of national rather than EU concerns. The European Commission is widely perceived as a remote technocracy. The ECJ, with fifteen appointed judges, is unusually powerful by the domestic standards of most European countries. Most powerful among Brussels institutions, the Council of Ministers assembles national ministers, diplomats and officials, who often deliberate in secret. Right-wing critics believe the EU is infringing on personal liberty. Left-wing critics view the EU as a throwback to the fiscally weak, neo-liberal state of the nineteenth century, which legally constructed markets with a limited range of balancing social policies.

Legitimacy has two meanings with regard to the contemporary EU – one philosophical and one practical. Some use it to designate the extent to which the EU is consistent with basic democratic principles, others to refer to the level of support and trust for the EU among European publics. The conventional view is that the EU has a 'double' legitimacy crisis, and that crises in each of the two areas are related, because the weakness of public support follows from the lack of philosophically defensible democratic credentials. Critics of current EU institutions, both among Europhiles and Europhobes, argue that EU decision-making is both unstable and illegitimate because it is not based on direct democratic consent. For the past half-decade, this has been the most widespread public argument for fundamental constitutional reform of the EU. It was on the basis of such beliefs, more than anything else, that the recent constitutional convention was called.

Yet the criticism that the EU is democratically illegitimate rests on questionable foundations. As regards abstract democratic legitimacy, most critics reach negative conclusions by comparing the EU to ideal forms of deliberative democracy, rather than the real-world practices of the national democracies they replace. Abstract democratic legitimacy must be judged using reasonable and realistic criteria. No existing government lives up to abstract, utopian standards of imaginary republics. It is far more reasonable to adopt the following standard: is EU governance as democratic as the (presumptively legitimate) domestic decision-making procedures of its member states in dealing with similar issues? When we rephrase the question this way, the claim that the EU is democratically illegitimate is unsupported by the evidence. This conclusion holds, I argue, no matter what mainstream philosophical conception of democracy one starts from: libertarian, pluralist, or deliberative.[89]

### Libertarian democracy
The *libertarian* conception of democracy, dating back to John Locke and others in early modern Europe, views it as a means to assure limited government by

checking the arbitrary and corrupting power of the state. For libertarians, the European Constitutional Compromise has created a Brussels 'superstate.' This is not just a figment of the tabloid imagination. Arbitrary rule by national and supranational technocrats – 'bureaucratic despotism' in Brussels, as Oxford academic Larry Siedentop puts it in *Democracy in Europe* – is a widespread concern among free marketers and libertarian conservatives.[90]

Yet the European superstate is an illusion. The European Constitutional Compromise imposes exceedingly tight constraints on policy – combining elements of the consensus democracy of the Netherlands, the federalism of Canada, the checks and balances of the US, and the reduced fiscal capacity of Switzerland. We have already seen that the EU, broadly speaking, does not tax, spend, implement, coerce or, in most areas, monopolize public authority. It has no army, police, and intelligence capacity, and a miniscule tax base, discretion on spending, and administration. As for constitutional change in the EU, it requires unanimity, often with public ratification, in the member states – a standard higher than any modern democracy except perhaps Switzerland. Such a system is deeply resistant to any fundamental transformation to basically alter the 'regulatory' nature of the European state without broad consensus among a wide variety of actors. This is why the EU only influences between 10 and 20 percent of European policy-making. And it is unlikely to change.

Even more importantly, from the Lockean perspective, the EU's ability to act (even where it enjoys unquestioned legal competence) is constrained by exceptional checks and balances among multi-level institutions. The EU is not a system of parliamentary sovereignty but one of separation of powers, with political authority and discretion divided vertically amongst the Commission, Council, Parliament and Court, and horizontally amongst local, national and transnational levels. The Commission must propose (by majority), the Council of Ministers must decide (by supermajority), European parliamentarians must assent (by absolute majority) and, if the result is challenged, the European Court must approve. National parliaments or officials must then transpose directives into national law, and national bureaucracies must implement them. Overall, this makes everyday legislation as or more difficult to pass as constitutional revision would be in most advanced industrial democracies. Only the exceptional interdependence of European states, which creates important convergence of interest, makes legislation possible at all.

It is important not to go to the opposite extreme and argue that we need not worry about European integration because the EU is so weak. The EU is in fact quite strong in many areas, as in market regulation, monetary policy, trade negotiation, anti-trust and anti-subsidy policy, agricultural policy, industrial standardization and environment policy – in which regulatory activity in Brussels, Luxembourg or Frankfurt dominates European policy-making. Are these activities under legitimate democratic oversight? This query leads us to the next conception of democracy.

*Pluralist democracy*

Many criticize the European Constitutional Compromise from the perspective of a *pluralist* conception of democracy, which stresses the need for EU activities to be accountable to and representative of popular views. To them, the EU policy process, even if under broad constraints, seems unduly to favor national *bureaucrats* and *ministers* at the expense of *parliaments* and *publics*. In some matters, moreover, semi-autonomous supranational authorities, such as the ECJ, the European Central Bank (ECB), and the Commission's Directorate-General for Competition, wield considerable autonomy and discretion. Long chains of delegation dilute the impact of public pressure. Overall, the lack of direct democratic participation seems to imply that the EU is an insulated cartel of supranational and national technocrats bent on regulating citizens free from public scrutiny.

Yet the EU employs two robust mechanisms of democratic oversight: *direct* accountability via the EP and *indirect* accountability via elected national officials in the Council. Over the last two decades, the EP has been supplanting the Commission as the primary interlocutor *vis-à-vis* the Council in the EU legislative process. The EP now enjoys the right, late in the legislative process, to accept, reject or amend legislation in a manner difficult for the member states to reject. The EP is directly elected by proportional representation within nation-states, and often acts independently of ruling national parties. The EP, which tends to reach decisions by large majorities, is most active in precisely those areas where public preferences are strong, such as environmental policy, oversight of the Commission, and social policy.

Indirect accountability, exercised through the European Council, the Council of Ministers, and national implementation, plays an even more important role in assuring accountability. In the European Council, now consolidating its position as the EU's dominant institution, elected national leaders wield power directly – setting the agenda for the EU as a whole. In the Council of Ministers, which imposes the most important constraint on everyday EU legislation, permanent representatives, officials and ministers act under constant instruction from national executives, just as they would at home. In countries that have made it a priority, such as Denmark, national parliaments consider many EU policies before they are legislated. All countries are free to do the same and, as we have seen, member states enjoy considerable discretion as regards implementation of EU rules.

A corollary of accountability is openness. In contrast to the impression of a cadre of secretive Brussels gnomes, EU officials in fact work under transparency and public scrutiny more intense than that found in almost any of its member states. With twenty commissioners and their staffs, fifteen national delegations, over six hundred parliamentarians, hundreds of national ministers and thousands of national officials, *ex ante* parliamentary scrutiny in some countries and *ex post* parliamentary scrutiny in nearly all, and the ultimate need for domestic implementation, there can be no such thing as a monopoly of information in the EU. The EU legislative process works slowly and openly, with no equivalent to ruling by executive decree or pushing legislation swiftly through a friendly parliament. Recent comparative research reveals that the EU's regulatory process is as transparent and open to pressure from interested parties as those of either the US or Switzerland.[91] The EU system may be unfamiliar to its citizens, but it is hardly closed. 'Sunshine' reveal documents, newspapers widely report deliberations, and the near total absence of discretionary spending or bureaucratic adjudication almost eliminates common incentives for corruption. Constant scrutiny from fifteen different governments similarly renders the EU less corrupt than almost any national government in Europe. Recent scandals, often cited to demonstrate the extent of EU corruption, are exceptions that prove the rule. When appointed a commissioner some years back, for example, Edith Cresson – a former French prime minister with a record of sleaze – was unceremoniously removed from office when she could not withstand the glare of Brussels' transnational political culture.[92]

Some pluralists might object that the EU relies too much on technocrats and judges in order to resolve essentially political questions involving the sensitive apportionment of cost, benefit and risk – as in the case of the central bank and constitutional court. Yet there is little that is distinctively 'European' about this pattern of delegation. Political commentators agree that the late twentieth century has been a period of the 'decline of parliaments' and the rise of courts, public administrations and the 'core executive.' Democratic accountability in such bodies is imposed not simply through indirect control through majoritarian institutions, but also through complex systems of indirect representation, selection of representatives, procedural norms, and precise balances among branches of government. The key point for understanding European integration is this: EU judges and technocrats enjoy the greatest autonomy in precisely those areas – central banking, constitutional adjudication, criminal and civil prosecution, technical administration and economic diplomacy – in which many advanced democracies, including EU states, also insulate themselves from direct political contestation.

The functional similarities between delegation in domestic and EU settings suggest that political insulation of certain decisions is no historical accident. Most non-majoritarian institutions have been created in the EU and elsewhere for compelling reasons. Some non-majoritarian institutions are designed to provide greater efficiency and expertise in areas where most citizens remain 'rationally ignorant' or non-participatory, as in the case of expert bodies. Other non-majoritarian institutions dispense impartial and equitable justice, rights, and entitlements for individuals and minority groups, as in the case of constitutional courts, which are often seen as defending individual or minority prerogatives against the immediate 'tyranny of the majority.' This tendency has spread in recent years as increasing numbers of governmental functions have been recognized as human rights that are judicially or administratively enforced, often at the international level. Some delegated or non-majoritarian institutions help redress biases in national democratic representation, particularly where government policy can be captured by narrow but powerful interest groups who oppose the interests of majorities with diffuse, longer-term, less self-conscious concerns. Free trade is the most obvious example. Many of the same Europeans who criticize the democratic deficit also call for the US to retain 'fast track' authority to pass trade liberalization – nothing less than empowering the US executive to act with minimal legislative constraint. In such cases, the EU is *more* representative of public preferences precisely because it is *less* directly democratic. On this account only one major EU institution stands out as problematic: the ECB. The ECB enjoys more political independence than any national exemplar, even though the technical (optimal currency area) justification for the bank itself is weaker. This implies that some counterweight to the ECB might be justified.

The accountability of the EU is not simply theoretical; it is manifest in the absence of evidence that the EU imparts an illegitimate bias on European policy-making. Pluralists may quibble about this or that quality of EU institutions, yet to judge by the output, it is difficult to find places where the resulting bias is significant. The EU appears to act largely consistently with mobilized mass public opinion. Where such opinion is engaged, as on environmental issues, genetically modified organisms, foreign policy, and other issues, the EU appears responsive. The scope of its activities, save for a defense policy many Europeans favor but appear reluctant to fund, also conforms to their views.

Consider, for example, the social democratic claim that the unaccountability of the EU creates a strong neo-liberal bias. Here the concern is not that the EU is too strong, as libertarians fear, but that it is too weak. This social democratic critique – drawing on a tradition that dates back to Joseph Schumpeter and Karl Polanyi – begins by noting that most Europeans favor maintaining current levels of welfare spending, as demonstrated by the tendency of member states to spend increasing percentages of GNP on welfare as per capita income increases. This ideal cannot be realized today, it is alleged, because of the tendency of market competition to generate a 'race to the bottom' in regulatory protection between countries. Such fears of 'social dumping' underlie much anti-EU sentiment, especially in the social democratic polities of Scandinavia and northern Europe.

While this criticism is at least more plausible than the libertarian fear that the EU is a regulatory superstate squelching markets and growth, it is nonetheless exaggerated. Where the EU is active, there is little evidence of a regulatory race to the bottom. Instead it has tended to set standards for environmental and consumer protection at a high level. Even where the EU is not active, the best analyses of this question, such as that of German social scientist (and Social Democrat) Fritz Scharpf, conclude that there can be such a race to the bottom in only a few areas, that there is little evidence that it has yet occurred, and where it may have, the effects are limited. Overall, the level of welfare provision in Europe remains relatively stable. National welfare systems are no longer moving strongly in the direction of greater redistribution, but neither are they imploding. Perhaps most importantly for the social democratic critique, the bulk of recent research suggests that the adverse impact of globalization on social spending in Europe (pensions, medical care and labor market policy) is not great. Far tighter constraints on social spending are imposed by domestic economic, demographic and fiscal trends: the shift to a postindustrial economy, lower productivity growth, declining demand for less skilled workers, and rising costs of health care and pensions. In sum, given the current preferences of European electorates, the EU and national governments, taken together, appear to provide an accountable and representative multi-level system of policy-making.

*Deliberative democracy*

This leads us to a final democratic ideal on the basis of which criticisms of the EU are advanced: *deliberative democracy.*[93] Even those who concede the existence of limited government and democratic accountability in the EU often criticize the European Constitutional Compromise for failing to promote the transnational political parties, identities and discourses that might help render European political participation more active, extensive and meaningful to the citizen. This view is related to widespread support among political philosophers for more 'deliberative' or 'strong' democracy in the belief that it will reconnect to the political process an apathetic and passive citizenry.

The deliberative democratic critique of the EU rests on the curious premise that the creation of more opportunities for direct participation or public deliberation would automatically generate a deeper sense of political community in Europe or, at the least, muster greater popular support for EU institutions. As a general claim, there is good reason to doubt that this is the case. No correlation exists between the democratic pedigree and popularity. 'Insulated' institutions – constitutional courts, some regulators, police forces – are often the most trusted and popular with the public. Legislatures are generally disliked, to put it charitably. And the EU itself has not increased in popularity with the significant expansion in the powers of the EP over the past five years.

Even if increased participation were desirable, it is unlikely to occur. European voters do not fully exploit their current opportunities to participate in existing European elections. Nor have they shown much interest in efforts to include 'civil society' in the workings of the constitutional convention. Research suggests that this is not – as the deliberative critique implies – because they believe that their participation is ineffective or that institutions like the EP are unimportant. Institutions are not the problem. One is forced to conclude that it is because they do not care.

Why are they apathetic? The most plausible reason for such apathy is that the scope of EU regulatory activity tends to be inversely correlated with the importance of issues in the minds of European voters. Of the five most salient issues in European societies today – health care, education, law and order, pension and social security policy, and taxes – none is primarily an EU competence. Amongst the next ten issues in the minds of the public, only a few (managing the economy, the environment, and the issue of 'Europe' itself) could be considered major EU concerns. In contrast, the affairs of the EU – trade liberalization, agriculture, removal of non-tariff barriers, technical regulation in environmental and other areas, foreign aid and foreign policy coordination – tend to be of low priority in most European polities. Monetary policy lies somewhere in the middle.

The central problem of deliberative democracy is thus to give voters sufficient incentive to care about EU politics and deliberate about it intelligently. In a world without salient issues, new institutional avenues for participation, such as referendums and constitutional conventions, do not necessarily encourage rich deliberation by an engaged population. Instead they can lead to unstable plebiscitary politics in which individuals have no incentive to reconcile their concrete interests with their political choices. This is the lesson of referendums on recent treaties. Consider the Irish referendum on the Nice Treaty, in which public opinion shifted by dozens of percentage points in response to offhand statements by the Commission president, driving citizens in one of the countries that benefits most per capita from EU membership to vote against an innocuous document. Ignorance was so great that the slogan 'If you don't know, vote no' carried the day. This is no way to inspire serious democratic deliberation – or a perception of legitimacy.

The recent episode of constitution-making can be seen as a grand political experiment to test whether democratization of the EU is required, or whether the European Constitutional Compromise is stable in the face of criticism. The explicit reason for holding a constitutional convention was precisely the hope that it would circumvent haggling and national vetoes and activate instead a broad public mandate. European federalists in the Spinelli tradition hoped finally to realize their dream of an active and engaged pan-European citizenry. Pragmatists hoped to combat rising apathy and cynicism towards the EU by radically simplifying the Treaty of Rome, more clearly delineating national and central prerogatives, and creating opportunities for democratic participation. Everyone gambled that an open, web-savvy twenty-first-century reenactment of Philadelphia in 1787 would engage citizens and politicians of all stripes, sparking an epochal public debate on the meaning and future of the EU.

It is increasingly clear that this democratic experiment was a failure, despite the utterly reasonable content of the resulting constitutional draft. The constitutional convention attracted little public interest, the result was modest, and the political costs now threaten to sink the entire project. Few Europeans were aware of the convention's existence, and only a handful could explain what happened there. When testimony from civil society was requested, professors showed up. When a conference of European youth was called, would-be Eurocrats attended. So the task of preparing a constitutional draft was left, as tasks so often are in EU affairs, to parliamentarians, diplomats and Brussels insiders. Two hundred *conventionnels* came, they deliberated and, sixteen months later, little had changed.[94] The resulting document is conservative: a constitutional compromise that consolidates a decade or two of creeping change. European governments took few steps toward democratizing the EU, beyond a continued expansion of the powers of the EP. Those who mobilized were disproportionately extreme Euroskeptics with intense anti-European feelings, who exploited public ignorance to breed conspiratorial suspicion among largely apathetic but broadly pro-European publics. And now, despite the modesty of the constitutional treaty, politicians are being forced to pay back their borrowed public support with interest, as they guide the proposed document through national referendums.

To transform the EU into an active participatory democracy, it would be necessary to give Europeans a far greater stake in creating new political cleavages based on self-interest – as occurred historically in past episodes of democratization. Amongst the most plausible proposals of this kind is that by Philippe Schmitter of the European University Institute, who proposes that agricultural support and structural funds should be replaced with a guaranteed minimum income for the poorest third of EU citizens, a reform of welfare systems so as not to privilege the elderly, and a shift in power from national citizens to immigrants.[95] This is a coherent scheme for reinvigorating European democracy targeted at the groups most dissatisfied with European integration today – the poorer, less well-educated, female, and public sector populations. Yet Schmitter's proposals have a Swiftian quality about them. (No wonder he coyly calls them 'modest proposals.') Such schemes would surely succeed in 'democratizing' the EU, but only at the expense of its further existence. The impracticality of such schemes demonstrates the lack of a realistic alternative to current, indirect forms of democratic accountability. Proposals of this kind would achieve prominence – but only at the cost of the EU itself.

## CONCLUSION: THE EU'S CONSTITUTIONAL MATURITY

The multi-level governance system of the EU is the only distinctively new form of state organization to emerge and prosper since the rise of the democratic social welfare state at the turn of the twentieth century. Recent events suggest that it may now have reached, through a characteristically incremental process, a stable political equilibrium. This 'constitutional compromise' is unlikely to be upset by major functional challenges, autonomous institutional evolution, or demands for democratic accountability. There is, moreover, an undeniable normative attraction to a system that preserves national democratic politics for those issues most salient in the minds of citizens, but delegates to more indirect democratic forms those issues that are of less concern, or on which there is an administrative or legal consensus. Contrary to what Haas and Monnet believed, the EU does not (or no longer needs to) move forward to consolidate its current benefits. This is good news for those who admire the European project. When a constitutional system no longer needs to expand and deepen in order to assure its own continued existence, it is truly stable. It is a mark of constitutional maturity.

This conclusion takes us back, finally, to Ernst Haas. Neofunctionalism may be incorrect about the preeminence of endogenous economic change, political entrepreneurs, unintended consequences, and continuous movement toward centralization in the integration process. Yet at a deeper level it is valid, indeed visionary. In the 1950s Haas correctly perceived that the EU would not become a success by pursuing the federalist strategy of public debate, elections, and other techniques for building popular democratic legitimacy. Nor would it succeed by building up an army and taking strong positions on the military-political issues of the day, as realists have always recommended. Instead, as we now know, it established itself by helping to meet concrete functional challenges within the context of the power that national governments delegated to or pooled in it. In this Haas has been proven correct. Moreover, that strategy has not only been successful but has created more popular legitimacy and geopolitical influence than more direct federalist or realist strategies might have been expected to generate. In an era in which the federalist and realist temptations have resurged, both among scholars and politicians, we would do well, even when we criticize its precise claims, to embrace the modernizing spirit of Ernst Haas's *magnum opus*.

**Address for correspondence:** Andrew Moravcsik, European Union Program, Princeton University, Department of Politics, Woodrow Wilson School, Robertson Hall, Princeton, NJ 08544, USA. email: amoravcs@princeton.edu

## NOTES

1 Professor of Politics and Director, European Union Center, Princeton University. More information, and copies of work cited here, are available at www.princeton.edu/~amoravcs.

2 Andrew Moravcsik, 'Striking a new transatlantic bargain', *Foreign Affairs* 82:4 (July/August 2003): 74–89.

3 Haas is quite explicit. See, for example, the last sentence of his classic book: 'To this extent the vision of Jean Monnet has been justified by events.' Ernst Haas, *The Uniting of Europe* 3rd edition (Stanford: Stanford University Press, 2004), 527.

4 Larry Siedentop, *Democracy in Europe* (London: Penguin Press, 2000).

5 This conclusion could also be reached from other theoretical starting points. A 'liberal intergovernmentalist' might argue, for example, that exogenous shifts in functional demand arising from issue-specific interdependence will continue to press for integration. The difference is that neo-functionalists saw this as an inevitable and endogenous process. For further discussion see notes 17 and 18.

6 'European federalism, an explicit ideology heavily indebted to Proudhon and Sorel, proved a failure largely because its language proved so peripheral to the objectives of a great majority of active citizens.' Haas, *Uniting of Europe*, xxix.

7 Haas, *Uniting of Europe*, xxxiii.

8 'Military threats,' Haas believes, are insufficient to explain the phenomenon of regional integration. Haas, *Uniting of Europe*, xv.

9 Integration, Haas argued, was launched because it 'offered a multitude of different advantages to different groups' rather than 'identical aims on the part of all the participants.' Haas, *Uniting of Europe*, xii, xxxiii.

10 The essentially economic nature of such interest groups explains why integration is only likely to progress in a region with 'an industrialized economy deeply enmeshed in global trade and finance,' 'interest groups and parties,' and democratic institutions. Haas, *Uniting of Europe*, xxiv–xxxvi, also xiv, xix. The neofunctionalist view of underlying preferences is ambivalent in only one sense, namely that political entrepreneurs manipulate economic policy, at least early in the integration process, to achieve political ends such as 'peace' as well as 'welfare.' Haas, *Uniting of Europe*, xx.

11 Haas, *Uniting of Europe*, xii.

12 Haas, *Uniting of Europe*, xxi.

13 For a succinct overview, see Charles Pentland, *International Theory and European Integration* (New York: The Free Press, 1973). More up-to-date but less subtle and reliable on major theoretical schools is Ben Rosamond, *Theories of European Integration* (London: Palgrave Macmillan, 2000).

14 Haas, *Uniting of Europe*, xxxiii. Note that the essence of the claim is that new functional challenges arise as an unintended function of the solution of old problems.

15 This is the direction that Haas's later work on international organization would take. See Haas, *Uniting of Europe*, *xii–*lvi.

16 'Though not federal in nature, the consequences [of supranational institutions] are plainly federating in quality merely because it activates socio-economic processes in the pluralistic-industrial-democratic milieu in which it functions, but to which conventional international institutions have no access. And to this extent the vision of Jean Monnet has been clearly justified by events.' Haas, *Uniting of Europe*, 527.

17 It does not follow, however – as many of Haas's followers incorrectly claim – that theories based on exogenous changes in economic interdependence are incapable of explaining change, which is incorrect on its face. Martin Saeter perpetuates the canard that exogenous theories of preferences, interstate decision-making and delegation are 'predominantly static,' 'cannot explain the transformation of the system into a more integrated one,' and 'disregard the transfer of competences ... following treaty obligations ... i.e. the *acquis communautaire*. Explaining European integration during the 1990s clearly requires a broader approach.' Martin Saeter, *Comprehensive Neofunctionalism: Bridging Realism and Liberalism in the Study of European Integration* (Oslo: Norwegian Institute of International Affairs, n.d.). Elsewhere Saeter contradicts himself on this point. 'A supplementary hypothesis would be that the greater the external, or international, challenges are, the more pressing will be the need for deepening.' He then ends up taking refuge in indeterminacy: 'Of course no theory can possibly pretend to provide a basis for prediction about political choices of such a kind.' Saeter, *Comprehensive Neofunctionalism*, 90.

18 A point often missed in glosses on these theories is that the essential difference between neofunctionalist claims and those of more classically regime theoretical theories – often termed 'liberal intergovernmentalist' – is not that the former explain dynamic change and the latter are static. It is that neofunctionalism explains dynamic change (as opposed to moving to a new equilibrium) primarily through endogenous spillover, while LI explains it as a response to exogenous pressures or intended consequences of previous agreements. For a useful discussion see Ben Rosamond, *Theories of European Integration* (London: Palgrave MacMillan, 2000), 68–73. Oddly, Haas remarks in his introduction to the 2004 edition of *Uniting of Europe*, in which he argues that liberal intergovernmentalism 'conforms exactly to the main ideas of neo-functionalism.' Haas, *Uniting of Europe*, *xvii. This is obviously not the case, as shown by Haas's discussion immediately following, which leaves liberal intergovernmentalism behind and focuses on work by determined critics of LI. For a discussion of the use and abuse of the distinction,

see Donald Puchala, 'Institutionalism, Intergovernmentalism, and European Integration: A Review', *Journal of Common Market Studies* 37:2 (June 1999), 317–31.

19 Haas, *Uniting of Europe*, *xii–*lvi. In his book Haas seeks to explain the deepening of integration from 1950 to 1957, leading to the founding of the EEC. In later work he seeks to explain integration in the 1960s as a consequence of earlier decisions, rather than as a continuing response to external pressures.

20 Haas, *Uniting of Europe*, xxiii. 'Once established,' he argued in 1958, 'the central institution will affect political integration...if it is willing to follow policies giving rise to expectations and demands for more – or fewer – federal measures.' Haas, *Uniting of Europe*, xxxiii, also xii. Haas quite arbitrarily discusses integration as if exogenous factors can matter only as preconditions at the time integration is launched, not at any subsequent decision point.

21 There is no reason why an adequate explanatory theory need be predictive. A prediction about the future based on a claim 'If A then B' depends not only on knowing the causal relationship, but knowing the value of A. Often we can measure the value of A in the past, but not in the future. In this sense, most social scientific theories are more explanatory than predictive. Haas, perhaps consistent with his Monnetist ambitions, was the reverse; he was more interested in prediction than explanation. I am indebted to Philippe Schmitter for pressing me on this point.

22 Robert O. Keohane and Joseph S. Nye, 'International Interdependence and Integration', in Fred Greenstein and Nelson Polsby, *Handbook of Political Science* (Andover, MA: Addison-Wesley, 1975), 363–414.

23 Here I follow the analysis in *Choice for Europe*, Introduction, Chapters 1 and 7.

24 For a summary of a decade of work, seePhillippe Schmitter, 'A Revised Theory of European Integration', in Leon N, Lindberg and Stuart A. Scheingold, eds, *Regional Integration: Theory and Practice* (Cambridge, MA: Harvard University Press, 1971); Leon N. Lindberg and Stuart A. Scheingold, *Europe's Would-Be Polity: Patterns of Change in the European Community* (Englewood Cliffs, NJ: Prentice-Hall, 1970).

25 Ernst B. Haas, 'International Integration: The European and the Universal Process'. In *International Political Communities: An Anthology*, 93–130. New York: Doubleday, 1966; Haas, 'The Study of Regional Integration: Reflections on the Joy and Anguish of Pretheorizing', in Leon N. Lindberg and Stuart A. Scheingold, eds., *Regional Integration: Theory and Research* (Cambridge, MA: Harvard, 1971), 23ff; Haas, 'Turbulent Fields and the Theory of Regional Integration', *International Organization* 30, no. 2 (Spring 1976): 173–212.

26 Haas, *Uniting of Europe*, xxvi–xxviii. To be sure, neofunctionalists did analyze other efforts at regional integration – generally concluding that the potential for integration was slight. For a subtle treatment, see Joseph S. Nye, *Peace in Parts: Integration and Conflict in Regional Organization* (Boston: Little Brown, 1971).

27 Donald Puchala, 'Of Blind Men, Elephants, and International Integration', *Journal of Common Market Studies* 10:3 (March 1972), 267–85. Also Pentland, *International*, 189–94; Carole Webb, 'Theoretical Perspectives and Problems', in Helen Wallace, William Wallace and Carole Webb, eds., *Policy-Making in the European Community*, 2nd edition (Chichester: Wiley, 1983), 32ff.

28 Janne Haaland Matláry, 'Beyond Intergovernmentalism: The Quest for a Comprehensive Framework for the Study of Integration', *Cooperation and Conflict* 28:2 (1993): 181–208; Linda Cornett and James A. Caporaso, '"And It Still Moves!" State Interests and Social Forces in the European Community', in James N. Rosenau and Ernst-Otto Czempiel, eds., *Governance without Government: Order and Change in World Politics* (Cambridge: Cambridge University Press,

1992), 248; Michael O'Neill, *The Politics of European Integration: A Reader* (New York: Routledge, 1996), 5.

29  Haas, *The Uniting of Europe*, xii–xiv. The passive voice in the title *The Uniting of Europe* captures the spirit of the enterprise.

30  See note 18 above.

31  Haas, 'Study', 26; Haas, *The Obsolescence of Regional Integration Theory* (Berkeley: Center for International Studies, 1975), 86. On the links between interdependence, governance and learning, see Haas, *The Web of Interdependence: The United States and International Organizations* (Englewood Cliffs, NJ: Prentice-Hall, 1970).

32  Henry R. Nau, 'From Integration to Interdependence: Gains, Losses and Continuing Gaps', *International Organization* 33 : 1 (Autumn 1979), 119–47; Keohane and Nye, 'International Interdependence and Integration', 363–414; Stanley Hoffmann, 'Reflections on the Nation-State in Western Europe Today', *Journal of Common Market Studies* 21 : 1–2 (September–December 1982), 21–37.

33  James Caporaso and John T.S. Keeler, 'The European Community and Regional Integration Theory', in Carolyn Rhodes and Sonia Mazey, eds., *The State of the European Union: Building European Unity?* (Boulder: Lynne Rienner, 1995), 43; Likke Friis, 'Challenging a Theoretical Paradox: The Lacuna of Integration Theory' (Copenhagen: CORE Working Paper 2, 1995), 2.

34  This lies behind the criticisms of scholars like Milward and Ludlow that a 'social history' of integration is required. The neofunctionalists did stress the role of economic transactions. Ernst B. Haas and Philippe C. Schmitter, 'Economics and Differential Patterns of Political Integration: Projections about Unity in Latin America', *International Organization* 18 : 4 (Autumn 1964), 707, 709–10.

35  There is a tendency in neofunctionalist theory to argue that they do not have to engage in any rigorous theory testing against *any* alternative, since their theory *subsumes* those alternatives. Yet this sort of relabeling misses the point, which concerns mid-range theory. In order to explain why feedback is important, one needs to know what factors influence static decisions and how they do so – since it is these latter factors that feedback would need to alter. Thus, in order to analyze feedback, we require an explicit micro-foundational theory of how societal pressures, national bargaining power, and transaction-cost incentives are transformed into policy outcomes – a theory whose empirical validity we can test. Similarly, in order to show that the sources of long-term change were endogenous consequences to previous integration decisions, rather than responses to exogenous trends and shocks, one needs to theorize and evaluate (as an alternative baseline theory) the exogenous influences on basic elements of state behavior, such as preferences, bargaining power, and transaction-cost incentives to institutionalize policies.

36  Ernst B. Haas, 'The Study of Regional Integration: Reflections on the Anguish and Joy of Pre-Theorizing', in Lindberg and Scheingold, eds., *Regional Integration*; Ernst B. Haas, *The Obsolescence of Regional Integration Theory* (Berkely, CA: Institute of International Studies, 1975).

37  Lindberg and Scheingold, *Europe's Would-Be Polity*, 284; Joseph S. Nye, *Peace in Parts: Integration and Conflict in Regional Organization* (Boston: Little, Brown, 1971), 64–75; Philippe Schmitter, 'A Revised Theory of Regional Integration', in Lindberg and Scheingold, eds., *Regional Integration*, 232–64; Ernst B. Haas, 'Technocracy, Pluralism and the New Europe', in Stephen R. Graubard, ed., *A New Europe?* (Boston: Houghton Mifflin, 1964), 62–88. Neofunctionalism failed, Haas argued, to capture the real decisions facing governments, for example the choice – repeatedly critical in the evolution of the EC – whether to engage in regional or global cooperation.

38  Ernst B. Haas, *Beyond the Nation State: Functionalism and International Organization* (Stanford, 1964), 34–5, 81; Haas, 'Turbulent', 173.

39  Hoffmann, 'Reflections', 31, 33–4; Haas, *Beyond the Nation State*, 23, 30, 32–5, 77. Ultimately Haas moved in a different direction, seeking to reconceptualize 'learning' through a process of trial and error and the application of expert knowledge, though he conceded a greater role for learning occurred as actors assess whether integration 'enhances the original purposes of the actors.' Late in his career he flirted with constructivism as a means to pursue the research agenda further.

40  For the link, see Robert O. Keohane and Stanley Hoffmann, 'Institutional Change in Europe in the 1980s', in Keohane and Hoffmann, eds., *The New European Community: Decision-Making and Institutional Change* (Boulder: Westview Press, 1991), 1–39.

41  Rosamond, *Theories*.

42  Theoretical analyses of integration theory tend to mistake debate over theory for empirical ambiguity. Ben Rosamond, for example, points out that there are competing positions in integration theory, but makes little sustained effort to weigh them empirically, let alone offer a critical analysis of the empirical evidence. Diversity of opinion, it seems, is more important than empirical progress. Compare, Rosamond, *Theories of European Integration*, with superior treatments that seek to incorporate empirical data, such as John Peterson and Elizabeth Bomberg, *Decision-Making in the European Union* (London: Palgrave Macmillan, 1999).

43  Characteristic is Jeppe Tranholm-Mikkelsen, 'Neofunctionalism: Obstinate or Obsolete. A Reappraisal in the Light of the New Dynamism of the EC', *Millennium* 20 : 1 (Spring 1991); Wayne Sandholtz, *High-Tech Europe: The Politics of International Cooperation* (Berkeley: University of California Press, 1992); Paul Pierson, 'The Path to European Union: An Historical Institutionalist Account', *Comparative Political Studies* 29 : 2 (April 1996), 123–64.

44  See Alan S. Milward, *The European Rescue of the Nation-State* 2nd edition (London: Routledge, 2000); Moravcsik, *Choice for Europe*.

45  Moravcsik, *Choice for Europe*, Chapter 1, supersedes Andrew Moravcsik, 'Preferences and Power in the European Community: A Liberal Intergovernmentalist Approach', *Journal of Common Market Studies* (30th Anniversary Edition) (December 1993).

46  Moravcsik, *Choice for Europe*, Chapter 7, finds that in eight of fifteen cases geopolitical concerns and federalist ideology played an important secondary role, and in three cases, all including Germany, agreement might have been impossible without them. He concludes also that certain elements of the EU, perhaps even including the agricultural policy and the quasi-constitutional structure, may have reflected geopolitical and ideological concerns.

47  This is not to say, of course, that all cooperation in the EU is economic. The essence of the LI position is *not* that economic issues dominate political ones. It is that: (1) states pursue national interests formulated as preferences across outcomes; (2) these national preferences reflect concrete issue-specific concerns more than general ideological concerns or linkages to other issues. This does not exclude, of course, that bargains would be reached across issues.

48  He did glimpse, however, that the founding of the EEC was in most respects a *repudiation* of the ECSC, which was viewed by European businessmen, notably in Germany, as unacceptably *dirigiste*, and by policy-makers as a noble failure. For the latest historiography, see Gunnar Skogmar, *The United States and the Nuclear Dimension of European Integration* (Basingstoke: Palgrave Macmillan, 2004).

49  Exogenous is used here in the social scientific, not geographical sense. I do not mean pressures from outside Europe, but pressures causally independent of prior integration.

50  Here is the passage in its entirety: 'One plausible explanation [for the success of cooperation among the Six and not in the OEEC] is that France, in ECSC, is face to face with four governments committed to common market thinking, while Italy is equally sympathetic in principle though sometimes desirous of arguing the case of her defensively-minded heavy industries. In OEEC, by contrast, the German and Benelux position enjoys no clear and consistent majority. But this fact alone does not suffice to explain the French refusal to use the veto power, and the good record of eventually complying with ECSC orders. It is suggested that the concept of "engagement," already introduced in connection with the Messina conference, provides a convincing explanation, combining institutional and ideological causes. The concept of "engagement" is developed as an adaptation from a similar principle in small-group psychology.' Haas, *Uniting of Europe*, 522. Haas provides no evidence that this shift is endogenous to past integration, nor any reason why exogenous interests cannot explain the French veto. For his prior evidence of the positions of national governments at Messina, consistent with the political economy approach, see also pp. 268–70.

51  Haas, *Uniting of Europe*, 512–27. This implies that *any* sort of interstate agreement demonstrates the 'supranational principle' at work.

52  See the discussion in notes 17 and 18 above.

53  See Jeffrey A. Frankel, Ernesto Stein, Shang-Jin Wei, *Regional Trading Blocs in the World Economic System* (Washington: Institute for International Economics, 1999).

54  Haas neglects the quiet but essential role of agriculture in the founding of the EEC. Concern about agriculture, and the notion that agricultural problems could be solved by finding neighboring export markets, were not created by the EEC. There is overwhelming evidence that French leaders would never have secured the votes to ratify the treaty without the votes of the agricultural bloc. François Duchêne, *Jean Monnet: First Statesman of Interdependence* (New York: Norton, 1995), 291. Craig Parsons (in an interesting and informed, if one-sided, analysis) seeks to defend the even more radically neofunctionalist thesis that French policy-makers did not think about agriculture in the context of Europe until induced to do so by EEC discussions in 1962 or 1963. See *A Certain Idea of Europe* (Ithaca: Cornell University Press, 2003). Empirically, this is an utterly unsustainable position, as the evidence above suggests. It gains credibility only because it conflates a state having a preference with an item being prominent on international agendas. Agriculture was not discussed in detail in the EU before the early 1960s, for tactical reasons, but it played an important role in French thinking throughout.

55  For a summary of evidence, see Milward, *Rescue*; Moravcsik, *Choice*, Chapter 7.

56  This case is argued in detail in Moravcsik, *The Choice for Europe*.

57  Fritz Scharpf, 'The Joint-Decision Trap: Lessons from German Federalism and European Integration', *Public Administration* 66 (Autumn 1988): 239–78. Fritz Scharpf, 'Europäische Demokratie und deutsche Föderalismus', *Staatswissenschaft und Staatspraxis* 3: 296–306.

58  See the discussion in Moravcsik, *Choice for Europe*, Chapters 2–3, 7 and Andrew Moravcsik, 'A New Statecraft? Supranational Entrepreneurship and Interstate Cooperation', *International Organization* 53(2) (Winter 1999): 267–306. This is not the result of short time horizons, as the lack of any subsequent effort to reverse these subsidies, as well as the similar behavior in this period of non-EU members like Switzerland, Austria, Japan, Ireland and most of Scandinavia illustrate.

59 Here I summarize the findings from Moravcsik, 'A New Statecraft?' which develops the theories presented here, and tests them using data in *The Choice for Europe*.

60 Wayne Sandholtz and John Zysman, '1992: Recasting the European Bargain', *World Politics* 42 (Winter 1989): 95–128; George Ross, *Jacques Delors and European Integration* (Oxford: Polity Press, 1995), who writes: 'the political lucidity of the Commission's proposals and the shrewdness with which they have been presented have been central variables in Europe's forward movement . . . In contrast to ordinary international organizations, the EC was set up to contain a supranational "motor" which would constantly press forward towards more integration – the Commission was not designed simply to be a "delegated agent" of EC member states' (pp. 3–4).

61 Most studies, even those that seek to establish neofunctionalist claims, concede that exogenously motivated state behavior explains most of the outcome. For an overview of more recent cases, see Andrew Moravcsik and Kalypso Nicolaïdis, 'Explaining the Treaty of Amsterdam: Interests, Influence, Institutions', *Journal of Common Market Studies* (March 1999); Finn Laursen, ed., *The Amsterdam Treaty: National Preference Formation, Interstate Bargaining, and Outcomes* (Odense: Odense University Press, 2002); Paul Magnette and Kalypso Nicolaïdis, 'The European Convention: Bargaining in the Shadow of Rhetoric', *West European Politics* 27(3) (May 2004): 381–404.

62 Milward, *Rescue of the Nation State*, Chapter 6.

63 Even his sympathetic (and best-documented) biographer, former Monnet collaborator François Duchêne, attributes to Monnet the idea of regional integration in 1949–50, but little in subsequent years. See his *First Statesman of Interdependence*. Haas also underestimates the independence of mind of Dutch diplomats, led by Willem Beyen, who were far more skeptical of sectoral integration than Haas's account suggests. See Haas, *Uniting of Europe*, 269–70. Cf. Moravcsik, *Choice*, 139–50.

64 Moravcsik, 'A New Statecraft?'.

65 Here I do not address neofunctionalism's presuppositions about institutional delegation, which imply: (1) centralization will occur across the board, and notably in areas of the most intense national regulation; (2) evidence that governments are overruled by central authorities is evidence for 'supranationalization' of politics. Neither is adequate. The first claim is not empirically accurate. Modern theories of international regimes assume that delegation to international institutions is a rational means of making credible commitments to further cooperation. This implies that centralization of authority is required primarily to manage the transaction costs. It would be interesting to test these claims against one another. The second claim is underspecified, since regime theory also predicts that governments will sometimes be outvoted or overruled. For further discussion of delegation see Moravcsik, *Choice for Europe*, pp. 67–77, 485–489.

66 Consider, for example, Simon Hix's uncommonly intelligent and sophisticated advanced introductory textbook on the EU, designed to reflect 'state of the art' theory and research. Hix devotes nearly dozens of pages to the Parliament, Court, and autonomous actions of the Commission, far less to the Commission in the legislative process and the Council of Ministers, and only a handful to the European Council and to national implementation. This strikes me as a distribution that perfectly reflects current scholarship on the EU, but also one inversely proportional to the respective importance of these institutions in shaping the overall trajectory of European integration. Simon Hix, *The Political System of the European Union* (New York: Palgrave, 1999). Cf. for a more balanced presentation, Mark

Pollack, *The Engines of European Integration: Delegation, Agency, and Agenda Setting in the EU* (Oxford: Oxford University Press, 2003).

67  See Mark Pollack, *Engines of European Integration*. Anne-Marie Burley and Walter Mattli, 'Europe before the Court: A Political Theory of Legal Integration', *International Organization* 47: 1 (Winter 1993): 41–76. Karen J. Alter, *Establishing the Supremacy of European Law: The Making of an International Rule of Law in Europe* (Oxford: Oxford University Press, 2001). For further empirical testing, see Alec Stone Sweet and Thomas Brunell, 'Constructing a Supranational Constitution: Dispute Resolution and Governance in the European Community', *American Political Science Review* 92(1) (March 1998): 63–81.

68  One would not want to make a rigid distinction here, as many forms of policy-making combine the two. Yet we can still usefully discuss how centralized European policy-making is.

69  Some – including reviewers of this article – find it surprising or objectionable that I compare the EU to a state rather than to an international organization. One hears this sort of dichotomy – often expressed as a spurious distinction between conceiving of EU politics as 'comparative politics' and 'international relations,' or conceiving the EU as a 'state' and the EU as an 'international organization.' But is this distinction helpful? In social science there are fundamental theories of political economy, non-coercive bargaining, and institutions. Properly specified and applied, they explain politics regardless of the level or sub-discipline; any restrictions follow only from the precise institutional setting. This sort of misunderstanding would be less important but for the fact that it dovetails with 'paradigmatic' formulations such as a tension between 'liberal intergovernmentalism' and 'multi-level governance.' In my view, these sorts of dichotomies are unwelcome legacies of the parochially EU-specific 'grand theoretical' language Haas and others introduced to the study of the EU (and carried on today in some textbook writing on the EU). In fact such claims are not mutually exclusive. Far from denying that the EU is a multi-level governance institution, 'liberal intergovernmentalism' (LI) dictates that it must be such an institution. Recall that LI models interstate negotiations to amend the EU's constitutional treaty basis as a three-stage process of national preference formation, interstate bargaining, and institutional delegation. In the third step, governments delegate to EU institutions as credible commitment mechanisms, within which further decisions are taken. This in turn implies that there is substantial uncertainty about precisely what decisions will be taken within the treaty arrangements, otherwise governments would simply negotiate the subsequent agreements *ex ante*. Such delegated institutions empower national governments to outvote their counterparts; social and bureaucratic actors to act as litigants, lobbyists or representatives; European citizens to vote for elected representatives; and supranational actors to render decisions. *All this is implied by LI itself.* If institutions were unimportant, then governments would not need to negotiate over the delegation to them set down in treaty-amending negotiations, and LI would not need to theorize how they do so. All this, moreover, is utterly consistent with the transaction-cost basis of the 'regime theory' developed by Robert Keohane and others, now a quarter-century old and the explicit basis of LI. To draw a contrast between 'liberal intergovernmentalist' and 'multi-level governance' frameworks as stark alternatives is, therefore, profoundly misleading. For a more nuanced approach, see Pollack, *Engines of European Integration*.

70  Martin Saeter's reformulation, for example, is cited approvingly by Haas. He sets up the central issue as follows: 'European integration is seemingly moving along a continuum, without any logical end stage, leading from the present, predominantly

The Constitutional Compromise and neofunctionalism   169

confederal, type of system towards increasingly federal-type, supranational mechanisms and structures.' Saeter, *Comprehensive Neofunctionalism*, 90.

71 This is not to say, as Niall Ferguson, Martin Feldstein and others have speculated over the past decade, that the EU will decay or dissolve. See Niall Ferguson, 'The End of Europe' (address at the American Enterprise Institute).

72 'En 1988, Jacques Delors avait annoncé que "dans dix ans, 80% de la législation économique, peut-être même fiscale et sociale, applicable dans les Etats-membres seront d'origine communautaires"', Michel Barnier, 'Le grand secret de la présidentielle', *Libération* (12 February 2002): 15.

73 For example, see Simon Hix, 'A Union that is a System, not a State', *Financial Times* (9 May 1998), 10; 'The Omnipotence of Brussels', *Financial Times* (8 August 1995), 13; Martin Walker, 'Walker's World: The New Enfeebled EC', *United Press International* (5 August 2004); Briony Warden, 'The Floundering Fathers of Europe', *The Sun* (1 March 2002); Bernard J. Mulholland, 'Personally Speaking', *Global News Wire – Europe Intelligence Wire* (26 February 2002); Eric Zemmour, 'La fin d'une fiction franchise', *Le Figaro* (17 June 2004), 9; Thomas Ferenczi, 'Plus de la moitié de la législation française est d'origine européenne', *Le Monde* (14 June 2004). One leading government minister, who often uses the EU as an excuse for legislative proposals, has recently argued that 60 percent of domestic legislation originates with the EU. Barnier, 'Le grand secret', 15.

74 For example, Annette Töller, 'Dimensionen der Europäisierung – Das Beispiel des Deutschen Bundestages', (unpublished paper, Hamburg, 2003).

75 Giandomenico Majone, *Regulating Europe* (London: Routledge, 1996).

76 Virginie Guiraudon, 'Immigration and Justice' (Paper presented at conference on The European Union and the New Constitution – A Stable Political Equilibrium?, Princeton University, November 2004).

77 Gráinne de Búrca, 'The Constitutional Challenge of New Governance in the European Union', *European Law Review* 28 (2003): 814.

78 Charles Sabel and Jonathan Zeitlin, 'Active Welfare, Experimental Governance, Pragmatic Constitutionalism: The New Transformation of Europe' (May 2003, available at http://www2.law.columbia.edu/sabel/papers.htm).

79 Jürgen Habermas, 'Why Europe Needs a Constitution', *New Left Review* 11 (September–October 2001).

80 For a leading and very optimistic scenario, see Paul Pierson and Stefan Leibfried, eds., *European Social Policy* (Washington: Brookings Institution, 1995).

81 For a recent empirical assessment that, despite the strongest possible effort, finds little evidence of progress, see Jonathan Zeitlin and Philippe Pochet, with Lars Magnusson, eds., *The Open Method of Coordination in Action: The European Employment and Social Inclusion Strategies* (Brussels: PIE-Peter Lang, forthcoming).

82 Fritz Scharpf, *Governing in Europe: Effective and Legitimate?* (Oxford: Oxford University Press, 1999).

83 For a critique of Scharpf addressing this and other points, see Andrew Moravcsik and Andrea Sangiovanni, 'On Democracy and Public Interest in the European Union', in Wolfgang Streeck and Renate Mainz, eds., *Die Reformierbarkeit der Demokratie. Innovationen und Blockaden* (Frankfurt: Campus Verlag, 2002), 122–48.

84 Ferguson, 'The End of Europe'.

85 Scharpf, *Governing in Europe*.

86 For full citations see Moravcsik, 'In Defense of the Democratic Deficit: Reassessing Legitimacy in the European Union', *Journal of Common Market Studies* 40 : 4 (November 2002); 'Federalism in the European Union: Rhetoric and Reality', in Kalypso Nicolaïdis and Robert Howse, eds., *The Federal Vision: Legitimacy and Levels of Governance in the US and the EU* (Oxford: Oxford University Press, 2001).

87 Majone, *Regulating Europe.*
88 This does not imply, as Majone has argued and others have incorrectly attributed to me, that EU policies have no important redistributive consequences. Obviously they do.
89 Here again I follow the analysis in Moravcsik, 'In Defense of the Democratic Deficit', which provides full citations.
90 In a curiously anachronistic reading of EU history, Siedentop sees the EU as a scheme imposed by France – in the manner of Louis XIV and Napoleon – to propagate the French administrative state across the continent. Siedentop, *Democracy in Europe.*
91 Thomas Zweifel, 'Who is Without Sin Cast the First Stone: The EU's Democratic Deficit in Comparison', *Journal of European Public Policy* **9**(5) (2002): 812–40.
92 More recent Commission administrative slip-ups generally stem from the Commission's lack of staff, which requires many tasks to be outsourced to semi-private groups. They have triggered an immediate public and parliamentary response.
93 Again, this analysis follows Moravcsik, 'In Defense of the "Democratic Deficit"', and 'Is there a Democratic Deficit in Global Governance?', where full citations are provided.
94 See Peter Norman, *The Accidental Constitution* (Brussels: Eurocomment, 2004). Norman, it is fair to note, believes that the consequences of the convention were unintended and represent a sort of spillover. For a contrasting view, which makes the most positive case for spillover that is empirically sustainable, and nonetheless falls short, see Magnette and Nicolaïdis, 'The European Convention'.
95 Phillippe Schmitter, *How to Democratize the European Union ... and Why Bother?* (Lanham, MD: Rowman and Littlefield, 2000).

# Notes on contributors

**Tanja A. Börzel** is Professor of European Integration at the Otto Suhr Institute for Political Science, Free University of Berlin, Germany.

**Gráinne de Búrca** is Professor of EU Law at the European University Institute, Florence, Italy.

**Henry Farrell** is Assistant Professor in the Department of Political Science and the Elliott School of International Affairs, George Washington University, Washington DC, USA.

**Adrienne Héritier** is Joint Chair in the Department of Social and Political Science and the Robert Schuman Centre at the European University Institute, Florence, Italy.

**Walter Mattli** is a Fellow of St John's College, Oxford University, UK.

**Andrew Moravcsik** is Professor of Politics and Director of the European Union Program, Princeton University, USA.

**Mark Rhinard** is a postdoctoral fellow at Leiden University, The Netherlands.

**Thomas Risse** is a Professor in the Centre for Transatlantic Foreign and Security Policy, Otto Suhr Institute of Political Science, Free University of Berlin, Germany.

**Ben Rosamond** is Reader in Politics and International Studies and Associate Fellow in the Centre for the Study of Globalization and Regionalization at the University of Warwick, UK.

**Philippe C. Schmitter** is a Professor in the Department of Social and Political Science at the European University Institute, Florence, Italy.

**Beatrice Vaccari** is Senior Lecturer at the European Institute of Public Administration, Maastricht, The Netherlands.

# Index

CPSIA information can be obtained at www.ICGtesting.com
Printed in the USA
LVOW10*0158090614

389141LV00001B/7/P